Arguing with the Crocodile

Gender and Class in Bangladesh

Sarah C. White

Zed Books Ltd
London and New Jersey

University Press
Dhaka

Arguing with the Crocodile was first published by Zed Books Ltd,
57 Caledonian Road, London N1 9BU, UK, and 165 First Avenue,
Atlantic Highlands, New Jersey 07716, USA; and in Bangladesh
by the University Press Ltd, 114 Motijheel Commercial Area,
PO Box 2611, Dhaka 2, in 1992.

Typeset by EMS Photosetters, Thorpe Bay, Essex.
Cover designed by Sophie Buchet.
Cover photograph by courtesy of the author.
Printed and bound in the United Kingdom by Biddles Ltd,
Guildford and King's Lynn.

A catalogue record for this book is available from the
British Library.

ISBN 1 85649 085 8 Hb
ISBN 1 85649 086 6 Pb

Contents

Tables

Figures

Maps

Acknowledgements

In Bangladesh, the notion of *apon lok*, one's own people, is extremely powerful. For me, the experience of field research, writing it up for a PhD and subsequently rewriting it as a book, has been perhaps above all a growing sense of this, of finding my 'own people' in the warmth and generosity of the many people who have helped me on my way.

My study is one of four produced at Bath University concerning different aspects of life in rural Bangladesh. My thanks thus go first to the other members of our informal 'research team': our supervisor, Geof Wood; and the other researchers, Marion Glaser, Allister McGregor and David Lewis. Their personal support and the academic discussions we have shared have been, and continue to be, invaluable to me.

My times in Bangladesh have been greatly enriched by those who welcomed me into their homes. The sensitivity and kindness of 'Dhiren' and 'Sukhi' (I retain here the fictional names I have given to them in the main text) with whom I stayed in Kumirpur, and Mrs Tudu and her family, who offered me a second home in Rajshahi town, made a vital difference to me in both personal and practical terms. My other 'homes' belonged to Erik and Tia Wijlhuizen and Lynne and Bernadette Cogswell in Rajshahi; and in Dhaka, to Colette Chabbott and Jane Anderson. I shall always be grateful for their generosity and support.

Many other friends gave me practical help, advice or encouragement. Among the many I can name are: the staff of the Christian Commission for Development in Bangladesh (CCDB), especially those in the Tanore office under Bijoy Tudu, who introduced me to Kumirpur; M. A. Hamid and Jharna Nath of Rajshahi University; M. Asaduzzaman of BADC Rajshahi; Anthony and Ingeborg Bottrall, then of Ford Foundation, Dhaka; Tricia Parker, then of Oxfam, Bangladesh; Bruce Currey of Winrock International; and, of course, the people of Kumirpur, particularly those who became my case study households and bore my interminable questions with considerable patience, courtesy and good humour. Amongst these, special mention is due to 'Asha', my interpreter, whose vivacity, affection and good humour did much to bring the interviews to life.

For reading and commenting on drafts of this book I am grateful to Farida Akhter, John Holmwood, Roger and Patricia Jeffery, Ursula Sharma, and especially B. K. Jahangit, whose insightful suggestions first launched me on the process of deconstructing my thesis and constructing a book.

My thanks are also due to the Economic and Social Research Council, London, for the grant which made the initial research possible. A small grant from the British Council enabled me to make my first return visit to the village in 1989.

I am grateful to Virago Press for permitting me to quote the passage from June Jordan's *Moving Towards Home* (1989).

Lastly, I wish to thank my parents, Barrie and Margaret, for their constant love and support. Their encouragement and concern have always sustained me; it is they who first and most fully have made me welcome in their home.

Sarah White

Bangladesh, showing the research area

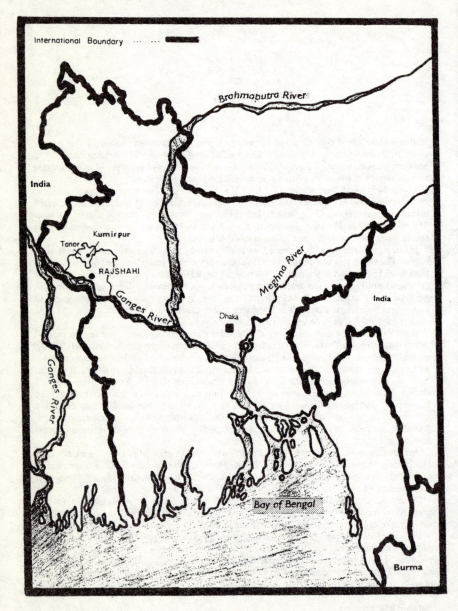

1. Penelope's Web

Introduction

Mention women in Bangladesh and you are likely to conjure up one of three sharply contrasting images. Predominant is the picture of urgent need: women with pleading hands outstretched, desperate in the wake of the latest disaster. Next is the picture of submission: sari-shrouded women clinging to the shadows or hunched mutely over laborious work. Alternative pictures show women working, demonstrating, in groups or defiantly alone. Again the message is clear: these women, though poor, are militant and strong. They claim solidarity, not pity; support, not charity.

Faced with these different views, the simplest reaction is to ask which is true. The next, perhaps, is to suggest that each image holds a fragment of the truth. Beyond these, however, arises a deeper question: how are such contradictory images produced and sustained? Each picture, then, says something not only about women in Bangladesh, but also about the people, or organization, or system, by whom or in which it was drawn. The differences become not accidents or inadequacies, but an index to the political interests which the images represent.

In this book, I aim to question these images. I lived in a village in Bangladesh between 1985 and 1986, and began then to doubt how well writings on 'the situation of women' fitted the ways in which people themselves experienced their lives. I saw how their experience differed from the conventions about what was supposed to happen. In talking with people I often found my concerns and assumptions turned upside-down. The heart of this book concerns the observations I made at that time and on shorter visits since then.

This experience having made me critical of the texts I had read, I began to look beyond the images to the circumstances in which they were produced. No picture or piece of writing stands alone. It is linked, first, with other pieces of work that have dealt with the same subject or taken a similar style. It shares with these certain assumptions, certain points of reference, certain values. Second, in and through this, it expresses something more, something about the social relations that surrounded its production and that underlie the family of works to which it belongs. In technical terms, it belongs to a 'discourse' that defines the kinds of things that can be said, who is speaking and to whom. Such discourse is not neutral: it arises from and reproduces certain relations of power.

An historical example makes this clear. Current debates on gender in Bangladesh are successors to discussion of 'the status of women' in Indian society which emerged as an issue in the context of British colonialism. This drew attention to 'barbaric' acts against women (such as burning of widows after their husbands' death) and the 'backward' state of women's education and integration in public life. A crude (but widely read) example of this was Katharine Mayo's book, *Mother India* (1927). In 1932 Frieda Hauswirth Das, a British woman married to an Indian, published a passionate refutation, sharply satirizing the book itself and the public response that it produced:

A few years ago an occidental woman went all over India in a mad scramble for 'material'. She covered her field kangaroo-fashion in great erratic leaps; she searched dark corners; her eyes saw just what they wanted to see, her heart found just what could quicken it. The rest she, for her purposes, ignored.

This investigator stopped whenever she came across an evil cesspool, pounded the ground with booming noise, turned up her eyes and called the heavens and the wide earth to witness and to condemn such appalling, unparalleled iniquity. "Behold, O my white people. Compared to these Indian sinks our Western cesspools are indeed but heavy-perfume phials!" And a good deal of truth her indictment indeed contained.

The earth listened to her ominous thumping. Breathless shivers of mingled horror and pharisaical delight ran up and down the spine of the entire reading world. Then up rose a mighty cry of vociferous sympathy for the poor far-off victim of this exposed iniquity – for the downtrodden, long-suffering, helpless womanhood of India. More and more emphatic, increasing in credulity and volume grew the asseverations that the kind hand of Western protection and interference could alone mitigate this awful state of suffering, could restrain, guide, and redeem the guilty men and race of India.

Yet a mere three years later, over five hundred of these very women, these much-abused, defenceless, weak creatures, gathered together in Bombay to give the world a drastic little demonstration of just how cowed they were and how abused they felt. But while millions in the West had listened to the kangaroo's resounding indictment and been swayed by it, hundreds only were reached by the direct voice of protest of these Indian women themselves.

Strange to note, the demonstration of these assembled women took the form of protest not against the Tyrant Male of India, but against the Broad Protecting Western Hand. Their timidity wore the garb of sheer defiance: on a certain day they braved the white-officered Bombay police for twelve hours on end. (Das, 1932:1–2.)

As Das so forcefully expresses it, concern with the 'status of women' in Indian society was used to assert British superiority and justify colonialism. The elements she identifies in this are worth noting. Fundamental, is the radical division between those who write and read and those who are written about. On this is built a framework of comparison, whereby (Western) 'we' are contrasted with (Indian) 'them', and the difference is expressed in moral terms. Into this comes a newly arrived Westerner with a pre-set agenda and selective vision, who makes an exaggerated presentation which is immediately accepted by a large (Western) readership. The response of outraged sympathy is hypocritical; it serves to legitimate the West's intervention as self-styled saviour. The ideological character of this is emphasized by the juxtaposition of a large number of actual Indian women, making a protest not against their men, but against colonialism. This is all but ignored, because, first, they lack the same access to publicity; second, their message is not welcome to the people in power; and third, because they are assumed not to be the appropriate people to represent their own interests.

These oppositions are brought out forcefully by Edward Said in *Orientalism* (1985), which shows how the production of Western knowledge about the (Arab) Orient has been intimately tied up with the will to establish and maintain empire. Orientalism, Said says, constitutes: 'a Western style for dominating, restructuring, and having authority over the Orient.' (p. 3)

Mother India is a particularly crude example of this. In general, however, to see writings as belonging to a discourse is not to assume such a simple political instrumentality. Nor does it mean denying individual authors' creativity or the quality of their work. Rather, it is to contest the way literature and culture are presumed 'politically, and even historically innocent' (Said, p. 27). If they are to be understood, texts and the society in which they are written should be studied together. For the writers in that tradition, Orientalism thus represents: 'a set of constraints upon and limitations of thought.' (p. 42) which might be artistically productive, not simply inhibiting (p. 14). What is produced, however, are representations of Oriental culture and society which depend more upon the traditions and conventions of the discourse than on any external point of reference in the Orient itself (p. 22). Above all, the discourse restricts the possibilities for human encounter (p. 328).

I believe that the characteristics Das and Said identify remain present in much writing on Africa, Asia and Latin America today, especially as it relates to women. In this book, these characteristics are explored in relation to debates on the position of women in Bangladesh. The dominant discourse can be challenged in two ways. First, by opening discussions up to allow more women of diverse backgrounds to speak for themselves. Second, by developing a critique of the existing literature, to uncover its bias and make explicit the power relations in and through which knowledge about women is produced.

Ursula Sharma (1985:45) likens social science research to shining a torch around a darkened room: as one object is lit up, others are cast into shadow. I argue that the dominant discourse on women in Bangladesh means that the shadows thrown are not haphazard, they reflect a predominant set of values and interests. There is need, therefore, both to question what is said, to address the debates as they are presented; and to trace the shadows, all that is not said, not even seen, if an understanding of gender in Bangladesh is to move forward.

This book is a contribution towards this. I begin by describing my research in the village, and so the roots of my own sense of 'the situation of women in Bangladesh'. In chapter 2 I introduce the literature on women in Bangladesh, focusing particularly on debates concerning women's work and status. I argue that public discourse concerning gender in Bangladesh is heavily influenced by the national context of aid dependence. 'Women' have a symbolic significance both for international aid agencies and for the various groups that compete for power within the Bangladesh nation state.

By highlighting the politics of discussions of gender in Bangladesh I aim to do three things. First, to break down the artificial focus on 'women', as separate from the broader village community and 'mainstream' debates about rural Bangladesh. This means breaking down the 'separate spheres' of academic discussion and looking at connections across different aspects of village life: how the activities of men and women relate to class and gender divisions and how closely the economic and social are intertwined. Second, in and through this, to consider established debates on women's work and status and to question how well they represent people's own priorities and how they themselves interpret what they do. Third, to argue for a shift of focus from 'women' to gender, seeing gender as a 'contested image' (Poovey, 1989) the content of which is not fixed but variable, continually being defined and redefined by context and interest.

The village case study presented here is an attempt to put these aims into practice. Five chapters describe in turn: the composition of the village community; changing relations between rich and poor with respect to access to land, labour and credit; the trend towards small businesses and involvement of women in market transactions; marriage practices and kin-based links; and women's work, rights and responsibilities in their households. In the final chapter some of the 'shadows' cast by my own study and how it, too, suppresses a number of alternative perspectives are identified. This broadens the focus once more to the wider discourse and indicates how severely this constrains the questions that are asked. Of course, the 'voided questions' I point out have no kind of epistemological priority: there are many more questions that could be asked. This chapter concludes with a more general reflection on the future of gender as a critical focus and a basis for action.

The field research

I was in Kumirpur, ('the village of the crocodile') from October 1985 to July 1986 and a further month in November–December 1986. Before this I spent ten weeks at language school in the south of Bangladesh, and several more weeks deciding on an area and finding a place to stay. While I was out of the village I was able to visit other areas of Bangladesh, including some with women's projects, where I could talk with the staff and learn their perceptions of gender issues. I made short visits back to the village in February 1989 and July 1990.

My original aim was to assess the impact of agricultural development on village women, taking small scale irrigation as an index of technological change. This combination of women and irrigation was aimed to span the divide between 'mainstream' and women-oriented studies, by showing that women, as members of households, are affected by irrigation just as men are. The difficulty in actually operationalizing this focus leads me to suggest a new category – 'desk-sound': to capture the radical disjuncture between the 'logic' of the academic desk and the practicalities of field research.

Being clear that there was no such thing as a 'representative' village, I decided fairly arbitrarily the *upazila* (sub-district) where I would go: there happened to be background data on irrigation there (a study by the Water Master Plan Office which, however, I hardly used) and it suited my main wishes to research in an area without a strong regional dialect, away from a town, or a major road, and without a women's development programme. I was helped to find a place to stay by the non-governmental organization working in irrigation in that upazila. Their logic in this was quite different to mine. Their priority was my safety; their first concern the family, not the village, where I would stay. In fact their selection was in many ways ideal. I stayed with a doctor whose profession meant he had a wide acquaintance; he was of a lower-middle landholding, with some influence in the community but not too strongly engaged in factional disputes; he was Hindu, but had good relations with Muslims; he was a person who commanded wide respect so I was well-protected by being identified with him. In both work and personal terms, the help and care I received from him and his wife were invaluable (they appear as Dhiren and Sukhi in the text).

I began by making an informal survey in an attempt to orientate myself and as a way of meeting people. It was so informal that I had to re-do it three months later. Then I tried to focus more particularly on the effects of irrigation. Unfortunately I found the village women could not see the point of my questions. Anyone could see the crops that were growing. And everyone knows that is men's business. Also, women did not remember how much or when they had done what work. I did not have the resources for a detailed time-use survey, which would have been the only reliable way of gaining the kind of data my research topic required. Rather than give up too easily, however, I spent several months pursuing ingenious strategies for generating material. If they would not tell me how work had changed, I thought, then I should go and sit with them and write down the work they do all day, and interpose the odd 'spontaneous' question, like: 'Did you do this before irrigation?'

This was the first of many steps I needed to retrace. The question I was facing was one that dogged me throughout my research: How do you know what you need to find out before you have found it out?

Penelope, the wife of Odysseus, was troubled by suitors during her husband's absence. She announced that she would marry none of them until the web she was weaving was completed. Each night she then unpicked part of the work she had done during the day. This, above all, is my experience of research. With each stitch what was done earlier unravels, as these new findings show the further questions that needed to be asked, in order to understand more fully the material already gathered.

This applies very much not only to the techniques, but also to the research topic itself. The final argument is a negotiation between the original agenda and the data that is gathered. For example, many sleepless nights were spent worrying that I had gone to the wrong village: that it was too big; too complex with four, different, major communities and a lot of migration; too Hindu, when all my reading had been about Muslims; and showing no evidence of Bengali women being drawn into paid field labour, which the literature told me was the main issue concerning women's work. Over the months of fieldwork, and again in writing it up, I gradually adjusted my thesis to take this into account. Thus the social disruption of migration became an opportunity to view how social relations are constituted; the absence of women working in the fields a chance to avoid the area bias and thus constrained agenda of many studies on women and work.

The research topic contained two quite strong assumptions that I came to question. The first is that technology is the actor, with people the objects acted upon. The second is that the situation of women as it had been was known, all that was needed was to learn how it was changing. I became increasingly critical of the first of these assumptions, and the way it reproduced passive images of women. I came to see irrigation as a resource to which people have different access and which they use in different ways. It is only in this very weak sense that irrigation can be said in itself to have an 'effect'. In the second place, I increasingly realized that: 1) while the 'traditional' situation is assumed as known in much of the literature, there is little rigorous analysis of the relations involved in it; and 2) my reading of the literature had given me no idea of how it felt to be a woman in Bangladesh. Even if the factors of change could be isolated, I could not begin to assess their significance. A much fuller basic understanding was needed before any analysis could be attempted. I needed to get to know some people.

It was this that was the main outcome of my strategy to track down the elusive information on irrigation: staying the whole day with one woman and trying to help with what she did. This was how I got to know Asha, who later worked with me as a research assistant. While she spoke no English, she would chat to ease any strain, laugh, translate my broken Bengali into something intelligible, explain afterwards what in people's answers I had been unable to understand, fill me in on background I would otherwise never have heard about. Her patience, reliability and good humour were a vital support to me – personally as well as in the work. Also, Asha came from a different class (landless) and community (Muslim) than the family with whom I stayed. This clearly helped to balance the composition of my 'natural' social network.

Trying to join in with women's work was thus important to my research, but in no way amounted to 'participant observation' in the classic sense. My foreignness and obvious inabilities – imagine a grown woman who can't wash, change, cook, eat, or even talk properly – made this impossible. Just as important were my sense of time constraints and anxiety to accumulate data. To the end of my stay I was asking questions or at very best directing conversations. It is not easy to make casual remarks in a language you have been learning for a matter of months.

From April 1986 I selected 30 households for more detailed case studies. After spending six months in the village I was able to choose the households in five 'clusters' which were closely related socially and economically. In this way I hoped to analyse both parties in key linkages of employment, share-cropping, loans, and so on, and so get a fuller sense of the relationships between them. This would help identify the different kinds of resource to which different individuals have access. The resources considered were: 'material' – livestock, goods, property; 'personal' – education, business sense, skills; and 'social' – relationships with other people. Putting these together, I aimed to build up gradually a picture of the household spreading outwards to significant relationships with other households, and backwards through time. Through asking questions about women's natal families and daughters who had married away I tried also to get some idea of changes across the generations. In a few cases it was possible to follow this up with visits to daughters in their marital villages. The case studies also differed by class, community, household structure and occupation to give a cross-section of households with whom I had an easy relationship.

For analytical background I drew both on the literature on women's work, outlined in chapter 2, and on the wide-ranging discussions about the local form of class relations in South Asia. These centre on 'the mode of production debate', which attempts to locate the South Asian situation in the terms of Marxist analysis.[1] This debate is not rehearsed here, but its influence has been so dominant in rural social studies that it inevitably forms part of the background to my argument. Out of it arise three key questions: 1) what is the local form of class relations, how significant are vertical (patron–client) and horizontal (class-based) ties? 2) do these links result in the gap between rich and poor widening or narrowing? And 3) to what degree are cross-class and intra-class relations founded in co-operation, and to what degree in conflict?

I approach these questions from the perspective of the household, which typically contains both males and females, in exploring the relations through which it gets its business done. This shows how closely interrelated are social, personal and economic relations and how both men and women participate in each. In this way it shows interdependence between male and female activities, and class and gender relations. Also, by concentrating on how women exercise power, rather than their 'status', the hope is to replace a passive, negative stress on how women are perceived with an active, positive one on how they act, taking account of women's own perceptions and descriptions of what they do.

In the course of a month I worked with a young Hindu man from a nearby village, interviewing owners of irrigation devices and asking the male household heads about land, crops, irrigation, loans, and so on. During this time I also began working with Asha, usually talking primarily with one woman in each household (typically the wife or elder daughter-in-law). I had a check-list of items rather than a form to fill in and this often led on to unexpected discussion – and a gradual evolution of the list.

I planned eventually to cover most aspects of all the items for each of the case study households. This was not always possible: sometimes women were unwilling to discuss some questions; at other times they were constrained by the presence of others, particularly the mother-in-law. We very rarely held a private interview as is the Western research text-book ideal. To some extent of course, the fact that Asha and I were present together meant there was always a kind of 'group' situation. On the whole this probably led to an easier atmosphere than the intensity of one on one. A group gathering often ensured the use of humour, which could be confusing, but was often interesting. Humour between husband and wife, for example, showed a lot of 'consciousness' about underlying patterns in their relationship which direct questions rarely brought out. Humour was also used fairly often to make me realize that my questions were out of line!

As time went on I became increasingly aware of the need for intuition, to be sensitive to the implications of what was said, the framework of understanding which it expressed. What I needed to know – to understand – were not things I could ask about. The use of humour is an obvious example of this: in a very real sense it cannot be explained. I could not ask because what I wanted to know involved attitudes and ways of experiencing things that people were unaccustomed to reflect on, that were in a sense pre-discursive. This is described very well by Giddens (1977:169) in his discussion of ethno-methodology:

> In the active constitution of interaction as a skilled performance, the "silences" are as important as the words that are uttered, and indeed make up the necessary background of mutual knowledge in terms of which utterances "make sense", or, rather, sense is made of them. Tacit understandings are drawn upon by actors as ordinary, but unexplicated, conditions of social interaction.

To a foreign researcher, the usual of 'tacit understanding' seems particularly well-developed in Bengali. A selection of general terms – 'inconvenience' (*osubidha*), 'spoiled' (*nosto*), 'trouble' (*kosto*) – can be given in answer to practically any question, without conveying anything at all to the uninitiated. It is very rude to probe further and usually unproductive (I tried). None the less it is possible to acquire sensitivity. When I returned for my last month in the village I set up group sessions with women in clusters of households, to check back with them my perceptions and have a chance to observe interaction between them. In many cases I could guess the kind of answer that would result from a particular way of pursuing a question.

Overall, then, I tried gradually to build up a picture of women's lives, following lines suggested in the literature, but widening them to get a sense of how things happen, and what that means. Perhaps my key assumption was that it is important to know what really happens, not just what is supposed to happen. This means finding out what happens when things 'go wrong'. This can be extremely sensitive: with women it often relates in some way to sex and so to 'scandal'. This makes such questions difficult for an outsider to ask ('impolite'); and for people to answer (not wanting to show their society in a bad light; a sense that such cases are exceptional; disapproval of 'gossip'; fear that the people concerned will hear that they have told).

Also, it is very difficult to assess the accuracy of stories that are told. Of their nature, the details of such matters are known for sure by only quite a small group. Recommendations of 'street-wise' researchers to check over with others what you have been told become unrealistic and irresponsible. Much of what I heard about things 'going wrong' I stumbled across while concerned with something else. I judged its reliability according to how it was told and by whom, or sometimes by asking someone whose word and discretion could be trusted. In such areas the 'researcher effect' becomes very strong – who you are, who you know, and how you are perceived, result in radically different fieldwork findings.

This goes much deeper than the question of fieldwork techniques: it is an indicator of the conditions of production of the text. First there are academic conventions which favour internally consistent presentations. This weights attention towards culture, 'rules', which people are happier to discuss, are less controversial, and are less contradictory than actual behaviour. Alongside this is a set of unwritten rules (much challenged by feminism) about what constitutes 'proper' topics for discussion. It is therefore not only difficult to ask about 'scandalous' matters 'out there'; it is also problematic to write about them 'back here'.

These underlying features are compounded by specific factors affecting women researchers in a purdah society. There is an anxiety to 'discover the rules' of social behaviour, not just as a social scientist, but also to avoid giving offence while living there. This anxiety – and relief at having got away with it – is very clear in accounts of fieldwork by women researchers in Bangladesh (see, for example, S. Islam, (ed.) 1982). At the same time, doing research necessarily involves activity which is inconsistent with purdah norms – such as moving from house to house – and so produces anxiety about those norms. This affects both Western women concerned to counteract local assumptions of their 'shamelessness', and Bangladeshi women on whom pressures to conform can be particularly acute. The danger is that attention is so focused on the rules that activity which does not obey conventions can be discounted as exceptional – or that the researcher's concern to be 'proper' constrains the kinds of information that people pass to her.

In practice, of course, actual behaviour does not simply reflect what custom or religious texts say ought to happen. Knowing the 'rules' is important, but not because what goes on follow their prescriptions in any simple way. Rather, the rules represent a vital guide for interpreting what happens and for grasping its meaning for the people involved. Social life is about negotiating between cultural rules and calculating options and interests in a series of practical situations. Of course the 'rules' define and circumscribe options, but they do not comprehend them. It is important to recognize the range of actual behaviour and the extent to which the 'rules' themselves are matters of debate within the society studied.

As will be clear from this account, my research combines informal and formal methods. This is not I think coincidental, or something specific to me, but rather reflects the ambiguous position of development studies. This both prescribes the need for quantitative data (such as details of landholding) and values anthropological methods of a more participatory style. The two aims are to some extent contradictory: the drive to get quantitative data can be alienating as people may be unwilling for you to know details, or be unable to remember precisely and become frustrated. On the other hand, fuller 'participation' may preclude the kind of 'hard' data which development studies expect.

Even taken separately these two traditions contain their own contradictions. Precise questionnaire surveys appear to provide a 'strong data-base' but there is often a great gap between this and the means of its production, particularly when these involve collection by 'enumerators' in the researcher's absence. There are many ways to fill in a form! On the other hand, the stresses of being an outsider and the sense of one's own agenda ensure that the researcher is always an observer, rather than participant. I would therefore defend my ambidextrous research strategy, while recognizing that it involved many losses and compromises. On the one hand I was not able to collect the precise data that I should have liked; on the other my externally formed focus clearly alienated me from all sorts of other findings.

Notes

1. For descriptions of this debate see Banaji (1972); Rudra (1978); and Thorner (1982). Key contributions on Bangladesh have been Bertocci (1972); Abdullah et al. (1976); Wood (1978; 1981); A. Rahman (1979); Jahangir (1979; 1982); Adnan (1984). While not participating in the debate as such, Van Schendel (1981) and Jansen (1986) are also written partly in critical response to it.

2. Targeting Women

Introduction

In her study of Victorian England, Mary Poovey (1989) shows brilliantly how gender may be a 'contested image' in society. Ideals of gender are not fixed but variable, they are a matter of debate in themselves, and these debates may also serve as the site of other conflicts. An example she gives of this is how notions about 'woman's nature' served as the currency for exchanges in intra-professional rivalry amongst medical practitioners, in the course of debates about the proper form of attendance at childbirth.

The notion of 'contested image' is an extremely useful one in understanding discussions of women and gender in Bangladesh. There are three dimensions to this, which are often intertwined but need to be distinguished for analysis. First, there are changing ideals of 'woman' which serve as flags for different factions. Fundamentalist Islamic parties' ideal of Bengali womanhood is thus very different from that of the liberal intelligentsia. At one level these differences are about gender. At another, however, gender is simply one means through which the struggle to define Bangladeshi nationhood and, perhaps, capture power in the state, is played out.

Second, there is the use of masculine and feminine imagery in characterizing the nation, or particular groups within it. Examples of this are given by Tanika Serkar (1987) in relation to the movement of Bengali nationalism against the British in the late nineteenth and early twentieth centuries. Serkar shows how British taunts about Bengali effeminacy were nicely inverted as Bengal was invoked as mother, in opposition to the masculine imagery of the British empire as a lion (p. 2011). This was further strengthened as a nationalist icon through recovery of the Bengali tradition of reverence for the goddess Kali, the image of resurgent and anarchic feminine power.

Third, there are the changing parts that actual women and men play in social and political life. As Serkar again shows, the boycott of British goods made the personal political, breaking down conventional divisions between the public and private, so that women spinning yarn for home use became a political act (p. 2013). In the movement of Bengali nationalism against Pakistani dominance in the 1960s, women's dress (*saris*, rather than *shalwar-kameez*),[1] cosmetics (the 'tip' on the forehead which Pakistanis considered to have Hindu associations)[2] and cultural activities (singing, which is disapproved of for Muslim women in Pakistan) similarly became political issues (Kabeer, 1989:8–9). As Serkar points out, men and women moving into unconventional roles tends also to foster reconsideration of the conventions themselves.

In this chapter, gender is considered as a 'contested image' in the public discourse of Bangladesh since Independence was gained. After outlining the ways in which gender issues have figured in Bangladesh state policy, I turn to research on 'the situation of women' in Bangladesh. In both cases consideration is given to how statements need to be read not only for their substance, but also for the ways they express struggles for power in Bangladesh, between the state and different groups in society, and between self-determination and domination from outside. The environment in which these debates take place is one of aid dependence. My contention is that this context has had a highly significant impact on the kinds of issues that are identified, the ways they are treated and the solutions that are proposed.

The second part of this chapter deals with two key substantive aspects of these studies. First, the model of 'separate spheres' which pervades texts on 'the situation of women' is considered. As noted in chapter 1, I argue that the abstraction of 'women' from the wider context significantly obscures the analysis of social inequality. Secondly, the predominant concerns of these texts with 'women's status' and 'decision making' are criticized as being both internally contradictory and extremely difficult to apply in practice. This section thus sets out the framework within which the five case study chapters which follow are presented.

Gender and the Bangladeshi state

After centuries of colonialism under the Moguls (from the sixteenth century to 1757), the British (1757–1947) and the Pakistanis (1947–71), Bangladesh became an independent state in 1971. Now, however, it is overwhelmingly reliant on foreign aid. The Annual Development Plan for 1989/90 was budgeted to have 87 per cent aid funding (Economist Intelligence Unit, 1990:9). The real extent of aid financing may be even greater, since even domestic revenue budgets are reliant on aid: between fiscal 1974/5 and fiscal 1983/4 more than one-third of total revenue earnings came from customs duties and on average more than one-half of imports are funded by aid (Sobhan, (ed.) 1990:7). Aid takes many forms, from generalized 'programme' support to provision of specific commodities. At one extreme are massive projects of multilateral and bilateral donors to strengthen or extend the national infrastructure of roads, bridges or electricity, and at the other hundreds of smaller organizations taking foreign funds to work for the welfare or development of disadvantaged groups.

While couched in the language of human need, aid is a highly political resource for both donors and recipients. Donors allocate aid in accordance with their political and commercial interests; amongst groups as diverse as government ministries, foreign consultants, local contractors and village factions there is fierce competition for access to aid resources.

The relationship between the international donors and the Bangladesh state has been contradictory. In the first place, aid has undoubtedly played a central role in the stabilization of the state, as it eases the need to extract domestic revenues and furnishes the Bangladesh state with resources which can be used to neutralize potential opposition (Hossain, 1979). At the same time, some of the main challenges to the Bangladesh state have been external. Donor 'target group' ideologies, for example, aim to combat the tendency for aid to be used as patronage and to use the administrative system to effect (limited) redistribution of resources (Jahangir, 1989:72).

Post-liberation suspicions in the Planning Commission that aid was likely to compromise Bangladesh's independence quickly gave way to the recognition that the state could not function without it (Faaland (ed.) 1981). The fears were well grounded: aid has undoubtedly played a part in the redirection of Bangladesh away from the early ideals for national autonomy. The commitment of new Bangladesh to its original 'four pillars' of nationalism, secularism, democracy and socialism, was shortlived. Nationalism split into competing interest groups within the country and came under the force of donor pressures from outside. Moves towards socialism – nationalization of key industries and measures to introduce more equitable distribution of assets – were toned down or reversed. Democracy crumbled as the state became more authoritarian, with the presidential militia and then the military taking an increasingly central role. Secularism was the only state principle to survive the first president of Bangladesh, Sheikh Mujibur Rahman, who was assassinated in 1975. This, too, was soon reversed: in 1977 Islam was introduced into the Bangladesh Constitution.

As noted above, discussion of gender can serve as an index to other relations of dominance. Over gender issues, the Western aid community is openly critical of Bangladeshi society, and is deliberately aiming not only to raise economic standards of living, but also to change basic social relationships. Even at the level of symbols there is direct opposition: aid-inspired studies and projects aim to 'bring women out', to redress their 'invisibility'; while the purdah culture (see p. 22) of Bangladesh holds seclusion to be the highest ideal for women. That Bangladesh accepts this intervention is indicative of its client status: consider, for example, the degree of national subordination implied in high profile foreign funded population programmes claiming, as they do, the right to intervene in Bangladesh's most private place, its women's bodies.

The Bangladesh state's approach to gender has been opportunistic and contradictory, but with several constant underlying themes. The first of these is the primary identification of women as mothers and thus their association with biological reproduction. The major thrust of economic planning is still predominantly male oriented. Allocations targeting women's development still amount to less that 0.3 per cent of the total public sector development budget, and women appear primarily in relation to social and welfare sectors. Even in the 1980s, 55 per cent of projects which specify they will work with women are in the area of population control (Jahan, 1989:14).[3]

The second theme is the personalization of problems women face, which camouflages their political implications (Guhathakurta, 1985:84). An important exception to this was made shortly after liberation, when Sheikh Mujib shattered public/private divisions by declaring as *birangona*, war heroines, the thousands of women abandoned and disowned by their families after being raped by soldiers during and just after the liberation struggle.

Predominantly, however, gender issues in public discourse are treated as moral or personal matters. Guhathakurta (1985:83) cites how the minister of Women's Affairs attributed to 'unrequited love' a spate of incidents of acid being thrown in women's faces in the street. To effect their rehabilitation women prisoners are given hair oil and combs (unrestrained hair is seen to indicate moral laxity); a copy of the Koran; a sewing machine (a better way to earn a living); and have marriages arranged for them (ibid.:84). As the extent of prostitution became a public scandal in the 1980s, state programmes for their 'rescue' referred to prostitutes as 'Women in Moral Danger', or the 'Socially Handicapped' (Kabeer, 1989:21, 19). Guhathakurta repoliticizes the issues. Blatant violence against women by the police or army exists, she says, but more prevalent: 'is the tendency to subtly combine coercion with the cultivation of certain moral strictures . . . Decency thus becomes a weapon with which to attack women.' (1985:87).

The third continuing trend in the use of gender imagery in state discourse is the increasing significance of Islam. The second head of state, General Ziaur Rahman (1975–81), introduced Islam and a commitment to fostering international Islamic brotherhood into the Bangladesh Constitution (Jahangir, 1986:80). His successor, President H. M. Ershad (1982–90), followed this up in 1988 by declaring Islam to be the state religion. Women's organizations were foremost in opposition to this move: while debates about the true interpretation of gender in Islam continue, there is no doubt that its political expression in present day Bangladesh acts significantly to curtail women's room for manoeuvre.

The issue here is not primarily religious, but political. Eighty-five per cent of the population of Bangladesh is Muslim. The state secularism of Sheikh Mujib was a political commitment, he was a practising Muslim as a private individual. The shift towards Islam in politics reflects the increase in Saudi Arabian aid. It is also a move to assert a cohesive national identity, while appealing internally to Muslim ideals of *umma*, a religious community which obscures differences of class and interest, which might otherwise become rallying points for political opposition (Jahangir, 1986:78).

This trend towards Islam has been to some degree in tension with the fourth major tendency: the capitalization by the state on the opportunities afforded by the 'discovery' of 'women' by the Western aid community. At another level, however, these moves are congruent with one another: both are calculated to appeal to donors (the United States and Saudi Arabia respectively) and both were used within Bangladesh in an attempt to create a constituency for the party in power.

The 1972 Constitution recognized the principle of gender equality, but few practical steps were taken to achieve this. It was the launch in 1975 of the United Nations International Decade for Women, that made policy on gender a matter of priority. 'Women's issues' suddenly came to represent a new resource through which a range of individuals and groups could gain access to funds and/or social and political recognition. This coincided with the rise to power of General Ziaur Rahman. He signalled his openness to international capital by riding the women-and-development tide, so gaining legitimacy for his rule (Guhathakurta, 1985:81). He established a Ministry of Women's Affairs, a National Women's Organization and increased the number of jobs and official positions reserved for women.

The outcome of these measures serves as a useful warning about the implications of a commitment to women's development being used to advance other agendas. The seats reserved for women in the National Assembly – 15 initially, increased to 30 by Ziaur Rahman – are not open to direct election but are filled by nomination, and have simply been used by the ruling party to increase its majority. The reserved seats have served to launch some women into public life, but their primary impact has been to consolidate the existing political élite. Women are allocated a constituency which covers ten of the men's, so female members of the National Assembly are actually further removed from their constituents than are their male colleagues. Overall, these seats have led to pressure against women standing for general seats, intensified women's dependence on male patronage and meant that women are not taken seriously as National Assembly members of equal value. So blatantly did the Ministry of Women's Affairs and National Women's Organization become vehicles of General Zia's own party interests that they were restructured and sidelined after his death in 1981.

Research on women in Bangladesh

It is not only for the Bangladesh state that 'women's issues' represent a potential resource, but also very much so for the non-governmental organizations (NGOs). The availability of funds for groups working with women clearly affects those groups' activities and philosophies. While the views and commitments of the people working on the ground make a great difference to the impact of funds, whatever the donors' intentions, those views and commitments may themselves change as funds become available. This has various implications. On the one hand, it may strengthen groups already committed to working for gender equality which find funds to take up development activities. On the other hand, NGOs for which gender has not previously been considered an issue find in 'women's issues' a means to expand their programmes and gain access to new sources of funding.

Sometimes these NGOs' commitment on gender remains instrumental. There are many examples of women's programmes that reproduce, rather than challenge, the established pattern of male privilege in access to resources. Thus, the women's programmes have lower budgets overall than those for men. Their aims are modest, comprising 'soft' components, such as very basic instruction in health, culinary and sanitary practices, rather than 'harder' programmes to bring significant economic or structural benefits. Income-generation programmes that are undertaken confirm or introduce women into labour intensive, low profit sectors such as handicrafts or poultry rearing, using very simple – if any – technology. Such programmes can clearly be easily accommodated within an ideology that construes women's work as domestic. Within the NGOs also, the impression that women's development is not as serious or urgent as men's is also confirmed. In other cases women may be able to take advantage of the new opportunities that open up and begin to institute real changes. Amongst the NGOs there are some impressive examples of women's mobilization: women enabled to save themselves and their families from poverty who have gained new self-confidence and social respect; women who have come together to act against unjust legal cases, threats of divorce or demands for dowry, and violence against women, or to press for their rightful pay.

The same ambiguities are seen in relation to writings on the situation of women in Bangladesh. Aid has again had a predominant influence: to put this at its crudest, virtually every text on women in Bangladesh has been funded by foreign aid. A large number of studies arise directly out of or were commissioned directly to inform specific aid programmes. Aid organizations are key consumers as well as sponsors of research; an 'implications for policy' section is virtually obligatory in any study, whether or not it is a 'policy study' as such. This has almost a moral force: the 'need' is so great that any 'purely academic' discussion is self-indulgence, research must advise on what can be done.

Of course, research cannot be reduced simply to its funders' interests, any more than in practice can programmes, and different donors have different philosophies of development and different concerns in research. None the less, the context in which texts are produced cannot simply be ignored. Donors are motivated to sponsor research that will help them make their programmes more effective. Writers of studies on women in Bangladesh – who thereby become 'experts' in the field – have a direct interest in recommending more funding, more programmes, and more research. Studies therefore participate in and sustain aid discourse by their focus, concerns, priorities, the data they collect and the way they construe 'evidence'.

There are several direct implications arising from this. First, especially in the early years of women and development studies, expatriate names predominate. In part this perhaps reflects the donor networks, but more fundamentally it shows the standards of competence that operate. Knowledge of Bangladesh, or even Bengali language, is not a prerequisite for becoming an expert; familiarity with the international discourse is of far greater importance. This puts Bangladeshis at a disadvantage, as they have not had the same ease of access to publications, research funds or such forums as international conferences and journals where the issues are discussed (Alam and Matin, 1984). Even where

Bangladeshi researchers are engaged, they operate in broadly similar relations of production: relatively large funds (though larger for expatriates) available for relatively short pieces of consultancy resulting in a specific publication that relates ultimately to 'development' concerns.

The vast majority of studies are written in English – the language that policy-makers read – and these are disproportionately prominent compared with the smaller number of Bengali publications. As Bengali is now the usual medium of instruction up to university level, this means key studies can be read only by a small élite of Bangladeshi society. Compounding this, many studies are produced for the internal consumption of the agencies or universities that sponsored them, and so are circulated only within a privileged circle of policy-makers or academics. Lack of access to studies published overseas is being mitigated by joint publication between the University Press in Dhaka and various publishers in the West. Even so, the shelf life of small print runs is often short: relatively highly priced books are available in Dhaka in élite outlets for a short period and then cannot be found. All this undermines continuity and chances of a substantial body of knowledge being built up. It also restricts opportunities for the aid discourse orthodoxies to be challenged by indigenous voices with quite different perspectives.

Second, the aid context is shown also in the substance of studies. Many are taken up with presenting quite basic information: they read like an orientation course on women for newcomers to Bangladesh. They present Bangladesh as the world sees it, 'a litany of grim statistics' (Arthur and McNicoll, 1978) which becomes the more woeful when it deals specifically with women. Studies are predominantly descriptive, providing evidence to substantiate a selection of key themes. The stress of the literature is positivist, rather than hermeneutic; most aspire to science, rather than art. In general the thrust has been to develop more systematic techniques, rather than to produce sharper analysis. The primary concern is to quantify what is observed. This is part of a wider system, whereby the vernacular of poorer countries is translated into the international language of aid discourse. Diverse realities across the world are reduced to 'key indicators' which can serve as the basis of comparison to compound, for example, a World Bank league table of 'the poorest countries'. By systematically excluding extraneous factors of cultural specificity, this sustains the facade of 'development expertise' which can be applied the world over with only minor adjustments.

The focus of studies is women, or gender, used as a proxy for women. Here again the context of aid is significant: a focus on women is much more easily developed into a policy initiative. In terms of analysis, however, it means a significant sacrifice of sensitivity to the multiplicity of forms of identity and power relations that gender can express. In aiming to address specific debates studies bracket off a whole range of other social and cultural factors. Religion appears primarily in fairly crude terms as social control. Discussion of Bengali literature, art, media, popular culture or history is rare. There are two dimensions to this. First, it reflects the priority of policy concerns. Second, it reflects the predominance of expatriates, such that many writers do not know either the language or the culture well enough to widen their field of attention, even if they had the interest. As fits their commissioning by aid donors, the motif underlying studies is that of the social technician: if this is done then that will happen.

Development policy, then, appears like a super ego in virtually every work on women in Bangladesh. Views of development and the importance of relating it to women, however, vary substantially. The first view is a quite simple one: development is a good thing and women should have a share in its benefits rather than being simply passed by because of ignorance of their lives. This is the reason given for one of the earliest works in this discourse, T. Abdullah's *Village Women As I Saw Them* (1974:2).[4] She aims, she says, to learn about the 'life-cycle, customs and culture that are associated with the day to day activities of rural women' to bring into focus their 'fundamental problems' which development programmes can then 'be oriented towards solving'.

The theme of invisibility, which studies aim to remedy, is continued in the second view, which predominates now. This holds that the non-integration of women is impeding the development process. Women are an 'invisible resource' (Wallace, Ahsan, Hussain and Ahsan, 1987) the mobilization of which is crucial to the national economy. This approach is reminiscent of the one that says women are important as mothers, because they have responsibility for the next generation. Ideologies about the desirability of feminine self-effacement clearly pervade the development academy as well as the indigenous culture it studies. Thus Wallace et al. (p. 2) state: 'Our aim is not to argue for the emancipation of rural women – that can be left to the "philosophers and social critics".' Rather, 'Our primary aim is the documentation of the contributions, measured in time spent working, made by women in the rural economy.'

The policy implication of their work will stand on its own:

> If the power brokers in Bangladesh . . . have the argument of data rather than emotion available for their interpretation and they fail to better utilise and develop women's work, then they are simply following an outdated and inefficient economic policy.

This statement expresses clearly the ideological character of its avowedly neutral commitment to technical documentation. Its economic reductionism, assumptions of superiority, and the barely veiled threat implicit in it need no underlining.

A related argument, but one with a rather different tone, is presented in Abdullah and Zeidenstein's introduction to their 1982 study, *Village Women of Bangladesh*. Women here are not themselves the resource, but are the means to more efficient resource management: 'The attainment of the priorities of national development in Bangladesh and most developing countries depends on enabling rural women to change their behaviour' (p. 1).

The priorities are to increase food production and lower the birth rate. The achievement of both of these depends on women through, respectively, crop processing and contraception. Studies are needed because:

> programs directed towards rural women cannot accomplish their objectives unless they address the practices of rural women, recognizing what women want, what risks they cannot take, how these risks vary by status and class, and what their culture values. (Ibid:3).

Alam and Matin (p. 3) justly castigate this as: 'a basically manipulative stance towards Bangladeshi women'.

A third, less common perspective does not take such a benign view of development. This holds that the general effects of development are negative for women, as it tends to widen the gap between rich and poor, and involve various other kinds of social dislocation and disruption of traditional values. Lindenbaum (1974), for example, sees the displacement and devaluation of, first, women's work contribution (by labour replacing new technology, and rural to urban migration) and second, their role as mothers (by national aims of population control) as the danger of 'rice-monopoly minded' development strategies. Programmes targeted to women and the poor are needed to combat these negative effects.

The fourth view, and much the rarest, is exemplified by Florence McCarthy (1984a), and her many writings with and without Shelley Feldman over the years. Women become a 'target group', she says, because they remain a largely untapped resource, not yet fully exploited in the non-benign development process (Ibid.:50). The development process involves: 'collusive relations between donor nations and the local state in how to get the most out of a country' (Ibid.:50).

The thrust to incorporate women in the development process followed, first, the recognition that the supply of contraceptives alone was not leading to a reduced birth rate, and the belief that women going out to work or having higher incomes would help achieve this. Second, women's work became of interest because they represent new sources of labour and capital formation (through rural savings schemes) and new potential consumers of capital inputs. Third, targeted programmes may actually preserve social inequality by mitigating some of the negative effects of development, and so defusing potential opposition. Linked to this, the 'separate but equal' philosophy of the target group approach sets up an opposition between men and women which weakens the organizational base for class-based action in the countryside. It also imposes a gender perspective on problems which may not be essentially gender related and so may obscure the crucial problems (ibid.:55).

The changing imagery of Bangladeshi women – from a 'backward' sector 'left out' by development, through 'human resources' or 'resource managers' to the passive 'target' of programmes aimed to reduce their fertility and draw them into capitalist production – originates in the aid community, rather than in Bangladeshi society itself. A comparison with 'women in development' studies in other contexts makes this quite clear.

Caroline Moser (1989:1807) for example, characterizes changes in international development policy towards women as a perspective moving from social welfare, to gender equality, to anti-poverty, to efficiency, to empowerment. In some cases the stages follow one another chronologically, but in most there is a jump from welfare to efficiency. Like other writers (Blumberg and Hinderstein, 1983; Butler Flora, 1983; Buvinic, 1986; 1989) Moser considers the main impulse behind the Women in Development policies to have come from North American feminists. They were able to influence the United States Congress to pass the Percy Amendment, 1973, which specified US bilateral aid should give particular attention to programmes envisaging an economic role for women. They also placed development for women firmly on the agendas of the funding organizations (such as the Ford Foundation) in which they worked.

The Bangladesh story reads like an echo to this. The four approaches I distinguished above clearly arise from very different theoretical positions which have some independence from historical period. Nevertheless, there are three broad phases that can be distinguished in the discourse as a whole. First, from the mid-1960s to the mid-1970s, there were a number of general surveys to counter the perceived ignorance of Bengali women's lives. These tended to be anecdotal in style and to generalize statements rather than tying them to a particular region or economic class. The convention – that continues today – that the lives of women are unknown is itself an interesting one. There are numerous texts dating from the colonial period, on women in India and specifically Bengal. These, however, do not count. Admittedly, they have a predominantly urban and élite focus, but perhaps more importantly, they are outside the development discourse. None the less, it seems strange that 15 years on, Professor Muhammad Yunus, a prominent figure in the Bangladeshi development and academic community, can still write that:

> when it comes to our knowledge about the other half of our society, it is like knowing about the other half of the moon – we know it is there, but never felt an urge to know more about it. (1988)[5]

There is in fact no dearth of descriptions of those aspects of women's lives that aid agencies consider important: their economic activity; education; and health (particularly fertility). The primary problem is not to know more about it but to understand what that knowing means.

By the end of the 1970s the trend was towards more detailed studies of particular issues, or village studies which laid more emphasis on techniques and numerically precise field data. The category women is divided to assess variations by community, age, marital status, position in the family, economic group, region, and so on. Papers continue to discuss 'the situation of women' with relation to the law, religious texts, and education. Shadowing development concerns, however, the two major topics for field study are women's work and fertility; within these the theoretical preoccupations are with women's status and development. For this phase, which is in many ways still the dominant one, most studies therefore fall within the matrix shown below, testing one or more of the variables alongside one or more of the others.

Health (fertility)	Work (economy)
Status (purdah)	Development (policy)

This is, of course, a very reductive way of expressing it. The studies vary widely, with great differences in the degree of sophistication, the care taken in gathering and presenting data, and the degree of account taken of 'intervening variables' (or the wider social context). Also, writers differ in the judgements they make, from those who see women as essentially in harmony with their families and culture, and those who advocate change and see existing relations as founded in power and latent conflict. None the less, in terms of many studies' basic agenda, I think this reductive description is valid. There is a remarkable extent of agreement on what the issues are, and even how to go about approaching them. Data on time use and decision making, for example, are held to be significant across a broad cross section of studies.

In the third phase, gathering pace since the mid-1980s, the dominance of this narrow agenda seems to be beginning to break down – or, at least, crumbling at the edges. This has two aspects. First, studies are being produced on new topics: dowry, prostitution, violence against women, folk religion. The authors of all these works are Bangladeshi researchers (though the funding is still from aid). The second aspect is that there is beginning to be much more thorough-going critical reflection on the wider political context. In *Jhagrapur* (1977:1), Arens and Van Beurden implicitly raise these issues, when they state that they turned away from writing a 'scientific' study for the use of development organizations, government officials, social scientists, and so on, and decided to focus on issues: 'relevant to those who are trying to guide peasants in their own liberation.' (p. 2)

A thorough-going more recent attack is Alam and Matin's swingeing critique of the underdeveloped information base; institutional constraints and ideology of Western experts; and the class membership and ideological leanings of indigenous writers on women in Bangladesh. Writings by McCarthy and Feldman, R. Ahmed (1985), Guhathakurta and Kabeer similarly question the dominant discourse. Doubts and criticisms are, of course, also expressed by many people in a less formal way. Alongside these, there is a growing movement against the dumping of and experimentation with birth control techniques that are banned in the West. As it criticizes the exclusive targeting of women for population control, and the loss, rather than extension, of control that women can have over their own bodies, this clearly demonstrates connections between subordination of women and international domination. This points the way forward: the mystification of its own highly contradictory origins lies at the root of the insubstantiality and analytical weakness of most of the discussion about women in Bangladesh up to now.

Separate spheres?

To look at the politics of development discourse is to introduce the centrality of power to any analysis of social relations. It is in its avoidance of discussing power that the fundamental weakness of the literature on women and development lies. As Alam and Matin (pp. 5–6) state, the social contexts of both expatriate and élite Bangladeshi researchers militate against analyses which give power a central place, and so identify change in terms of conflict, rather than the essentially consensual paradigm of development. The model of separate spheres, which acts as a predominant motif in writings on women in Bangladesh, has played a crucial part in obscuring the political aspects of gender.

There is some variation in how the model of separate spheres is applied but essentially it relies on a number of polarities: men occupy the public sphere, women the private/domestic; men are concerned with the market, women with the family; men's roles are instrumental, women's expressive/affective; relations between men are political/economic, those between women personal/social. This has two dimensions. First, it is claimed to reflect the empirical reality of rural Bangladesh and the division between male and female worlds. Second, it has become the reality in academic studies, as mainstream development texts continue to focus on men and their lives outside the home – amended, perhaps, with a paragraph of apology – and research concerned with women, or even gender, virtually excludes men, and therefore wider debates on the constitution of society. The separate spheres model thus reifies perceptions of gender difference, but inhibits, rather than promotes, any investigation of how this is sustained.

The institution of purdah (literally, 'curtain', or 'veil') plays a significant part in sustaining separate spheres imagery. In purdah, the gender division of labour is grounded in values of honour (*izzat*) and modesty or shame (*lojja*) expressed in the ideal of female seclusion. Along with the organization of work and family, purdah exemplifies what Edholm et al. (1977:119) see as a key characteristic of gender divisions of labour: 'an affirmation and reification of difference, of otherness'.

Ideologically it is intermeshed with fear and distrust of women's powers of sexuality and fertility. This is expressed in Islam by association of women with *fitna*, disorder (Mernissi, 1984:44), and in the Hindu cult of *Shakti* which recognizes the feminine principle as the source of power, appearing variously as mother (as Shashthi) and destroyer (as Kali). In material terms, purdah legitimates and facilitates the use of female family labour and sexuality while also restricting women's control of what they produce. In Bangladesh it has historically been associated with a system of family farms where crop storage and processing work within the homestead was a vital part of subsistence production. This situation is now found only amongst middle stratum village households; which, accordingly, tend to be the most orthodox in purdah observance.

The ideal of seclusion could only ever be observed by a tiny proportion of women – those whose families could afford to keep a small army of domestic staff. The practice of purdah differs over space and time, and by religion, caste, class, family, education and age. In Bangladesh at present, change is occurring at both ends of the social scale: increasing numbers of women are being pushed by poverty to seek work outside the homestead; higher class women are attracted by new opportunities or rising aspirations for consumption into taking salaried employment. They say that: 'Purdah is a state of mind' (McCarthy and Feldman, 1984:954) and express their modesty by keeping to certain areas, covering their heads and bodies and behaving with decorum in mixed company. As material conditions alter, so forms of articulating purdah shift. It is important not to assume that this indicates a decline in the importance of purdah, although it may in some cases. Overall, the power of purdah is the power of a myth, not in the sense of being unreal or untrue, but as a symbolic expression of relations between male and female, with simultaneous ideological and material dimensions.

The purdah motif is replicated in social science studies: the veil is drawn between men and class on the one side, and women and status or gender issues on the other. This occurs at two levels. First, the closeness of fit between the separate spheres model and the culture of purdah means the model may itself be read as reality. The idea of the market and the form of male participation in it, for example, become so closely associated that women are simply not seen in the public sphere, or men in the home, because their involvement takes a different style. The model thus becomes self-perpetuating. Second, there is beyond this an unspoken assumption that empirical segregation and specialization of tasks by gender correlates to different kinds of meaning in what is done. Women are not only centred on the home, but this is where the significance of what they do lies – in terms of their status or decision-making power. The converse is true for men, who are characterized primarily not by their gender or family role, but by their class. While men are immediately in the arena of power and (at least latent) conflict, therefore, women are predominantly characterized within an apolitical framework.

In most of the discussion of 'the situation of women in Bangladesh', power is referred to only obliquely. Studies of the practice of power consider decision-making; theoretical concerns are with female status. The idea is that as women's status rises (typically with greater economic participation) they will have increasing decision-making power especially in relation to economic matters. Findings may thus compare before and after patterns, or contrast households where women are in paid employment and those where they are not. Tables are drawn up to show on which issues women decide alone, which men decide, and on which they decide together. Again, this is not specific to Bangladesh. The extensive USAID survey of the status of women in Nepal, for example, also relied on this framework (see, for example, Acharya and Bennett, 1983).

There are numerous practical problems with both status and decisions as foci for analysis. First, decisions are simply not accessible. They are made through complex processes, perhaps over an extended period, and may involve diverse negotiations of interest. It is very hazardous to weigh the importance of different factors, which are rarely all conveyed in the reasons given for what was done, and even the people involved themselves often have very different views on what took place. Methodologically, it is sounder to concentrate rather on what is done and how – livestock bought or sold or given to be tended by others; businesses managed; marriages arranged. . . . The key is to ask about particular instances, rather than general questions, which tend to produce just conventional answers.

Second, a stress on decision-making assumes that actions issue from choices by individual actors. This prejudges questions of social identity that should be a key focus for exploration in gender studies. Also, if true at all, this notion of choice holds only for a narrow, privileged sector, even in a society with considerable confidence in its technical competence to influence its environment. It clearly does not fit perceptions of fate which are so widely found in peasant societies. In village Bangladesh, reasons for action are more often expressed in terms of obligation than as matters for personal choice. Further, a stress on decisions fails to take account of the way that power determines whether and which decisions should be made, not only who does the deciding. Power inheres not only in open conflict but in manipulation, authority and the social construction of people's wants (Lukes, 1974). Whether or not there is a choice, or thus decision, is crucially prefigured first by poverty, and second by gender.

Theoretical discussion of women's position is similarly confused, as it derives from the fusion of two traditions. In the first place, its origins are in the status of women debates; in the second place it takes key reference from discussion amongst feminists in the West, which reflect Marx's and Engels' stress on the centrality of private property and 'productive' labour. The legacy of a concern with women's status has blunted gender analysis. First, as noted in chapter 1, it has been used as an index for making a moral comparison between different societies, and so has fostered racism and imperialism. Second, it renders women passive, by emphasizing how they are perceived, not what they do. Third, it lays stress on culture, on what society says about how things are supposed to happen, rather than looking at actual behaviour, which may be quite different. This gives a passive picture of women, as though their lives are simply determined by social norms. Fourth, it treats women as a single category. This writes in gender as the fundamental difference, and inhibits exploration of the differences between women, which strengthens their exclusion from class analysis. Underlying all these points is the identification of gender relations as ideological (status) rather than rooted in material conditions.

The addition of analysis derived from Engels has only served to heighten confusion. The key point is Engels' (1972:137–8) belief that women's entry into waged labour is a precondition for greater gender equality – though he does not state that all gender inequality will thereby automatically disappear. This has led to the conviction that women's low status results from their exclusion from productive labour, or more recently, from the lack of recognition that their productive work receives. Getting women out to work, then, becomes the key to raising female status in Bangladesh.

There are numerous problems with this. Not least is the point, well demonstrated by studies all over the world, that for women to enter the labour market does not automatically dissolve gender inequality. Rather, women typically enter the market on terms different from men's (because, for example, of continuing domestic responsibilities) and in any case divisions within the market itself reflect, reproduce and even intensify structural inequalities by gender. There are further difficulties specific to the purdah culture of South Asia. As noted above, seclusion of women represents the cultural ideal. At least until recently, women going out to work has been evidence of – and a factor contributing to – the low social status of their households. Partly because of this, women themselves would typically choose to work within their own homesteads – except for a middle-class, mainly urban minority, women go out to work only when they are too poor to care about this mark of social status.

Analytical use of the term 'status' is thus in direct opposition to its practical usage: the factor that analysis interprets positively as signifying higher female status (women going out to work) is seen by women themselves and their communities negatively as indicative of low social status. In terms of policy, some striking double-think results from this assumption that going out to work is, in itself, good for women. In 1989, an NGO newspaper, for example, featured a picture of women squatting at the roadside breaking bricks in the burning sun for a pittance, and heralded this as a sign of progress.

There is a further aspect to this confusion between two traditions. The reasoning goes as follows: 1) women's outside work is an indicator of higher female status; 2) it is mainly women in poorer households who work outside; 3) therefore there is more gender equality (higher female status) in poorer households (lower social status). Assumptions about household structure back this up. Joint households, which are more common amongst the rich, are seen as more restrictive for women. The greater specialization of tasks possible within them is assumed to mean women are more excluded from major decisions, which is a second factor taken as a proxy for female status. None of this results from the careful exploration of actual cases of poor and wealthier households and the room for manoeuvre that their members have, let alone those people's own estimations of what is desirable. However, the contradiction that female status is higher in poorer households is widely noted. At the very least this suggests a tension between the interests of gender equality and of economic advancement. At worst, the implication may be drawn that, in some sense, poverty is good for women. This alarming implication has never, to my knowledge, been seriously brought out and challenged.

Conclusion

To maintain that foreign aid has had a highly significant impact on the way that gender has figured in public discourse in Bangladesh is not to assume any simple opposition between outside intervention and some kind of indigenous culture. On both sides there is considerable diversity, controversy, conflict and manipulation of the issues to suit particular ends. It is not true that local gender relations are set and specifiable, as many 'women and development' approaches assume. Rather, gender is a 'contested image' also within Bangladesh society, and external intervention articulates and integrates with this.[6]

To view gender as a contested image moves the focus away from women and on to the ways in which women and men can shift and manipulate definitions of identity in accordance with their own interests. This breaks down the categories of 'women' and 'men' conceived in essentialist terms as either complementary or in opposition to one another. It also resists any identification of women as passive victims, and frees the study of power in gender relations from its predominantly negative associations. In place of seeing people as individuals or in gender groups this approach makes space to recognize the flexibility of identity, where people may conceive of themselves primarily in relation to others, including on grounds of love and affection. In addition, it brings gender out of the family (and so does the same for women) and into the politics of community and nation state.

To redirect analysis of gender in this way is not simply a matter of academic integrity. Nor is it only a question of political concern, that the apparently radical commitment to gender issues should not be a means for expressing and reinforcing relations of domination, as in historical status of women debates. It is also central to sound development policy. The subservience of academic to policy discourse weakens both: it severely narrows the basis for distinguishing which issues are locally significant and how. Much of the argument here is applicable also to studies without a gender focus: the women of Bangladesh stand for their country as a whole in its widespread promotion as a 'development problem'.

Notes

1. Loose trousers and a long shirt worn by adolescent girls in Bangladesh and by adult women in Pakistan and parts of North India.

2. Combined with red colouring in the centre parting of her hair, a red tip indicates marriage in the case of Hindu women, but a tip is often worn simply for ornamentation by Bangladesh unmarried Hindu girls or women as well as Muslims and Christians.

3. Rounaq Jahan is here quoting Teresita Schaffer (1986) *Survey of Development Projects and Activities for Women in Bangladesh*, Dhaka, USAID.

4. Bengali edition 1966; English translation (Ford Foundation) 1974.

5. Foreword to Khan (1988) *The Fifty Percent: Women in Development and Policy in Bangladesh*, quoted by Westergaard (1989a:3).

6. See also McGregor (1989).

3. The Village of Kumirpur

Introduction

It took a while to find my way around Kumirpur. At first, it seemed like a random collection of houses, all solid mud structures, some larger than others, some with two storeys, most with thatched roofs and some with tin. The large pools, used for bathing and washing clothes and dishes, were key reference points, as was the road which flanked the village to the north, a broad mud track running roughly parallel with a canal a few hundred metres further away. Otherwise, all seemed variable. I arrived in October, just as the monsoon was ending and each day, it seemed, new paths appeared as small pools shrank and dried to nothing. As moving around became easier, the village seemed much more open and spacious. At the same time, I came to see just how many households fitted into the areas between the few houses which I had come to know; how densely people were living together. There was a sharp contrast between the closed compounds behind high mud walls within which people lived and how, passing through a sparse fringe of trees and bamboo, I would suddenly find myself out in the open, surrounded on all sides by fields thick with brilliant green paddy (rice).

As the puddles dried away and the land became firmer, so different boundaries of the village gradually became clearer. There was no centre of the village as such, but a number of different centres around which I came to see houses were clustered in *paras*, or neighbourhoods. Socially, each had a quite distinctive character, despite the fact that spatially they overlapped and ran into each other. Figure 3.1 shows a map of the village.

This experience of the village gradually emerging as I came to understand more of the divisions between people and the ways in which they were linked continued throughout my stay. At the same time, however, the village was itself changing. There were five new houses built while I was there, and three households left to move elsewhere. Loss of land or the death of the male household head (quite often the second is followed by the first), quarrels or scandal, push households to move; availability of employment or share-cropping land pull to in-migration, usually where there is already some kin connection. New people are constantly joining the village on an individual basis, usually women, and some men, at marriage. There are also a few men

Figure 3.1
The village of Kumirpur

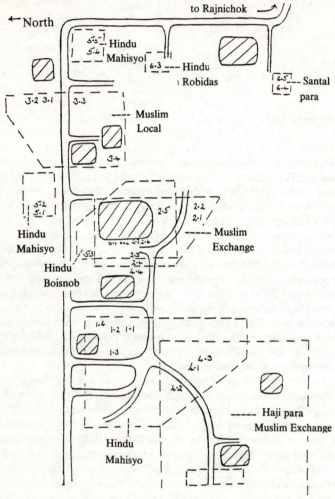

Key   ▨ = Pool   ⌐ ¬ = Community

Numbers show location of case study households

who have come to Kumirpur for business and then married into the village. Not all migration is permanent of course – migrant labourers come for the harvest, students or masters at the local schools stay as lodgers with wealthier households.

Alongside these individual moves, the underlying political balance between the different communities was also shifting. There are in the village four major communities: two Muslim (one of local origins and one of migrants from West Bengal); two Hindu (one agricultural and one artisan caste). There are also a small number of lower caste Hindu households, and some Santal households (a non-Bengali ethnic group) who live just outside Kumirpur, but have extensive economic links in the village. Economic and social mobility of particular households is tied up with the history of their community, and this in turn, with developments within Bangladesh as a whole. To describe the neighbourhoods as I came to know them, therefore, it is necessary to sketch something of the wider historical background in which they have taken shape.

Historically, the Kumirpur area was dominated by Hindus. Up until 1962 it was ruled by Hindu *jomidars*[1] (large landlords), and tales are still told of their vices and virtues, the splendour in which they lived. A generation ago, Kumirpur was a Hindu village, with one small Muslim neighbourhood. In 1947, however, when India was divided, East Bengal (the area now known as Bangladesh) became part of the new Muslim state of Pakistan. Following Partition there was large scale migration between the two countries and many wealthy East Bengal (then East Pakistan) Hindu families moved across the border into (Indian) West Bengal. This communal migration still continues, though now it has slowed to a trickle. For Kumirpur, the crucial period was 1965–67, when a government programme encouraged Hindus to leave East Pakistan, and exchange their land with Muslims from West Bengal. The prime migrants were the richest households. All Kumirpur's richest Hindus were thus replaced by *ripozi* (refugee) Exchange Muslims. While they form only 44 households or 19 per cent of the village population, they have become the wealthiest and politically most dominant community in Kumirpur.

More recent developments have reinforced these patterns. The shift towards Islam at state level has made itself felt locally also. In the parliamentary elections of 1986, Jamaat-i-Islam (a fundamentalist Islamic party) was elected to represent the constituency to which Kumirpur belongs. At the same time, each successive government has aimed to increase national integration with a stronger state presence in the rural areas. In 1982, therefore, the basic administrative units were upgraded from thanas (police stations) to upazilas (sub-districts) and endowed with a new sub-stratum of local government offices. Although cynics say that the main impact of this has been to introduce a new level of corruption into the state apparatus, there is no doubt that it does represent new resources coming to the rural areas, and so new opportunities for the wealthier (particularly) to exploit.

The state has also drawn in the rural areas through economic initiatives. Particularly since Independence the national objective to increase grain production has brought new technology in the shape of mechanized irrigation and rice hullers, chemical fertilizers and pesticides and high-yielding varieties of seed into the villages. The implications of these in Kumirpur society is discussed in more detail in subsequent chapters. The point to note here is that these developments have broken down the relative autonomy of the rural areas. Farmers have come to rely on agricultural inputs from outside: state suppliers (such as the Bangladesh Agricultural Development Corporation, BADC), non-governmental agencies or private merchants. In the 1980s the aid community under the leadership of the World Bank put pressure on the state to hand more of its functions over to the private sector. The part played by private suppliers is thus increasingly important. Whether private or public, however, all of these serve to integrate the villages more closely into the nation state and the systems of international capital which it embraces.

This expansion of traffic between the village and the town is quite tangible. Kumirpur lies in Tanore upazila in Rajshahi district, in north-west Bangladesh, 25 miles to the north of Rajshahi town. Until recently, Tanore has been a relative backwater, not somewhere you go to on the way to anywhere else. For the past generation, the promise of a metalled road has been the most frequent pledge of visiting dignitaries. Even now, the upazila centre has the feel of a wayside stopping place, glorified by the few new blocks of government offices. During my stay, however, the main road from Rajshahi was bricked over up to the upazila headquarters (four miles south of Kumirpur). When I arrived in October 1985, only one person in Kumirpur had a motorbike, by the time I left, three more had been bought. In 1985, there were two buses a day to the upazila, when I returned in 1989, buses were going hourly.

Neither is increased communication limited to the road. During the rainy season, both passengers and goods travel by the Shibonodi river. The relatively established launch service is now supplemented by country boats powered with irrigation pump engines. A single electricity line runs parallel to the road as far as the upazila centre (and its government offices). There are two televisions in Kumirpur (run on car batteries) and radios can be found even amongst the very poor. Increasingly, developments at the local level are closely articulated with currents that move within the nation state.

The influence of this is not restricted to the public sphere. Changes in dress also reflect the state's reliance on international capital and the shift towards Muslim dominance. Women still wear the traditional saris, though the cloth is less coarse than it used to be. Western influence is more evident in men's and children's clothes. Little boys wear shorts, and little girls, knickers or dresses. Younger, educated men usually wear trousers outside their homes, as do most men with office jobs. Most men wear a tight vest, and then perhaps a Western style long, loose fitting shirt (*punjabi*). As the state becomes more Islamic, so punjabis are becoming more common. Almost all Hindu men in Kumirpur have now stopped wearing the traditional Hindu dress (*dhoti*) for general use, and instead wear the *lungi* on their lower halves – a garment formerly common only among Muslims.[2] After childhood, girls wear the formerly Muslim *salwar-kameez*. Perhaps due to the history of Hindu dominance, still only a small minority of (wealthier) women in Tanore wear a *burqa* (long Islamic overdress, covering head to foot) even for travel.

Poor diet, exposure to the elements and accidents mean that health problems are very common: more than one in four children die in childhood.[3] Many still rely on the folk healers who seek to divine causes rather than make a physiological diagnosis. A charitable dispensary for the area was set up in the nineteenth century by a beneficent local jomidar, but since the mid-1960s there has been a gradual expansion of health services, with an upazila (formerly thana) health complex, a growing number of 'quack' doctors (three in Kumirpur) with a mixture of homeopathic and allopathic remedies, government clinics – including for birth control – and private dispensaries. Of course, access to these facilities varies according to class and gender. Although government hospitals are formally free, in practice patients have to pay to receive treatment and this (and their poor reputation) certainly keeps people away. Drugs are often over-prescribed, they may be very expensive and have no guarantee of success. Jorgensen (1983) states that women are less likely to receive formal medical treatment, both because their problems are not thought of as 'disease' and due to a sense that they are not worth spending on. Women's access to medical care is also restricted by modesty norms which limit their mobility and make it difficult for them to approach male doctors.

There has also been significant expansion in formal education. In 1975 literacy in Bangladesh was measured at 29.9 per cent among males, and 13.7 per cent among females. At all levels enrolment in schools is lower for girls than for boys and the drop-out rate is higher (Ahmad, 1985). Explanations in terms of purdah are clearly undermined by the flexibility of purdah practice. Probably more serious have been ideals of girls' ignorance and submission, their early marriage, and limited opportunities for employment while still in their parents' home. There are, however, marked changes over time. Of the senior generation in the case study households (grandparents), only two men studied up to Matriculation (Class 10, GCSE) and one woman up to Primary Pass (Class 5). All of these are in the wealthiest class. No one of this age group in the other classes has more than basic education.

In the present middle generation of the wealthier households (parents) the picture is significantly different. Most men are educated up to Matriculation, and most women to Primary level. Three of the men have studied to Bachelor degree level. All school-age children go to school, though girls are often withdrawn earlier, for reasons including to be married. Many of these wealthier households engage a private 'master' (often a boy studying at the local Intermediate college) to give their children extra tuition. Very few parents amongst the poor have any education. Their children are still less likely to go to school, and drop out earlier. Those who are a little better off, however, typically place a high priority on education for their children.

Reflecting this increased demand, during my stay the local Intermediate (sixth form) College was upgraded to BA level, and the principal was working very hard to get government recognition. Registration for Matriculation (GCSE) and Intermediate examinations rapidly increased. This is certainly evidence of the growing importance of formal qualifications, but does not necessarily reflect a rise in education: as throughout the education sector in Bangladesh, students rely on lax adjudication to consult notes, or even friends outside the hall, in order to pass their examinations.

All this means that the coming of the Exchange Muslims to Kumirpur coincided with the coming of new resources to (and the expansion of means to extract resources from) the rural areas of Bangladesh. When they first arrived, the Exchange Muslims made overtures of alliance to the Local Muslims. They were hostile to the newcomers and the two still live quite separately, and worship in separate mosques. There are three particularly prominent kin groups among the Exchange Muslims, who each come from a different district of West Bengal. They are: the Hajis; the Mondols; and Sajjur's. Each of them has used a somewhat different strategy to strengthen their position in the village. The first element of this is migration. To a greater or lesser extent, all of them have gathered around them a number of satellite households: people who had been dependent on them in India and others who, knowing of them, came to Kumirpur when they fell on hard times elsewhere. As a result the class structure of the Exchange Muslims is relatively polarized. The dominant households are very wealthy and almost all the middle income households were formed by sons separating off to set up households of their own. The poor form a sharp contrast: many have virtually nothing of their own, they are dependent on their patrons even for the land on which their houses are built.

In South Asian social science, the term 'community' is typically reserved for Hindu/Muslim communal difference. My usage is less restricted: in general I use community to refer to a clear social group such as the Exchange Muslims, or a Hindu caste group, emphasizing Hindu/Muslim dynamics as such only when these seem particularly important. This comes midway between the social science usage and the Bengali word for community, *somaj*, which refers to the unit which regulates social order, by means of its leaders and community hearings – *bichar* or *salish*. For Hindus this normally corresponds to their caste group, for Muslims those who come from a certain area, recognize a common leader, or worship in a common place. It is difficult to be more precise than this – as in any such group, functions vary and disputes may lead to sub-divisions or new alignments. Somaj in Kumirpur are very unstable – as one elderly villager remarked: 'One day they're together, the next day they separate'. This is particularly true among the Hindus. The predominant (Mahisyo) caste have now divided into three somaj, all with a different leader, and none without internal dissent. The Exchange Muslims are also divided into two.

Although their community is an important part of people's identity, it does not necessarily define their economic and social relationships. The closest this comes to being true is in Haji para, which over the last 20 years has become almost exclusively occupied by the Haji *gusti* (patrilineal kin group) and its dependent households. In 1986 three Hindu households actually moved from this neighbourhood to another part of the village, because they felt so uncomfortable at being communally isolated. Another Hindu household sold up to an incoming member of the Haji gusti and migrated to India. The Hajis themselves are two elderly brothers (a third died but his wife and family remain) who have earned the honorific title by making the Haj pilgrimage to Mecca. This indicates the priority they give to Islam: they have founded a mosque, one of their sons is in charge of its finances, they also pay the salary of a religious teacher and two of their other sons teach in religious schools. Their mainstay is still agriculture – they have, together, the largest landholding in the village. Alongside education, however, they are now branching out into business enterprises. Except for harvesting times, virtually all the Hajis' employees come from their own community. Within the village, Haji para is a byword for militant Islam.

Sajjur's kin group is made up of his own joint household – his parents, he and his brother and their families – plus his two sisters and their husbands and families. Sajjur himself is basically a landowner, but his (less wealthy) brothers-in-law and their sons have taken up small businesses and clerking jobs. They do not belong to the Hajis' somaj. In India their somaj stretched over three villages and when they migrated they grouped themselves in a similar way in Kumirpur and two neighbouring villages. As a result, though they keep close relationships with some dependent households from their India days, there are rather few client households from their own somaj in Kumirpur. To compensate, they have formed close links with the Hindu households which live around them. In effect, they have inherited the relationship cluster of the Hindus who used to live where they live now. In one case, Sajjur even provided land for a destitute Hindu family who claimed him as their *Mama* (maternal uncle) as Sajjur's predecessor in the house had been. This does not mean the absence of communal feeling – Sajjur's somaj all supported the Jamaat-i-Islam party in the 1986 Parliamentary election. This is rather an anomaly though; in general, Sajjur's group have the reputation for being devout, rather than militant, in their adherence to Islam.

The Mondols' strategy is different again. They belong to the Hajis' somaj, though they conflict on most issues. In Kumirpur, there are two senior brothers, plus their families and a nephew, Tozimember. As his name suggests, their nephew is a member of the Union Council, the committee for local government.[4] This reflects their orientation towards the wider area: their power base lies beyond the village, with more of their kin elsewhere in Tanore, and two sons in Rajshahi town. They draw a great deal of strength from these wideranging links, and are much in evidence in all local affairs. Within Kumirpur, the Mondols have made considerable efforts to foster links with the Hindus, to the extent even of adopting one as their fictive son.[5] While still deriving the main part of their income from their extensive land-holding, they are primarily interested in seizing the new opportunities for agriculture-related businesses. As a result, they have much looser patronage links than either of the other two.

While the Exchange and Local Muslims operate quite separately, to some extent the shift towards Muslim dominance has carried the formerly embattled, small Local Muslim community in its wake. There are now 38 Local Muslim households who make up 17 per cent of the village overall. They have a long tradition of petty trading (such as spices) and have expanded into new technologies. Their community is the nearest to the traditional type, with a close fit between social and economic links and somaj ties. Amongst the Local Muslims, the dominant household is Akhbar's, his father is head of the somaj and its major patron. While they belong to the gusti that has long been dominant, it is only in this generation that their branch has been in the ascendant. Their gusti is less cohesive than the others, they relate to each other more as rivals than with a joint strategy. Akhbar's father began quite humbly but was lucky in inheriting land from a childless uncle. He strengthened his bid for centrality by marrying his daughter to her cousin, who was the son of the former leader of their somaj. Akhbar's household has since further consolidated its wealth by taking full advantage of opportunities to exploit new technologies, irrigation and rice mills. As his father now draws away from centre stage, Akhbar moves in to it.

This shift is an interesting example of how leaders emerge. It has two main dimensions. On the one hand, Akhbar is working to establish himself: turning his back on his wild youth, he shows respect to influential neighbours and cultivates a new gravity of manner. On the other hand, the other community leaders give him responsibilities (such as chairing a community hearing) which show that they recognize him as one of themselves. Even in the community which has been least disrupted by migration, dominance is thus achieved, not simply ascribed. Although the vertical links of patronage relationships are very important in the establishment of power, the horizontal dimension of acceptance by the other rich and powerful should not be forgotten. Though they may conflict on specific issues, there is undoubtedly some level at which these men have interests in common. At the very least, their mutual recognition helps sustain the patterns of dominance by which they all profit. The analogy between dominance by gender and by class is clear here – relations between the rich sustain inequalities of wealth, just as relations between males sustain those of gender. As in this case, relations between those who are both rich and male help reproduce both forms of dominance.

Since the coming of the Exchange Muslims, the Hindus (62 per cent of households) have been in disarray. There are two major Hindu communities in Kumirpur and two much smaller low-caste Hindu groups. The largest community is the Mahisyo caste; they make up 103 households or 45 per cent of the village population. Like the Exchange Muslim community, they depend mainly on agriculture but also increasingly take up small businesses. They are the only Hindu caste with sufficient wealthier households to have any significant internal patronage relationships. Even so, the Mahisyos have only one very wealthy household, that of Kangali Serkar.

Kangali Serkar began as a poor share-cropper, and has not made many friends in his accumulation of wealth. His only brother died young, and his parents also died before his marriage. The prime focus of his household is agriculture. Their strategy of self-exploitation – that is, work done by household labour whenever possible – is very different from the traditional style of the Hindu rich, in which status is expressed in leisure. Even so, Kangali Serkar's household position as the only one of the Hindus to have substantial resources means that he is looked to by the poor of his community. One of his five sons is a school teacher, and through him the family is spreading wider links and, in particular, aiming to become a focus for Hindu consciousness.

The second large group is the ritually higher but poorer, Boisnob caste, with a tradition of involvement in small businesses (mainly snack-making). They make up 31 households or 13 per cent of the whole. They have only one middle income household, and none that is very wealthy. While some households are more socially and politically dominant, the divisions between them do not have the same economic force as amongst the Mahisyos or the Muslims. For employment, most have to look outside their own community. There are, in addition, three Bhoimali metal-worker and four Robidas shoe-maker households – the women of both these communities work as midwives. Also included in my study are seven Santal households who live just outside the village proper but have employment links with Kumirpur villagers.[6] The Santals have their own language and culture. This particular group is very isolated and fragmentary, with a fluctuating community that swells at key labour times around a stable core of two or three households. There are more Santals in other villages nearby, and particularly to the west of Tanore where they include some major landowners. The Kumirpur group, though, is very poor, and all its adult members work as agricultural labourers.

In regard to gender relations, the differences between the communities in Kumirpur are not as great as might be expected. The culture of male dominance pervades them all, although it is less pronounced amongst the lowest caste Hindus and the Santals. There are some differences in Hindu and Muslim observance of purdah. Muslim women's mobility outside the homestead tends to be more constrained; Hindu women should practise strict avoidance of older male affines, even within the homestead.[7] The women in the Hajis' households are probably the most constrained. This reflects the very strict domination by the older Hajis themselves, over the younger men as well as the younger women in their family group. The mobility of the women in Akhbar's household is similarly very restricted, while those in the Mondols' and in Sajjur's kin groups are somewhat freer. Purdah norms tie Kangali Serkar's daughters-in-law less tightly to the homestead but the amount of work they have to do ensures that in practice they have little opportunity to visit other households.

While there are thus some differences by community, the most significant factors in shaping gender identity are age and stage of the life-cycle.[8] There is remarkable congruence in the relations these prescribe across class and community (see chapters 6 and 7). Beyond this, observance of purdah differs predominantly by class. Across all the communities it is women of poorer households whose work necessitates them going out of the homestead more and further away, and they consequently attract much less criticism both within their own households and from the community at large, when they do.

Classing the village

Cutting across communal difference, class distinctions in Kumirpur are very striking. I identified four classes in the village, on criteria of wealth and stability. At first I felt Kumirpur to be unusually wealthy, because almost all the houses that caught my eye were the larger, impressive ones of the more prestigious villagers. Perhaps initially (certainly not later) the wealthier were also more ready to make moves towards me and invite me into their homes. Differences in wealth are quite obvious through dress, manner and physical build (fatness stands for good health and prosperity in village Bangladesh). While the respect a person commands is to some degree a question of their family and individual character, significant political influence is very closely associated with economic strength.

The use of 'class' terminology to characterize rural society in South Asia has been a central issue in the dominant mode of production debate and other writings on rural society that have been influenced by it. While not entering this debate, it is important to note a number of points that have been raised. First, some writers maintain that household situations are too diverse to identify classes. Household social and economic mobility is very common. Even over the household life cycle significant changes in resource position may occur. Households are typically at their strongest economically when sons are old enough to earn an adult wage. Rapid economic decline, however, may result from the need to give dowries at daughters' marriages, ill health, fraud and division of the household when sons and their families leave to set up on their own. In his study of peasant mobility, however, Van Schendel (1981) points out the 'cumulative effects' of economic advantages and disadvantages. The high degree of inter-category mobility of particular households has not resulted in basic structural change. To put this another way, it might thus be that patterns of class relations remain relatively stable, although the position of particular households within them changes.

Another factor that may seem to undermine class analysis is that members of a rural household may engage in many different kinds of relationships in the course of a year – as tenant, creditor, employer, waged worker. For women-focused analyses this point appears particularly acute, as women not only do work different from men's, but crucially are in very different positions with respect to the means of production, rarely being themselves owners of key assets (land, new technology, draught cattle) as male household members may be. Wood (1981) however, stresses the importance of looking beyond the form, to the meaning of relationships. The terms on which a poor cultivator loans to a rich one, for example, are not the same as those between a rich creditor and poor client. Narrow focus on the transaction without reference to the wider context may mean mistaking its true significance. In relation to women, there is no doubt that their exclusion from direct control over the means of production is significant in their subordination. None the less, their household membership is a key element of their identity. The point is not to exclude women from class analysis or to identify them as a separate class, but to analyse points of relative autonomy and reinforcement in class and gender subordination.

Perhaps the most serious objection to using class terminology is the continuing dominance of patronage relationships which is taken as lack of class consciousness. The difference is between identifying a 'class-in-itself' – defined by relation to the means and relations of production; and a 'class-for-itself' – ready for class based action (Jahangir, 1979). There is no doubt that vertical links between richer and poorer households predominate in most parts of rural Bangladesh. For the poor, fostering particular links with a wealthier household is the most likely avenue towards upward mobility. While structurally they can be seen to have common interests (and these are sometimes overt, as noted above, in relation to Akhbar), from day to day households of a similar class are typically in competition with one another.

Wherever it is applied, class can only be a simplifying construct which reduces rather than expresses the complexity of experience. It can never present drawstring categories into which empirical cases can simply be bundled. The fact that conditions in Bangladesh do not conform to an ideal type of bourgeois–proletarian dynamics is not therefore a serious objection. The key to understanding social and economic inequalities is to grasp the relations through which they are (re)produced. There are, clearly, crucial differences between households, which are expressed in and result from their interaction. That interaction is predicated on those differences, and in turn sustains, intensifies, or mitigates them. To put it at its simplest, the poor are poor because the rich are rich. This is not captured by discussions simply of economic category. It is its stress on the relational quality of wealth and poverty that makes class a vital concept in the study of social inequality.

In identifying classes, I began by reflecting on the different opportunity situations of households which I came to know well. I was then able to recognize households of similar circumstances in the village as a whole. My approach was broad, taking account first of the material resources available within households – land and major assets – but also of their human and social resource positions – their members and skills and the strength of their social networks. At one level, households in the village are ranged along a continuum and it is to some degree arbitrary where the lines are drawn. Socially, however, there appear two broad status groups. The divisions can be seen by who is comfortable with whom, and who is deferential to whom. The economic indicator of this is the hiring out of labour. Males from households in the 'upper' group never do agricultural labour, males from 'lower' group households do. Hiring in of labour is not an equivalent indicator – many poorer households may hire in labour at peak labour demand seasons. In the upper group households have landownings of 150 to ten *bighas*,[9] in the lower group, 5 bighas to landless.

As noted above, diversity and mobility are key characteristics of rural Bangladeshi households. Despite this, most classificatory schemes are static. To capture some sense of the dynamic in household relations, I identify a further polarity within each of the two status groups, into 'strong' and 'vulnerable'. While this cannot perfectly present the mobility of particular households, it does convey some sense of the general disposition towards mobility. Within each status group, 'strong' households are typically upwardly mobile, or at least secure in their present position. 'Vulnerable' households, on the other hand, experience tension in maintaining and improving on their existing status and are potentially liable to decline. The patterns of mobility amongst Kumirpur households are discussed in more detail in the next chapter.

In broad terms, the upper/strong category comprises the very wealthy of the village who are dominant in both economic and political terms. Upper/vulnerable households have the status expectations of the upper/strong, but have considerably less resources with which to sustain them. Their say in village affairs depends in large part on personal factors: their wealth alone, unlike that of the upper/strong, is not sufficient to guarantee them a voice. The distinction between lower/strong and lower/vulnerable is much less marked in material terms, in part because their access to the major material resources is far less stable – it is mainly through short-term labour and share-cropping contracts. The differences show primarily in their human and social resource use: lower/strong households tend to have much stronger social networks and to maximize their labour through small business sidelines, and place a higher priority on sending their children to school. They generally have a little surplus for productive investment, while lower/vulnerable households suffer deficit over the year. Amongst the case studies there are four upper/strong; six upper/vulnerable; ten lower/strong and ten lower/vulnerable households. Comparative proportions for the village as a whole are ten u/s; 48 u/v; 64 l/s; 108 l/v.

In introducing the wealthiest households of the village, I described how each of them fosters its own patronage group. The village market is not 'free', but highly segmented, particular contracts are almost always expressions of longer-standing ties. I use the term 'clusters'[10] of households, to describe the unit of most frequent interaction. Clustering tends to take place between households that live near each other, and are of the same somaj, though this is not always the case. The cluster does not represent a new social unit, rather there is a tendency towards clustering: for multiple links to compound already existing relationships. The cluster is neither exhaustive nor exclusive: depending on the definition, any number of households could be identified as within the orbit of a particular cluster. A household may drift out of one and into another and, at the edges, two clusters may well overlap. The same idea is behind discussion of 'interlocked markets' or 'faction' groupings. I prefer, however, the greater openness of clustering to the overtly economic and political overtones of those terms.

The number of households and density of clustering depends in large part on the richest household's need for or ability to support others, but of course also includes horizontal linkages between households of a similar class. Links are of 'customary' form – they last longer than any particular contract. They may be expressed in labour, share-cropping, loan, short-term borrowing or lending, community and kin relations. A household's cluster relations thus represent a key aspect of its social resources. The opportunities open to a household will be different according to their cluster relations, and they are well worthwhile nurturing. In Bengali, the all-purpose *dol* (group, party, faction) is the nearest equivalent to cluster. Despite the lack of a more specific term, I was constantly aware of people identifying themselves (and others) as related in this way. In many cases it was so taken for granted that it would not be stated but still was a crucial part of the resources on which they knew they could draw. When I came to choose case studies I deliberately selected them in five clusters, each centred on a community leader. In this way I aimed to gain a better chance of seeing both parties in any interaction, and so a fuller sense of the relations between them.[11] Table 3.1 and figure 3.2 show the community composition of Kumirpur by class.

Table 3.1
Class and community composition of Kumirpur Community

	Muslim Exchange		Muslim Local		Hindu Mahisyo		Hindu Boisnob		Hindu Other		Santal		Total	
u/s	8	18%	1	3%	1	1%	0	0%	0	0%	0	0%	10	4%
u/v	8	21%	26	25%	1	3%	0	0%	0	0%	0	0%	48	21%
l/s	6	14%	14	37%	36	35%	6	19%	2	29%	0	0%	64	28%
l/v	17	39%	15	39%	40	39%	24	77%	5	71%	7	100%	108	47%
	44	100%	38	100%	103	100%	31	100%	7	100%	7	100%	230	100%
	19%		17%		45%		13%		3%		3%		100%	

Relationships within the household in many ways mirror these patterns in the community at large. The framework is similar: a hierarchical structure in which people's rank is expressed in access to key resources but within which there is certain room for flexibility through negotiation. The cultural norm is for young couples to live with the husband's parents until his father's death. In practice, however, many split away before this, particularly amongst the poor who have fewer common resources to hold them together. Division does not necessarily result in much physical change. Sons and their families typically continue to live in rooms within the same homestead (*bari*) but their wives will cook separately rather than together. Except where relationships deteriorate badly, this household separation is far from complete. Neighbours, for example, may continue to treat the father and sons as a unit, and laugh at their façade of formal separation. Land and other key productive assets may continue to be held and even worked in common. Obligations to look after one another also persist, and common identity is expressed in shared decisions over key issues such as major purchases, marriage and disputes.

The household is not a simple unit, but comprises many divisions of interest by age, gender and sub-family group. The significance of these points of contradiction and common interest are explored in chapters 5 and 6. None the less, the form of household to which they belong is significant for the work people do, the social and economic resources on which they can rely, their

Figure 3.2
Class and community composition of Kumirpur

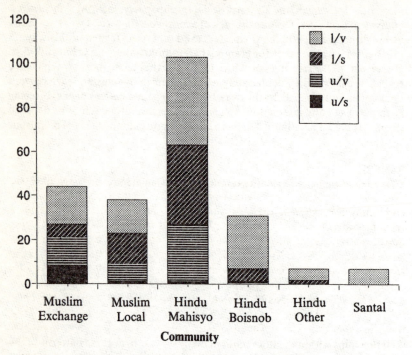

day-to-day authority and social strength. In Bangladesh, shared eating, particularly shared rice, is an important criterion of difference, with considerable symbolic significance. While Hindus and Muslims in Kumirpur share 'dry' foods (biscuits, puffed rice, even bread) it is still not acceptable (which does not mean it does not happen) for them to eat rice together. When a woman has a dispute with her husband and leaves his house, it is said: 'She would not eat her husband's rice' or perhaps: 'He did not give her any rice'. While other resources may be separate, those within a single household will share the same rice: it is the minimal statement of shared identity. This is therefore how I use the term household.

I identify four forms of household structure: joint, separate, extended, single. 'Separate' rather than 'nuclear' is used to avoid the associations of Western-style nuclear households. Extended households are those of separate pattern with some extra members – typically the mother or sister of the male head. Single households are those headed by a single person, almost invariably a woman. Table 3.2 shows the composition of village households by class.

As table 3.2 shows, separate households are most common in Kumirpur (62 per cent). There is also a clear association between richer households and more complex internal structure. This is in line with other observations across a

Table 3.2
Household structure by class

Household Type	*Class* *u/s*		*u/v*		*l/s*		*l/v*		*Total*	
joint	5	50%	16	33%	4	6%	7	6%	32	14%
separate	4	40%	22	46%	46	72%	70	65%	142	62%
extended	0	0%	8	17%	8	13%	8	7%	24	10%
single	1	10%	2	4%	6	10%	23	21%	32	14%
Total	10	100%	48	100%	64	100%	108	100%	230	100%
	4%		21%		28%		47%		100%	

broad spectrum of times and cultures (Netting et al., 1984:13). There are fewer extended households at both ends of the spectrum. Extended households are commonly formed after the death of the male household head when joint resources are divided. Amongst the richest, the households formed by this division commonly slip down from u/s to u/v. The low incidence of extended households amongst the poorest might reflect growing poverty overall, such that sons no longer feel they can afford to support their mothers. More significantly, perhaps, it can be difficult to incorporate a widowed mother into a son's household that has been separately established for some time. Within the 23 l/v single households, seven are older women who are living alone after their husbands have died. The others are households whose senior male has died leaving his wife with young children. The figures show the close association between fragmented household structure and poverty: households without adult males are acutely vulnerable both socially and economically.

I give each case study household a code to help in identification. For example, Sajjur and Rashida's household is coded 2.1 ME u/s j, which means: cluster No. 2; house No. 1; Muslim Exchange upper/strong; joint family. Dhiren and Sukhi's household is coded 1.1 HM u/v s, which means: cluster No. 1; house No. 1; Hindu Mahisyo; upper/vulnerable; separate. In each cluster household No. 1 is the wealthiest, thereafter numbering within the cluster follows (very roughly) wealth or density of interaction with that first household. To avoid breaking up the text I have put these codes into footnotes. A table showing the basic characteristics of the case study households is given in appendix B.

Divisions and alignments

In this chapter I have described the village of Kumirpur from two perspectives. First, I have emphasized how the village community is constantly changing – in the composition of its households and communities and in the relations between them and the outside world. Second, I have also identified categories such as class, community and household structure and so described the village in structural terms. The story of the building of the *madrassa* (Muslim religious school) brings these two approaches together.

The essential issue was the balance of power between Kumirpur Hindus and Muslims. The process of building the madrassa, however, involved a great variety of divisions and alignments, both within the communities and between them. Like the notion of gender as contested image, this example therefore brings out how apparently structural aspects of people's identity are not fixed but negotiable. Ultimately, the question of identity is a political one. People mobilize around different factors at different times, as serves their interests best.

A generation ago, in the centre of Kumirpur was a thick forest into which women never went, and a large black pool, in which no one ever bathed. It was a sacred place, a place of darkness and fear. Sixty to seventy years ago, a group of Muslims went to the local Hindu jomidar, in whose hands it was, and asked permission to build a burial shrine there for their religious leader (*pir*). This was granted. The years passed, and the shrine was grown over, the jomidar left for India, the pool passed to Aynuddin Mondol,[12] and the land beside it to Hasan Mullah,[13] an upwardly mobile Exchange Muslim, with a name for his strict devotion to Islam. After ten years, Hasan Mullah decided to cut down the forest and level the land for cultivation. The Hindus protested but he took no notice, claiming he could do what he liked on his own land. The Union Council judged that the Hindus should receive some land in compensation, but this was never observed.

Provoked by this, the Hindus looked into the land papers, and found from a 1972 survey that the land was set aside for religious purposes and did not strictly belong to Hasan Mullah at all. By this time, Hasan Mullah had irrigated the land and made it very profitable. So the community leaders, Hindu and Muslim, said that he should give up the land or at least give them half the crop on a share-cropping basis. Hasan refused. When the crops came to harvest, wheat and then paddy, the other villagers harvested it by force, and gave the land to someone else (an Exchange Muslim) to share-crop. They sold the crop and built a club house for the men of all the communities to use, beside the pool. After two years, in 1983, the share-cropper obtained a government lease for the land, but the village as a whole brought a case against him. In 1986, the case was still continuing, his crops suffered as he had to spend so much time in court, the other villagers (Hindu and Muslim) harvested his paddy and kept it for community use.

It is on the uncultivatable edge of this disputed land that the madrassa was built in 1986. In 1980, the mosque committee (prominent men from all the Muslim somajs and the local High School headmaster) decided to form a *moktob*, a religious primary school. Two years later, it was expanded into a madrassa, for which the Hajis donated three bighas of land. The madrassa was in Haji Para. When that site proved too limited, the committee decided to change location. The Hajis suggested another plot of theirs, on the southern edge of the residential area. The Mondols were reluctant for the Hajis to retain so much control, so suggested instead the disputed site. This site is right in the midst of a Hindu neighbourhood, and the move there represents a tangible expansion of the Muslim presence. No formal agreement was sought from the Hindus before building began.

Knowing their structural weakness, none of the Hindus wanted to be the first to protest. Finally, they made a petition to the upazila chairman, and the High School headmaster was commissioned to write a report. He called a public meeting, and amidst much rhetoric about the need to compromise and live together, it was decided that the Hindus should be given some land in compensation. Several months later, this agreement was still verbal only, and the Hindus sceptical of its force. On this issue, lines of division were strongly communal. Aynuddin Mondol's son is a close friend and fictive brother of Dhiren,[14] a middle-income Hindu Mahisyo. When Dhiren was ill, it was Aynuddin's son who took him several times to Rajshahi for treatment. They argued fiercely, as young leaders, Hindu to Muslim, about the madrassa construction. Finally, Dhiren made the claim: I could destroy it in 24 hours. And his 'brother' answered him: 'You could, but you could not live in this village afterwards.'

When the madrassa construction was well under way, it did finally spark off a communal response from the Hindus. In protest they built a temple nearby and in time for Kali Puja,[15] celebrating their new found unity with a communal meal (men only). Around this time there was in fact a general mood of Hindu revivalism in the area. Like the location of the madrassa, this both arose from conflicts within the community, and resulted in a shift in the balance of power, between Hindus and Muslims overall. One party amongst the Mahisyos was pressing for a new religious orthodoxy as a means to discredit another which had been in the ascendance. People were rebuked for slackness on Hindu customs, and there was a renewed impetus for religious and cultural meetings. By funding the temple, Kangali Serkar also made a further bid for centrality in the Hindu community, moving over into the more traditional patronage role of the Hindu rich. The net result was a resurgence of Hindu consciousness, though the bid for power was unsuccessful and the sense of communal identity short-lived. The statement signified by the madrassa, bringing children of the Muslim future into the midst of Hindu dwellings, remains.

In this summary introduction, it is possible only to give a brief sketch of the social composition of Kumirpur. This illustrates the flexibility of the situation, with a great deal of movement both between and within populations. It is a picture of activity, of continual establishment and reconstitution of relationships. As in the case above, this includes ways of defining reality, where contested images include such categories as the sacred and the profane. At the same time, there are clearly real differences of interest between rich and poor, by gender and community. The manipulation of identities is not random, but reflects the pursuit of quite definite interests. In the case of the madrassa, the outcome was a victory for the Muslims, and specifically for the Mondols' faction. To understand the significance of class and gender, it is important to keep in mind both the structural differences between people, and the space people have for manoeuvring within these. Ultimately, the process of defining and re-defining identities is about power. In the chapters that follow, I explore the significance of structural difference and the negotiation of identity in individual and household strategies for advancement and the implications these have for social inequality.

Notes

1. Jomidar is the local form of the term zamindar. The jomidars held large amounts of land from the government which they sub-leased to other categories of tenure-holders, stretching down to the cultivators themselves. They were given heritable rights to levy taxes at a fixed rate in 1793, which were abolished in 1950 (see Jannuzi and Peach, 1980).

2. A dhoti is a long piece of (usually white) cloth, wound around the lower part of the body giving the appearance of loose trousers. A lungi is a piece of cloth of which the ends are sewn together, which is knotted at the waist and worn over the lower body, to at least mid-calf length.

3. This is based on the case study households for which I had figures. There was a slightly higher proportion of female (31 per cent) to male (25 per cent) deaths, and among upper (33 per cent) rather than lower (26 per cent) status households, but the sample is too small to claim these as significant. Overall, this level of infant mortality (children under five) is consistent with findings of other surveys in Bangladesh and North India.

4. There are six unions in Tanore upazila. To denote his status, the honorific title 'Member' is used as a suffix to his name in place of Tozi's former title 'Uddin'.

5. Dhiren 1.1 HM u/v s. The code given here is explained on p. 41. The characteristics of the case study households are given more fully in Appendix B.

People form fictive kin links to celebrate a particular relationship or widen the circle of those with whom they have close ties. Fictive kinship is discussed more fully in chapter 5.

6. The village in Bengal is not a clearly defined entity (see Bertocci, 1970; 1972). Although the Santal group was nominally in another village, in terms of social community it was in neither: its ethnic minority status put it firmly in the category of outsiders.

7. Jacobson (1970) states that Hindu purdah emphasizes the opposition between kin by blood and kin by marriage, while Muslim purdah stresses the immediate kin group against wider society. Other writers (such as Vatuk, 1982) emphasize how purdah articulates gender inequality and see communal differences as less significant. This is the perspective I take.

8. This is also noted by Sharma (1980a) in her study in north west India.

9. One bigha is equal to one third of an acre.

10. The term 'cluster' is used in network analysis (see Mitchell (ed.), 1969) as 'segments or compartments of networks which have a relatively high density' (Boissevain 1974:43). While this study is not network analysis as such, this usage is clearly consistent with my own.

11. There are also six case study households which did not belong to any of these cluster groups, which were included because of particular features relating to agricultural practices or women's work.

12. 4.1 ME u/s j.
13. 6.1 ME u/v j.
14. 1.1 HM u/v s.
15. A Hindu festival in honour of the goddess Kali, involving folk drama and the ritual slaughter of a goat, which was celebrated in Kumirpur in June 1986.

4.   Scatter with One Hand: Gather with Two

Introduction

Despite moves towards diversification, agriculture remains the mainstay of the economy of Bangladesh. In Kumirpur, the availability of new agricultural technologies: mechanized irrigation, high-yielding variety (HYV) seeds, pesticides and chemical fertilizers, has led to an overall increase in prosperity. More land is under cultivation for more of the year, so that land values have increased and there is more demand for agricultural labour. There is also more land available for share-cropping, a form of tenancy in which a share of the crop is paid as rent. Although everyone in the village is affected by these changes and by changes in the environment more generally, the costs and benefits are not shared equally. Some poorer people find opportunities to improve their position, but it is clear that the major beneficiaries are those who were already relatively well off. Class and gender significantly structure access to resources, but there is no simple opposition between men and women, rich and poor. Instead, individuals and households use linkages between the different markets and foster alliances to secure their own advancement.

An important way in which inequality is structured in Bangladesh is through access to markets. In Kumirpur, the major assets are linked to agriculture: land, new technology, male labour and, often, credit. The markets for these resources are predominantly male: land is owned mainly by men, technology is operated and outlets are run largely by men, major loans are given on male authority and most field labour is open only to males.[1] By contrast, markets between women concern relatively minor resources: smaller animals, (barely paid) female labour and smaller scale loans.

The division between these two sets of markets is, of course, not complete: women may act as brokers in the 'major' markets, and men in the 'minor'. Also, since men and women come together in the household, their market activities are to some extent interlinked and predicated on one another. Thus the profit women make through goat rearing, for example, may be used as capital to buy inputs for men's agricultural production. Whatever the overlap and interconnection between them, however, there is no doubt that the overall segregation of markets by gender is at once a potent symbol and a prime means of sustaining male dominance within households and in the community more generally.

At the same time, transactions within each set of markets are highly significant for class relations. Entry to the different markets is clearly differentiated by class as well as gender, and class relations are in turn reproduced or shifted through them. Exploring how these markets work is therefore central to the questions identified in chapter 1: what is the local form of class relations; is the gap between rich and poor widening or narrowing; and how far are cross-class and intra-class relations based on co-operation, how far on conflict? Looking at the major and minor markets separately can highlight points of difference and similarity between them, putting them together at the household level helps to build up a fuller picture of inter-class relations.

The focus in this chapter on the predominantly male major markets is complemented by further discussion and more emphasis on the minor markets in chapter 5. Dividing the subject up in this way expresses something of the complexity of the social reality: the chapters belong together and cannot be read in isolation, but at the same time their segmentation is highly significant. Male domination of the major markets, for example, is significant in explaining why female-headed households figure disproportionately among the poor; women's entry into the major markets, particularly as labourers, signifies their households' extreme poverty, such that certain marks of status can no longer be preserved.

A changing environment

It was already getting dark as Asha, her brother and I made our way across the fields to the little cluster of houses exposed on high land at the edge of the village: Santal para. They laid out mats for us to sit on and gathered round, the light and shadow from my lamp flickering on their faces and on the mud hearths where a few were still cooking. We talked with them about their work and their customs, their links with other villagers and how their community had gathered. They watched as Bolai, one of the younger men, spoke, standing straight and assured, his expression open and direct:

"Listen, let me tell you something. It was the lean time, and we weren't getting work anywhere. I'd come back home and my kids were crying: Dad, I'm hungry; and I had nothing to give them to eat. So we went to Akhbar's father and asked if he had any work. He said he had some earth work that needed doing, how much would we take? So we thought: it's the lean time, there's no point in hustling and asking a lot. If we get six Taka[2] we can just about manage. So that's what we asked for.

"So he said: O, my son's just bought a Honda, six Taka, how can I manage that! So, there we are, listening to the tale of his woes. In the end he says: I'll give you three Taka. Three Taka for a day's work! So we thought and said, Give us one Taka more, give us four. And he said: O, how can I manage that? I'll give you three and a half Taka, take it or leave it, that's my last word. So we took it. What can we do? They know we have no choice.

"I tell you, if it weren't for the night times, the poor would have no happiness at all. You with your reading and writing, you can work on all night. But us, they can't make us work after daylight. That is our only comfort."

Not surprisingly, Akhbar[3] presents his role in the development of Kumirpur rather differently. His homestead is one of the largest and most spacious in the village, two two-storey buildings facing each other across a broad courtyard, a huge grain store and a roofed kitchen area against the far wall. As we talk, his mother, wife and sister-in-law squat nearby, cutting fish and vegetables for the evening meal. Akhbar is a heavy, dark man, who speaks with a strange combination of pomposity and half-mockery. It is he, he says, who is responsible for the changes that Kumirpur has seen. No one cares for development like he does. A few years ago there was just one rice crop, not cultivation all year round like there is now. But he saw the need there was, and out of pure public spirit brought a deep tube-well here to provide irrigation for the village, going through all the trouble of negotiating with the officers, organizing the management committee, keeping the books. Still now it is nothing but trouble, with people taking the water and then refusing to pay when the harvest is in. With the cost of the oil and parts he can barely break even. But he sees it does good, and that is his reward.

These two statements show how people reshape their own identities and the development of Kumirpur to tell their particular story. Bolai emphasizes employment relations at their worst, when in the lean periods ethnic discrimination intensifies his community's economic vulnerability to exploitation. In general, however, the Santals' circumstances have improved with the area's rising prosperity. They no longer have to migrate seasonally in search of work as they used to, there is now work locally for most of the year. Also, as more land is under cultivation for more of the year, Bolai has himself been able to gain a toe-hold in farming land, with a share-cropping contract for 1.5 bighas. None the less, their economic and social marginality clearly indicates a remaining underlying vulnerability: above all, they have no security, they eat so long as they can work, even the land that they live on belongs to someone else.

Akhbar's statement requires a good deal more adjustment. It is certainly true that the deep tube-well (DTW)[4] has significantly expanded agricultural opportunities and that these gains are shared – though not equally – by poor as well as rich households. For Akhbar to claim personal credit for the development that Kumirpur has seen is clearly, however, unjustified. Since 1974 shallow tube-wells (STWs)[5] have been supplied by the Bangladesh Agricultural Development Corporation (BADC) and by a non-governmental organization (NGO) operating in the area since 1979. In 1986 there were 18 STWs in operation in Kumirpur which were together irrigating almost 500 bighas, while even by Akhbar's estimates the DTW served only 150. Furthermore, the 'management committee' of the DTW, which is rented from BADC, is a fiction: Akhbar himself has sole control of it and has derived through it both substantial economic profit and political gain in terms of power within the village and extended links outside. As noted above, the story of development in Kumirpur is a familiar one: while many have seen some benefit, the major profits have gone to those who were already better off.

Tanore contains two very different land types and Kumirpur straddles these. To the west is higher land, looking towards the Borind Tract, with its high, relatively sparsely populated arid terraces. To the east is lower, fertile land, sloping down to the river which floods it each year. Villagers hold land in all directions, mainly outside Kumirpur *mauza*[6] itself. Paddy (rice) is the main crop, with different varieties grown at different times of the year on land of differing elevations. The main harvest is still the transplanted *amon* paddy, for which ploughing begins with the first monsoon rains in early June, and the crop is cut in November–December. In the past, most of the land then lay fallow for the rest of the year, except for the planting of a very few pulses in the cold season (December–early March) and some *boro* paddy (sown in mid-December and harvested April–May) on a fraction of the lower land. For cultivating boro paddy, the farmers used to build a dam across the canal which runs along the northern edge of Kumirpur. This had to be guarded night and day against sabotage from villagers downstream. The paddy could then be irrigated by *doon*, a long, canoe-shaped wooden conduit, by which water can be tipped from the source, at one end, to the land to be irrigated at the other.[7]

With mechanized irrigation, however, paddy can be grown virtually all year round. Cultivation of boro paddy (mainly *irri*[8] High-Yielding Varieties) is now greatly expanded, and some farmers grow an *aus* paddy crop (mid-May to early September) before they plant amon. Mechanized irrigation is also used to grow wheat, mustard, potatoes and onions in the cold season. A few of the more enterprising farmers also grow fruit and vegetables, such as cabbages, tomatoes, cauliflowers or watermelons from the cold season through to May. In 1986, there was virtually no jute grown in Kumirpur because of very low prices nationally in the previous year but in other years jute is also grown.

Such major changes in cropping of course have an impact on the environment as a whole. The new profitability of agriculture has meant forest areas have been cleared to provide more cultivatable land. With rising demand for fuel this has dramatically reduced tree cover. The land available for pasturing animals has similarly been reduced and numbers of milch cattle in particular have fallen sharply. This again means less proteins and vitamins in the diet as milk becomes scarce, and the loss of income for some of the poorer women who used to sell milk. Also, with wood and bamboo, cattle dung has been a key domestic fuel: dung sticks may be sold by women to generate income. The shortage of these sources has thus increased the time that poorer women spend gathering fuel, and pushes them towards more and more marginal sources, such as leaves and bark of trees, which hastens further the destruction of natural resources. In general, since the installation of the STWs and the DTW in Kumirpur, there are noticeably fewer common resources. The canal, which used to be a good source of fish, is now dried up much earlier in the season, by the use of STW engines as low-lift pumps (using surface, rather than ground-water, to give much lower running costs). Fruit and vegetables that used to grow with little or no tending, now give much lower yields, due to reduced soil moisture.

While these factors clearly affect all categories of household, they do not do so equally. The poorest households are disproportionately dependent on common resources to eke out income. Environmental changes therefore hit hardest those households which lack the means to purchase alternatives to hitherto free resources. Not all of the side effects of irrigation are negative of course. The increase in crops means for example that there is more straw available for fuel – though the new crops are predominantly shorter stalk varieties so the supply of straw has increased less fast than grain production. Use of straw for fuel has its own drawbacks, however. The fire has to be fed constantly so cooking time expands and quicker flames increase danger of injury. Also, straw leaves nothing but ash, whereas the charcoal left by burnt wood could be sold to local blacksmiths and so used to provide women with a marginal income source. Formerly, the lower straw left after the paddy was cut used to be burnt in the field. The shortage means it is now used as domestic fuel and this denies the soil restoration of some of its lost nutrients.

Even in terms of agriculture itself, therefore, changes since irrigation are not wholly positive. There are worrying signs of an overall decline in soil fertility since the increase in cropping intensity with irrigation. This shows most severely on the higher land, where there was a serious decline in wheat productivity from 8–9 *maunds*[9] a bigha in 1981, to 2–3 maunds five years later. The collapse in yields, made many (particularly poorer) cultivators stop growing wheat. To reduce the intensity of cultivation seems to have been the answer – by 1989 wheat yields had resumed their former higher levels.

It is in relation to drinking water that irrigation development in Kumirpur has had its clearest, and most contradictory, effects on the village environment. In 1986, everyone in Kumirpur drank safe water from a handpump. The handpumps are both important for health – though problems such as diarrhoea and dysentery remain common – and have reduced the time spent fetching water for women whose households own a pump, and for their close neighbours.

Most of these handpumps were bought during the previous ten years. Two-thirds of them (18) were supplied by the NGO. These hand tube-wells (HTWs) were intended for field irrigation, as an 'appropriate technology' for smaller landholders who could not afford and did not need an STW. As irrigation was available from shallow tube-wells and handpumping was hard work due to the low water table, however, people illicitly re-deployed the hand tube-wells, bringing them to the homestead for domestic use. Many are still outside the homestead walls to maintain the fiction that they are used for irrigation. This means neighbours have easier access to them than to those bought privately, which are usually installed within the homestead itself.

The NGO's HTW programme seems a classic case of male bias in development planning. The area is known for its lack of fruit and vegetables, and the HTWs were intended primarily to promote vegetable production. Vegetables are grown by women in and around their homesteads, and mainly eaten at home. Gourds are trained over the roof or bamboo frames, and some green vegetables may be grown in the rainy season. In Kumirpur as a whole, there are also 15 small vegetable plots nearby homesteads on which women do most of the work. Most women say that they lack the space to grow any more vegetables, though some cultivate remarkable gardens in a very small area. Very few women grow no vegetables at all: the exceptions are in wealthy households which buy in vegetables or grow them as a field crop.

The project design, however, envisaged field cultivation by male farmers, and saw the wish for domestic water as a problem. The NGO did not consider that siting HTWs near the homestead might mean they could be used both in the home and for vegetable production around the homestead site. Instead, metal pipes that could be taken up and sunk again elsewhere were replaced by plastic ones to stop HTWs being removed from the field. Demand for the NGO HTWs fell sharply. Instead of adapting the programme to give extension support to women for expanding their vegetable production, the re-siting of HTWs near the homestead was regarded as a failure, to which officers turned a blind eye. The shift of the handpumps to the homesteads thus meant that their productive potential was largely lost, but certainly improved the quality of life of Kumirpur women.

There is, however, another twist in the tail. When I returned to the village in 1989 it seemed that the STWs had been largely replaced by DTWs from a new area development programme. The drinking water handpumps were already – in February – running dry, and people were fearful of domestic water shortage as the hot season wore on into April and May. When challenged about this, the BADC chief engineer responsible for the DTW project initially took a cavalier attitude: irrigation was more important than drinking water. He denied that this reflected a gender bias in planning, disputing the point that it is men who work in the fields, but women who have responsibility for domestic water. All the women present, however, were unanimous that they had never seen village men carrying water for domestic use. Perhaps as a result of this, when I saw him again he agreed that it would be possible to provide pipes from the DTWs for drinking water in the villages, and claimed that he had incorporated this into the programme for the future.

This brief outline of the environmental impact of mechanized irrigation in Kumirpur shows that the 'random', unintended consequences of development programmes are in fact not random at all, but show a clear class and gender bias. This has been well documented in the gender and development literature.[10] The overall impact may be positive, at least in the immediate term,[10a] but it may be those people who are unable to take advantage of the new opportunities who are hit hardest by the negative effects.

It is easy to take mechanized irrigation as a background variable, and imply that it is a neutral agent of productive change. In fact, however, it is itself a resource, access to and use of which reflects local dynamics of power. Its impact on production depends on who has control over it and how they are using it; its use in turn affects social relations.

In 1986 there were 18 STWs in Kumirpur. All of the owners were of the upper category, and more than 50 per cent were from upper/strong households. This is not surprising considering the price of STWs, which ranged from Tk20–30,000, with an initial down payment of Tk2–3,000. All of the STW owners, the officers of agencies supplying irrigation equipment, the spare parts and machine oil dealers and mechanics are male.

In only one case was the STW being operated as a business with the primary aim of supplying water to others. More than 50 per cent of the land irrigated by the other STWs belonged to the STW owners themselves. The area irrigated was thus considerably smaller than the STWs potential capacity: in normal conditions, a 0.5 cusec STW should be able to serve up to 60 bighas, whereas the average area irrigated by a STW in Kumirpur is 27 bighas. In addition, there is a strong tendency for the area irrigated to decrease over time, as STW owners reduce their supply of water to other people. The STW that is run as a business is the only one that has actually enlarged the area that it irrigates. Owners explain this by saying, first, that they do not wish to put strain on their equipment: as many of the STWs are more than five years old, there is increasing danger of breakdown. Second, Tanore has a very low water table (particularly to the west) which may reduce water discharge in the hot, dry season. Third, most of the STWs are run on an *ad hoc* basis, with farmers requesting water when they need it. This involves considerable trouble to farmers as well as water suppliers – who also complain of difficulties in collecting payment.

The situation of STWs belonging to the rich and being used as an adjunct resource to improve their own land may clearly mean that poorer farmers have difficulty getting water. Farmers certainly do complain of this. There are, however, some more equalizing factors. Access to irrigation depends on cluster links as well as class – the area served by each STW is irregularly shaped, showing a selection of water users. Also, much of the land which shows as belonging to the STW owner is in fact not operated by him, but share-cropped out. In this case, the landowner/water supplier clearly has an interest in prompt and appropriate water delivery, so a poorer cultivator is assured good water access. As the share-cropper receives only a fraction of the product, the levelling effect of this arrangement should not be overstated – it depends on the terms of the share-cropping contract, and these are heavily weighted in the landowner's favour.

The relatively large number of machines in the area probably also improves the chances of a would-be irrigator. The potential irrigated area is set to increase further, with three new DTWs sunk in villages adjacent to Kumirpur in 1986. The danger, of course, is that in a situation where all forms of tube-well are competing for the same ground-water, the more powerful DTWs may displace existing pumps, by lowering the water table beyond their reach, rather than supplement the supply of water available. As noted above, on my return in 1989 it seemed that the STWs had largely been replaced by new DTWs, which were having a clear draw-down effect on ground-water resources.

Land ownership

Land has long been the key resource in rural Bangladesh and a central factor in households' social status and economic strategies. Land is much more than just another commodity, it represents security and is held in an almost mystical regard. To lose land is a matter of shame, as well as damaging to the household's longer term economic prospects. Accumulation of land may also have some shame attached: it is a matter of common conviction in the village that rapid increases in landholding cannot be made without some sharp practice. [11] In the longer term, however, the increased or decreased landholding becomes an aspect of its owner's identity and affects both his/her sense of him/herself, and how s/he is regarded in the community. With agricultural development and the new opportunities for profit it brings, demand for land increases still further, and this can mean pressures that squeeze out many poorer owners. Looking at structural changes in regard to landholding, therefore, is a crucial guide to shifts in the terms of exchange between richer and poorer households in the rural economy.

Sharp rises in landlessness in Bangladesh as a whole are reported in every major national review. The general trend is towards greater concentration of landholding, with overall a net downward shift. De Vylder (1982) estimates that 60 per cent of households in Bangladesh are effectively landless. In addition, landholdings are highly fragmented: the 1978 Land Occupancy survey found that almost 80 per cent of landholdings were less than 2 acres and the average plot only 0.15 acres. This is in part the result of inheritance rules according to which property should be divided equally between all sons. Strictly speaking, each plot should be divided, to ensure that each son has an equivalent share in terms of the quality, not just quantity, of land. Formally, Muslim law also provides for daughters to inherit land – at half the rate of their brothers' entitlement. Hindu women formally hold rights in property for life only, on death land reverts back to the male line. In practice, social factors and family politics inhibit women from claiming their formal rights (see chapter 7). Similarly, division of land between brothers by no means always follows the rules, and subsequent transfers and disputes show that power determines property rights, rather than the other way round (see Jansen, 1986, chapters 4 and 7).

In a situation of growing population such as Bangladesh, this recurrent division of landholding at inheritance must clearly introduce a strong downward bias. It cannot, however, bear the full explanation for trends in loss and accumulation of land. Land also changes hands as a result of marriage payments, mortgage, purchase, fraud, or litigation. This is borne out by the situation in Kumirpur. Table 4.1 and figure 4.1 show the significance of these other factors, as they show changes in landholding in Kumirpur under the present household head, excluding division of landholding on inheritance.

The overall fluidity shown in Table 4.1 and Figure 4.1 is striking – taking a weighted average across the classes, less than 30 per cent report no change in landholding. There are several households which had both gained and lost land

Table 4.1
Changes in landholding under current household head in numbers of households

	Class									
	u/s		u/v		l/s		l/v		Total	
increase	9	90%	36	75%	20	31%	9	8%	74	32%
no change	1	10%	11	23%	18	28%	56	52%	86	37%
decrease	0	0%	1	2%	26	41%	43	40%	70	30%
Total	10	100%	48	100%	64	100%	108	100%	230	100%

Figure 4.1
Changes in landholding under current household head

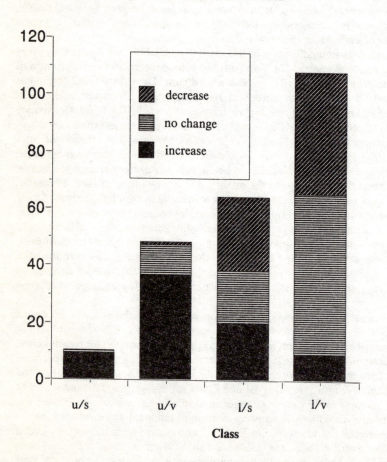

– only the net change is recorded here. It is the poorest who are least likely to move position. This is a sign of weakness – they start off with no land to lose. The likelihood of such poor households ever being able to buy land is decreasing, as with development the price of land has risen sharply in Kumirpur. In the late 1960s, 1 bigha of amon land sold at Tk1000, while the rate for boro land was between Tk2–400.[12] The combined effects of inflation and the rise in land values because of irrigation meant that by 1986, 1 bigha of amon land sold for Tk16–20,000; 1 bigha of boro land for Tk8–10,000. The pressure of demand for land was shown by a number of people who wanted to buy and yet could not find land on sale.

Land purchase is most significant for upper category households – at 90 per cent and 75 per cent of cases amongst the upper/strong and upper/vulnerable respectively. None of the upper/strong has lost land, and only 4 per cent of upper/vulnerable households have done so. Half of the u/v case study households have had to sell land at some point, but all except one later recovered the land and bought more. Large landholding both feeds and is fed by purchase of other major assets: in mid 1986, the four u/s case study households held four STWs, one DTW, two rice hullers, and three motorbikes. Gains on migration are also a significant factor amongst the Exchange Muslim households. The scale of changes is large: all of the u/s case study households now have over 100 bighas, none inherited more than 40, and some considerably less. As introduced in chapter 3, these wealthier households are able to consolidate and improve their position by a two-legged strategy of increased agricultural production and diversification into business enterprise.

Overall, the lower/strong class shows the most even balance between households gaining, retaining and losing land. There is a slight downward bias with 28 per cent who are stable and 41 per cent who have lost land, beside the overall averages of 37 per cent and 30 per cent respectively. What changes there are tend to involve relatively small amounts of land. None of the case study households of this class admits to buying more than 0.5 bigha. For this class as for the more wealthy, business activities and lending within the village supplement agriculture as a strategy for advancement.

Aside from share-cropping, the main means for the lower category households to gain control of land is through mortgaging. Three of the l/s case study households have invested in land on mortgage (two taking the land from relatives). These mortgages are of a type known as *khai kalasi*. A loan is given in return for the land for a set period during which the loan giver cultivates it. Each year the loan principal is reduced by a certain sum. This is now the predominant form of mortgage contract in Kumirpur. It has largely replaced the formerly common practice of *sudh kot*, under which the land is kept by the loan giver until the full sum is repaid to him/her. In the past, many families lost large amounts of land through mortgages that they were never able to redeem. Now, however, this seems less common in Kumirpur, as mortgaged land is mostly taken by lower households, either from others in their own class or from richer households, who need to realize cash or wish to bestow patronage.

The l/v class is striking for the low proportion of households that have gained any land – only 8 per cent of the whole. The case study households are no exception to this. Rather than gaining land, the majority have lost some, through a coincidence of improvidence and bad luck. In half of the cases, land was lost to near relatives, including through fraud. If the father dies while the children are still small, the young widow and her children can experience very rapid downward mobility.[13] Ill-health (including from over-drinking) particularly of adult males, is a major factor in land loss (and effective land loss, by mortgaging out) for poorer households. Class vulnerability underlies apparently random factors: a girl worker was accused of stealing a necklace from the u/s household where she was working, the necklace was never found, but in fear of violent attack her father sold 0.5 bigha to repay its value. For some of these poorest households, even the land on which their houses are built belongs to others. As Bolai – himself one of these – says: 'Those who have no land have no peace.'

Land loss is less predictable than land accumulation. While economic mobility takes an individual character in each case, there are also some factors that predispose towards change at the community level. Natural disasters such as the timing and heaviness of the monsoon or high winds that destroy houses and crops may push vulnerable households over the edge into land sale. Landholding is also affected by communal/political shifts. The most striking case of this occurred in the Independence war of 1971, when almost all of the Hindus of Kumirpur migrated to India for nine months. While they did not lose their land directly, their houses were stripped of all movable assets. Some land, and in many cases the women's jewellery, had to be sold in the re-establishment of their homes. The bitterness of that time is still very fresh in the minds of people in the Hindu community and underlines their present anxieties. Communal differences can still lead to land loss, at times backed directly by the state, as when Hindus' land is expropriated in their absence by declaration as 'enemy property'.

Other common reasons for land sale are the need to purchase cattle for draught power or to repair or build new housing. While it is relatively rare for land to be part of the wedding gifts, marriage constitutes, after inheritance, the most common reason for land transfer. Thus the peak period for the sale of Hindus' land coincides with the wedding season: February/March. The bride's household often has to sell land or assets to provide her with a dowry, and the groom's household receives assets which it may exchange for land. Amounts involved vary according to class and community, but amongst Hindus, receiving dowries can lead to land accumulation for the more prosperous. For all but the very richest and the very poorest households, the marriage of daughters may be an occasion for land loss.

Altogether, it is clear that small landholding means multiple vulnerabilities which predispose towards land loss, and large landholding ensures multiple strengths which enable land accumulation. This conclusion is supported by longitudinal studies which have observed changes in landholding across generations (Mukherjee, 1971; Van Schendel). It should be stressed, however, that this does not mean polarization of landholdings: it is not that large estates are growing ever larger while fewer households occupy the middle ground (Wood, 1981). Sub-division of landholdings through inheritance ensures a net downward shift in landholding is the strongest overall trend.

Share-cropping

The experience of Rohim and Karim[14] indicates clearly the interconnections within the major markets, and how these are centred in personal ties.

Rohim and Karim are brothers. Their parents were landless, so they went to live as boy workers in the houses of richer villagers. They therefore grew up in the ambiguity of belonging to, yet never being one of the family. Even now they are adult, something of this ambiguity remains in the households' continuing close ties. Rohim now share-crops and harvests amon and irri/boro for Akhbar, in whose household he used to work. He receives an interest-free cultivation loan (Tk3000) for the boro season from Akhbar. Rohim's access to the 5 bighas of scarce amon land for share-cropping is assured by a Tk1200 contract with Akhbar in the rainy season, to use his plough on Akhbar's land, as well as the land that he is cultivating himself.

His younger brother Karim also share-crops amon from Akhbar, and share-crops boro and harvests amon and irri/boro for Sajjur's brother-in-law, Mannan,[15] in whose house he worked as a boy. He also takes cultivation loans from Akhbar. Karim therefore began more closely in Sajjur's cluster, but is gradually shifting his patronage links to Akhbar, the head of his somaj, since Mannan is not sufficiently wealthy to offer him the same opportunities. Both of the brothers irrigate their land with water from Akhbar's tube-wells, and have the costs deferred until after the harvest as a favour. The bonds also stretch across gender: Rohim's wife rears a goat belonging to Akhbar's wife; Akhbar was the matchmaker for Karim's marriage.

In these examples it is very clear how elements of shared identity between rich and poor may both serve mutual interests and be rooted in contradiction. In being incorporated in richer households as children, Rohim and Karim developed ties of affection but were also open to extreme exploitation in the use of their labour for long hours for little or no pay. As these bonds have continued in adulthood the balance of power has shifted somewhat. There is no doubt that their patronage ties have served Rohim's and Karim's households' advancement in securing access to land and other resources on favourable terms. At the same time, cultivation of client households is clearly in Akhbar's interest as a means of strengthening his bid for dominance in the village community.

The examples of Rohim and Karim also demonstrate clearly the interlinkage of different kinds of economic activity. In the Indian literature this high degree of clustering in access to land, labour and loans is expressed in the term 'inter-locked markets'.[16] This has two dimensions. First, labour, share-cropping and loans are complementary aspects in a household's economic strategy and together contribute to the household's class position. Second, they also indicate 'multi-stranded' links between two particular households in a patron–client pair.

With land prices so high, share-cropping is the main way for poorer households to gain access to land. In the standard form of share-cropping in Bangladesh, the cultivator bears all the costs and gives one half of the crop to the landowner as rent. I use the term 'share in' to indicate share-croppers who take others' land for cultivation, and 'share out' those households which give land to others to share-crop. Overall, half the households of the village are involved in share-cropping. It is most significant for the middle classes: 50 per cent of lower/strong and 38 per cent of upper/vulnerable households share in some land, and a smaller porportion (16 per cent and 25 per cent respectively) share out. The poorest are least involved: 69 per cent of the lower/vulnerable neither share in nor out. All of the wealthiest households share out land, none share in.

The reasons behind apparently similar behaviour are very different for different classes. The wealthiest households, for example, share out land to cut cash outlays, bestow patronage and to minimize investment of household labour, particularly as educated sons are less interested in working on the land, preferring businesses or salaried jobs. On the other hand, upper/vulnerable households mostly share out land only when it is too far away for them to cultivate directly. Thirteen per cent of lower class households also share out their land, either because of distance or shortage of household labour. Many of these households are headed by widows, or have male members who are unwell or incompetent.

While for some sharing out land is thus an expression of strength, for others it is a statement of weakness. The market for share-cropping is not an open one for these lower households – often, they share out to a (somewhat wealthier) kinsman, balancing the social resource of his protection against the material resources that a more efficient cultivator might provide. Again, the terms of entry to the share-cropping market are thus clearly stratified by class and gender.

There have also, however, been significant changes in the share-cropping market over time. Historically, share-cropping was very widespread in the Kumirpur area, as wealthy Hindus considered it degrading to work on the land. This changed as the in-migrating Muslims preferred to cultivate their land themselves. Share-cropping contracts for amon land became so scarce that a payment or free services had to be given to secure them. A share-cropper might thus have to cultivate for free 2 bighas of the landlord's land, in exchange for a 10-bigha share-cropping contract. Some share-croppers still have to make such payments, either a large amount on (no interest) deposit, or a smaller straight fee. The majority of amon land share-cropped now in Kumirpur is the property of absentee landlords.

To some extent the situation has eased since mechanized irrigation has brought new land under (boro) cultivation. The large cash outlays involved in this cultivation mean that larger owners prefer to share-crop out – two of the four u/s case study households share out all their boro land. These new irri/boro share-cropping contracts, however, are not equivalent to the amon ones. They are short term, often lasting only a single season, with no security and involving small amounts of land. The relationship between landowner and share-cropper is thus much less dependable than those in former times. In the most common form of irri/boro share-cropping contract in the area, the cultivator bears all costs except half of the water and harvesting costs, which are shared by the landowner.[17] The harvest is then divided equally between them. A rarer alternative, is that the landowner bears no costs, just takes one-third of the total product (*tebhaga*).

In irri/boro cultivation, the profits for share-croppers are marginal, cultivation costs are high. For many poorer cultivators, the main benefit is that all the crop is available at once, while expenses are incurred more gradually, and so are less noticeable. When small amounts of land are involved – none of the lower/vulnerable households shares in more than 2 bighas irri/boro – share-cropping is compatible with agricultural labour, so it does not mean losing an alternative income source. Instead, it represents intensification of household labour use, resulting in a profit for the share-cropper only by discounting the cost of household labour. The share-cropper is therefore concerned with gross, not net, returns (Adnan, 1984:152). The picture for the landowner is very different. An average harvest on 1 bigha is 20 maunds (750 kg) paddy, selling at a minimum of Tk2400. This is shared equally between them, giving the landowner a profit of Tk950, for an outlay of just Tk250 (half the water cost). This profit will be much greater if, as is almost invariably the case, the landowner is able to store the paddy and then sell when prices peak. Rice prices can change by 50 per cent and more in the course of a few months. The landowner can also cut costs if s/he doubles as the water provider, pricing the water at the market rate which it does not in fact cost to produce.

While irri/boro share-cropping contracts do represent new opportunities for poorer households, their underlying tendency is to reinforce existing inequalities by awarding the richer landowner large profits, while the poorer share-cropper barely escapes loss.[18] The 'sharing' relationship which appears to reduce class inequalities in fact sustains them. These very low returns to the share-cropper appear to be the rule, rather than the exception, across India and other countries.[19] There is, however, considerable diversity in the forms of share-cropping contracts which again reflects who controls them. Put simply, the 38 per cent upper/vulnerable households share in more, better (mainly amon) land on securer contracts, than the 50 per cent lower/strong households. These in turn enjoy markedly better terms than the 19 per cent lower/vulnerable households, who without exception have access only to small amounts of irri/boro land on contracts that last a single season. The potential of share-cropping to reinforce or transform existing class inequalities thus depends on the terms on which different actors enter the (segmented) market.

This is not simply a matter of economics: terms of contracts vary greatly according to the wider relationship between the landowner and cultivator. It is not simply their wealth but also the upper/vulnerable households' better social connections, that underlie their preferential access. This applies to households in the lower group also, as the example of Rohim and Karim shows. For lower-class households in Kumirpur, regular labour through the rainy season (transplanting amon) is thus commonly linked with access to loans, share-cropping land and often harvesting contracts. The next two sections discuss these other aspects of labour and loans.

Agricultural labour

The cropping changes have expanded the market for agricultural labour in Kumirpur. Like share-cropping arrangements, labour is freer than it was, contracts are shorter term and most work is done by daily labour. No Bengali woman is hired as an agricultural labourer in Kumirpur. Again, benefits are therefore divided by gender as well as class: households without able adult male members are unable to take advantage of the new opportunities.

Santal women do, however, work as agricultural labourers. This is in addition to their domestic tasks – they rise early to cook breakfast, before the men go off to work in the early morning. They go themselves to the fields a little later, and often stay out all day, perhaps taking some lunch with them, perhaps going without, until they return home, maybe an hour before sundown, to begin getting the dinner ready. Their shorter day in the fields means they receive less money (usually by Tk2) than the men. All of the Santals work extremely long hours – outside the lean seasons, they are rarely in their homes except after dark. The women work the longest of all. Here, clearly, is a classic case of women's outside employment meaning they have to work a double day.

Changes in labour contracts indicate shifts in the local form of class relations. Regular work for a fixed term contract is less common now than it used to be. Only young boys still have year-round contracts (often as herdsboys). Otherwise, regular labour is hired on a seasonal basis. Rates for regular work vary by season, age and skill. In Kumirpur 1985/6, for a grown man, the lowest pay was Tk180, the highest Tk300 per month, with meals or 2 maunds of paddy per month – just under the wage earned by constant daily labour over a similar period. For boys on a paid annual contract, a year's work means 365 days – if they miss time through illness it has to be made up when the contract ends. Though boys may seek out the position for themselves, this does not mean that they do not resent the need to do so. When small, boys are employed on the same very exploitative terms (just food and clothes, or very minimal wages, as a 'family' member) as women are all their lives. They watch their contemporaries in the employing household able to study and play while their own health is broken through too hard work too young. In response, some refuse to let younger brothers go out to work as they did – a clear sign that boy workers feel as keenly as women the contradictions in their construction as a 'member of the family' and their exploitation as a low or unpaid household labourer.[20]

Seasonal contracts normally cease in the slack period before harvest, and the same worker often cuts the paddy as part of a group. I have given the term 'share-cutting' (by analogy with share-cropping) to the arrangement by which amon and boro are harvested in Kumirpur. I similarly use the term 'share-tending', to describe the arrangement whereby one person tends the animal of another and they divide any profits between them. In the share-cutting system, a labour gang (dol) is responsible for the entire harvesting process, from cutting and threshing the paddy and to putting it in sacks. The normal rate for this is 12.5 per cent of the crop total, though workers may be able to negotiate a rise depending on the distance of the land and weather conditions. This all-in system started relatively recently. Formerly, those who cut paddy received a share of the sheaves in the field and the winnowing and threshing was done separately.

The change in the cropping system has meant more labour demand for more of the year, but it has also brought a new, and much steeper, peak period of demand. The threat of early monsoon flooding means that the irri/boro crop has to be harvested with maximum speed – and the value of labour accordingly rises. Migrant labour comes in at peak times from Nawabganj (the district immediately to the west of Rajshahi) and, increasingly, from further to the west within Tanore upazila. News spreads informally – someone coming to Rajnichok land registry office hears of opportunities, someone married in the area hears talk while visiting kin. Many of the migrants, particularly those from elsewhere in Tanore, are young unmarried sons of middle class and smallholding households. The migrants also include a few Santal and other ethnic minority female groups.

The migrants see out the harvest in Kumirpur and then move on elsewhere, where the paddy ripens a little later. They live in gangs, typically in a room made available in a landowner's house. They cook and eat separately, one of their number coming back early from the fields to do this. Kumirpur women walk more carefully around the village during the time of the migrants' stay – incidence of attack is not extremely common, but far from unknown.[21] Some groups have stable relationships with a particular landowner, others just come on the off-chance. As these trends are very new, it is difficult to assess the forms that such relationships might take. It is clear however that personal linkages are again very important in these relationships – they are the means through which a gang comes to a particular area, and they often strengthen during the period of stay. The class significance of migrant workers clearly varies in different contexts. In Kumirpur, their social backgrounds and the tendency to develop links clearly cautions against identifying them as in other studies (such as Wood, 1978) as 'proletarian elements' in the countryside.

Despite the influx of migrant labour, the new availability of share-cutting employment is of considerable importance to the poorer households in the village. On 12 May 1986, in the height of the boro harvest, a survey of the village showed that of households harvesting that day, five were employing groups from Nawabganj, and seven groups from western parts of Tanore. Twenty-nine, however, were employing a group from within the village, and eight were harvesting in part of a group which cut mainly the members' own paddy. For the lower/vulnerable class as a whole, the amount of paddy gained through share-cutting is of comparable proportions to that gained from share-cropping. Even for the case study households in which share-cropping is more extensive than in the class as a whole, the amount of paddy gained through share-cutting was 57 per cent of the gross amount which they derived from share-cropping, and that with none of the overheads of cultivation. This aspect of increased employment availability should not be underestimated. An added advantage of share-cutting is that paddy is gained, as through share-cropping in block amounts rather than as daily wages.

Many studies have claimed a worsening in wage rates, particularly in the context of an influx of migrant labour.[22] In Kumirpur, local people of all classes say the wage rate has increased and that households dependent on agricultural labour are now more comfortable than they used to be. They indicate, for example, that loans between very smallholding or landless households are increasingly common and claim this as evidence that there is more money amongst the poorer groups than there used to be. This could, of course, be due to the increase in employment available, rather than a rise in rates of pay. On the other hand, there is evidence that the terms of exchange have shifted in the workers' favour: landowners now often seek out workers, rather than waiting for them to come and ask for work as in the past. Also, workers now usually take the food component of their wages as rice rather than eating in the landowners' house, and this certainly operates financially in the workers' favour. At the same time, this relieves from wealthier women the burden of preparing large meals for their agricultural workers, and appears an interesting gender implication (male cash displacing female work) of shifting class relations. This is, however, very localized: in a village studied by Marion Glaser, in the district to the east of Rajshahi, wealthier women's workloads had been substantially increased by the need to feed growing numbers of workers.[23]

I was unable to make an independent assessment of changes in wage rates, though the share-cutting system is clearly advantageous for the workers. Since people tend to report decline (the good old days syndrome), however, I am inclined to take seriously the view that there has been some improvement, though overall rates are still extremely poor. In 1985/6, the wage rate for agricultural labour was Tk10 daily, with meals or 1.5 *seer*[24] rice (worth about another Tk10). This is (very) occasionally exceeded, with wages going up to Tk12, but can also drop right down in the lean season: Bolai tells, for example, how he has sometimes had to work for just 1 seer wheat flour (Tk5–6) for a full day.

As the examples of Bolai, Rohim and Karim indicate, the state of the market in general is only part of the story: in practice much depends on the nature of the relationship between employer and employee and how the two parties can manipulate this to serve their own interests. While there is no doubt that vertical ties through labour are more mobile than they used to be, this does not mean that labour is fully 'free'. Labour is often part of a wider cluster relationship. It is very common for labourers to be pledged to work for one particular landowner first, and for the landowner in return to be bound to offer any work first to them. While labourers may perceive these links to be chiefly beneficial to the landowner, they also recognize the value of the security they give. At their best, these links may be the means of the advancement of the poorer party, so that over time the terms and content of the relationship changes.

Credit

As in the other markets, the market for credit in Kumirpur shows evidence both of changing patterns overall, and of considerable flexibility within the system. Credit is the mainstay of so much of village life that it is difficult to identify one class as more dependent on it than another. Different classes enter into various kinds of credit arrangements for different sorts of purposes – there is no simple contrast between solvency and indebtedness. Large debts do not necessarily indicate weakness: they also show the ability to mobilize credit. Here I am not concerned with institutional credit, but with loans between individuals as they express different relationships within the village.[25] As with share-cropping and labour relations, the market for credit is far from perfect: it is deeply entwined in people's other social relationships. In many ways, indeed, it represents the most perfect case of social capital being realized in material goods, and so a neat example of inter-household relations.

Loans are most commonly taken for consumption, cultivation, and wedding or funeral expenses. If possible, transfers within the household are arranged to avoid having to take credit outside. A lower/vulnerable Hindu household, that of Biso and Gouri,[26] provides an instance of this. Their eldest (married) son worked in a house-building team from February to June 1986, earning a total of Tk3869, which paid for their irri/boro cultivation expenses. In the amon season, the household borrowed Tk300 from his wife's dowry, for fertilizer, and repaid the young couple with interest after the harvest. This is clearly a striking example of the way sub-divisions can exist within the joint household.

Aid in the form of interest-free loans may be given between close relatives, particularly brothers and (married or widowed) sisters. Alternatively, expenses may be avoided by reciprocal arrangements. The dowry given to an elder brother may be used to marry away a younger sister. This is taken one step further in cases of double marriages, where one brother and sister marry another sister and brother, and so no dowries need to be paid. In one case in Kumirpur this was even organized between sibling pairs in three different (Hindu lower) households, in a multiple bridal exchange programme. Sometimes the community as a whole may respond to need. There were several cases while I was in the village, of a somaj holding a collection so that recently bereaved women should not have to ruin themselves bearing the expenses of their husband's/mother's funeral. This should not, however, be overstated. In another case, the daughter of a beggar woman was married and the ceremony put on by her somaj, but only one of the wedding gifts promised by the local rich households was in fact forthcoming.

Loans between people within the lower status group are a relatively new phenomenon in Kumirpur which is becoming increasingly common. As noted in the preceding section, these are cited by villagers as evidence of rising prosperity: workers would never have had the capital to lend before. Alternatively, they could reflect growing indebtedness amongst the poorest households, and their increasing dependence on the market for basic consumption needs. These loan relationships are not on a low interest reciprocal basis, but usually at the same (or higher) interest rates as those from the rich (typically 50 per cent per season). They may however represent for the poorer household a desirable alternative to accumulating dependencies on a richer patron.

The classic kind of loan relationship, of a richer patron loaning to a poorer client, is also evident in Kumirpur. This may be more or less formal, with interest or without. Usury is forbidden under Islam, and there are undoubtedly some who take this injunction seriously. More generally, however, the terms on which loans are available vary according to the nature of the relationship between the two participants. Employees often go to their employers for loans, and share-croppers to their landowners. It is, of course, in the interest of the landowner to supply the share-cropper with an input loan, and so ensure a better harvest. While it is difficult to be too definite about this, it seems that there is a move of richer patrons towards narrowing the circle of their patronage, refusing loans to those who do not have a current functional relationship with them. Akhbar, for instance, will give loans only to those who are either in his employment or sharing in his land. The terms of those loans differ, depending on the nature of the relationship that he has with the recipients. Where he has a fuller relationship, no interest may be payable, where not (e.g. with someone outside his somaj) Akhbar will charge interest.

Loans are not always given by richer patrons to poorer clients. While the norm is for employing households to give loans to their workers, loans may also be given by workers/share-croppers to employers/landowners. Usually this involves upper/vulnerable households, who can be under some strain to sustain the lifestyle appropriate to their status from their limited material resources. This is regarded as shameful, and kept very secret, so it is difficult to assess its extent. None the less there is sufficient evidence in my small sample to suggest that it is quite widespread. Some of these loans are taken quite formally, and may have interest paid on them. These loans are not however always 'free', or even open. Sajjur's brother-in-law Hakim[27] represents an example of this. He was due to pay a boy labourer Tk1000 for the monsoon's work in September 1986. Hakim paid Tk600. The boy's father said they could not manage, so Hakim took a loan from another of his workers for Tk200, to pay the wages. In early December 1986, Tk200 was still outstanding.

This example shows clearly the reciprocity of patronage relations. While in some cases poorer households may be coerced into lending to a richer patron, in others such loans are regarded without friction, as part of the give and take in cluster relationships. These loans clearly express the fact that power relations are always (at least!) two-way: each values the relationship and maintains it because the other party has something it needs. The relationships thus have typically both contradictory and solidary elements. As Foucault (1981:94) puts it, power is exercised: 'from innumerable points, in the inter-play of nonegalitarian and mobile relations.'

Households in the lowest class can be chronically in debt. The very poorest and least well connected among them are less so – there is a level below credit worthiness, who respond to the question of loans: 'Who would lend to us?!' Households without adult male wage earners are most often in this category. In most extreme cases they turn to begging. Of the seven households in Kumirpur dependent on begging, only one has an adult member, and he is very old and unwell. The others are either women whose husbands have died young, or widowed mothers from whom their sons have all split away after marriage.

The maxim 'who you are determines what you get' perhaps comes as close as any to summing up life in rural Bangladesh. This is well demonstrated in a final example. Suresh and Maloti[28] own 20 bighas and share in 10 more. The share-cropping contract is of the classic type now rare in Kumirpur: medium-high (amon) land, given regularly to Suresh for the whole year, by an absentee landowner. Suresh runs a business transporting paddy to Rajshahi during most of the year. They employ a regular male worker, and are looked to as a more prosperous household by the poor in their vicinity – as an employer and potential loan-giver. Conventionally, interest rates on institutional loans are considered more competitive than those in the village. For Suresh, however, this is not the case. After taking a bank loan one year, Suresh says he never will again. Instead he takes no interest loans from wealthy people within the village, in return for favours such as ploughing or transport. Their indebtedness is extensive.

Since building a two-storey house some years ago, Suresh and Maloti have had a Tk10,000 loan from other people in the village. They are also Tk3000 in debt to the paddy trader middleman with whom Suresh does business. In February 1986 they married their second daughter. For the wedding they borrowed Tk4000 from the Rajshahi owner of the land they share-crop. At the wedding they gave Tk5000 of the dowry, and promised to make up the total sum of Tk32,000 within the following year. Despite being unable to pay in advance, they secured good access to irrigation for their irri/boro land, with further informal loans in the form of deferred demands for water charges.

Suresh and Maloti give a prime example of the successful management of social resources and translation of these into material benefits. They manage to maintain widespread good relations on a relatively equal level which assure them preferential access to important goods that would otherwise be beyond their means. This is certainly facilitated by Suresh's paddy trading business, which gives him frequent contact with the town and so many opportunities to do favours.

Conclusion

Technological changes over the past ten years in Kumirpur have certainly increased the volume of resources that are exchanged through the major markets. More land is under cultivation for more of the year, and yields have grown. It is the already wealthy who are best placed to take fullest advantage of new opportunities. None the less, it would be mistaken to emphasize only those aspects of the situation which reconfirm existing inequalities. Increased availability of share-crop land and agricultural employment have loosened production relations and have given workers more options. This may not be entirely positive however: where personal networks are so fundamental to the social formation, it may be that more narrowly economic relationships are not in the long-term interests of the labouring households. Underlying trends towards loss of land by the poor confirm that while there may be some short-term gains, there is also a fundamental problem in lack of security.

The considerable social disruption during the past 20 years in Kumirpur has not undermined the tendency towards clustering of links. Ties may be less strict than they have been in the past, but the markets for land, labour and loans are still strongly interdependent. This means, first, that strength in one market tends to be mirrored by strength in another. Also, the clustering of relationships between particular households affects the terms on which they enter the market. Market relations are in fact highly personal and particular. While general patterns are set, actual transactions reflect the relationship between the two parties, as much as the terms of the rules. There is thus a great variety of meanings that households of different classes who are linked in different ways can give to apparently similar relationships. Each household thus crucially has relations not only to the means of production, but also to other households. They therefore draw not only on their material resources, but also on their human capital, and the social networks which they are able to sustain. These human dimensions are vital to the household's prosperity: adept management of quite limited resources can result in household advancement, while ill-health or poor social relations can drain even substantial material wealth.

Just as households may move between one class and another, so the relationships between them move between one form and another. At any point, a household may be shifting towards fuller or narrower cluster links, towards more functional or more broad-based alliances. As one gusti declines, it may no longer be able to sustain the functional links that it had built up with dependent households. Then the social relationship may remain, while the client seeks other households with which to develop economic linkages. The relationships between rich and poor households have aspects of both solidarity and contradiction. While they are in the interests of both parties, they are rooted in relations of inequality, and may reproduce, just as they may transform these.

This chapter concentrates on relationships between men. In fact, of course, women are also central to households' economic and social relations. Women's work sustains male participation in the major markets and the networks which women foster serve to convey all kinds of information, including some about transactions from which they are formally excluded. The following case gives an example of this.

In November 1986, while her husband, Dhiren,[29] is in Rajshahi, Sukhi hears that one of their neighbours (in the same cluster) wants to sell his heifer. He has been once to the market, but found no buyer. Sukhi tells him to wait: perhaps Dhiren will buy it. On his return Dhiren gives no direct answer. Sukhi says: 'I think he wants it'. Dhiren sees that she does. The asking price is Tk1700, but as Sukhi says: 'Who knows what will happen when we sit together?' That evening the neighbour comes and they agree to Tk1650. Dhiren will sell one of his rings. Sukhi is pleased. They bring the heifer into their yard the next day.

Sukhi was also the one who arranged for them to buy their HTW from a neighbour who needed to realize some cash, and on another occasion went to collect the paddy they were owed by a share-cropper on their land. It is also very common for women to act as intermediaries: requests for loans or share-crop land, for example, often go first to women in wealthier households, in the hopes that they will be able to influence their husbands. Where there is flexibility in the terms of a contract the role of broker is an important one, and in this way women in wealthier households may have considerable leverage over poorer men and women. The fact that women do not enjoy sole authority does not mean that they have no power.

It is when men are unwell or absent that women's role in the major markets is most likely to become overt: thus it is typically Asha[30] and her mother, rather than her old and lame father, who go and engage labourers to work in their shared in land. The two women substitute for him in other ways too, for example, by taking seed paddy to the fields. Strict segregation of actual men and women into the 'male' and 'female' markets depends on the household having the full complement of able-bodied and co-operative members of both genders that the culture assumes. In a large and perhaps increasing number of cases, this ideal is not fulfilled.

A final example illustrates the close interrelation between male and female activity in the major and minor markets and their articulation with structural positions by class and gender. Khalek and Kaniz[31] are landless. They share-crop land from Tozimember[32] and buy water from him for irrigation. Their son works on his land. Kaniz does various tasks around the Tozimember homestead. Her daughter works alongside Kaniz as a domestic servant, returning to their own home only to sleep. In December 1985 Tozimember came to know that Khalek and Kaniz had just sold paddy worth Tk3000 to a trader in the village. Tozimember demanded that they loan him Tk1500. They could not refuse: in lean times they depend on him. He repaid them no cash, but did not charge them for irrigation. A year later he still owed them Tk300, with no question of interest being paid.

The money had been for their daughter's dowry: they were having difficulty getting her married since she was seduced when working in the Mondols' house. During the two years she had worked for Tozimember, she had been given only her food and grain worth half the cost of one sari and petticoat. They finally decided that she should leave the job. Her mother, Kaniz, put it like this:

"In shame we didn't ask for more. We have shame, they have none. So my

daughter is coming home. Why work there, if we have to eat from home, buy
our own clothes, even a little oil to put on our hair? They say to me, we give
you paddy, hasn't that value? But can two people be employed for 4 maunds
a year? You tell them this in your country, they'll be amazed."

The forced loan makes clear the vulnerability in such a relationship for the
poorer party, but this should not lead to too monolithic a picture of power.
Kaniz's protest that they have no 'shame' shows her sense that the advantage
Tozimember's household took of their dependence was not legitimate. Also,
part of the reason the daughter could ultimately leave work was the additional
margin they had since her brother had begun to share-crop Tozimember's land.
More such interrelations between major and minor markets and the
ambiguities of power are brought out more fully in chapter 5.

Notes

1. This is true in Kumirpur, but not necessarily the case in other areas of
Bangladesh.
2. In 1986 the rate of exchange of the Bangladesh Taka (Tk) was 40 Tk to the
UK£.
3. This is reconstructed from a number of meetings I had with him, not his
verbatim speech on a single occasion.
4. A device for ground water irrigation, of in this case, 2 cusec capacity.
5. A device for ground water irrigation, of in this case, 0.5 cusec capacity.
6. Mauza is the name for the revenue unit, the area bearing the village's name on
the map. This often does not conform to the socially defined village, *gram*.
Kumirpur gram actually spreads across two mauzas.
7. The doon is still used to cut costs by supplementing mechanized irrigation.
8. The term irri is used locally to mean any kind of High-Yielding Variety (HYV)
paddy, not only the International Rice Research Institute's (IR) varieties. This local
usage is followed here.
9. A maund in Bangladesh is in general equal to 37.5 kg. In the Kumirpur area,
however, a maund of paddy is calculated according to the measurements of the
British period (pre-1947). This reckons weights at 75 per cent of the value elsewhere.
One maund of paddy in Kumirpur, therefore, is only 75 per cent the size of 1 maund
as generally calculated. This peculiarity applies only to paddy.
10. See, for example, Agarwal (ed.) (1988).
10a. The longer-term environmental impact of chemical-intensive agriculture is,
of course, a further matter of concern.
11. There may be a strong tendency for land transfers to be viewed as unfair, even
if they are formally correctly transacted, when they are clearly to the disadvantage
of one party and the gain of the other, and the two are living in close and continuing
proximity (Geof Wood, personal communication).
12. Prices then were low, as people were hesitant to purchase land after the
imposition of land ceiling legislation.
13. This should be less true since the reform of the Muslim Family Laws
Ordinance, 1961, which conferred statutory inheritance rights on the children of a

man who predeceases his own father. There is little doubt, however, that the vulnerability of a new widow and young children mean that they are not always able to claim their statutory rights, so land loss can still occur.

14. 3.2a ML l/s e and 3.2b ML l/s s.

15. 2.2 ME u/v j.

16. Bharadwaj (1979); Bhaduri (1973:83); Rudra and Bardhan (1978); noted by Adnan (1984).

17. In some cases the landowner shares the cost of seed also.

18. This discussion assumes that the landowner is wealthier than the share-cropper, which is true in the majority of cases in Kumirpur, but is not necessarily so.

19. Adnan (pp. 66–71) notes that (real) negative returns to share-croppers are shown by data collected by USAID and the Ministry of Agriculture in Bangladesh, by Bharadwaj and others in India; and that similar 'short-term production failures' are recorded for Bengal jute 100 years ago, as well as in parts of Russia and Poland at other times.

20. As far as I know, there has been no study made of the implications that this work outside the household in childhood might have for the solidarity within the poorer family unit. It would seem plausible that links might be weakened by it, and be a contributory factor to the earlier breakup of poorer households.

21. There was an attempted rape by a migrant worker in Kumirpur in 1985.

22. See Jansen; Khan (1977); Wood (1978).

23. See Glaser's thesis *Water to the Swamp* (1989).

24. One seer is a little less than 1 kg.

25. Access to institutional loans of course expresses relations within the village as well. This is beyond the scope of my study. It is comprehensively discussed by J. A. McGregor, forthcoming.

26. 1.4 HM l/v j.

27. 2.3 ME u/v j.

28. 5.4 HM u/v s.

29. 1.1 HM u/v s.

30. 2.5 ME l/v s.

31. 4.4 ME l/v s.

32. Aynuddin Mondol's (4.1 ME u/s j) nephew.

5. An Enterprise Culture

Introduction

An image which pervades virtually every recent text on poor women in Bangladesh shows them as eager entrepreneurs, ready to launch new businesses to lift themselves out of poverty with the availability of capital as the only significant constraint. This clearly reflects the penetration of donor concerns: not only for the alleviation of poverty, but also for the fostering of private enterprise.

The imagery is common to both development agencies and women-focused studies. Some studies openly merge policy reflections with their more general presentation of women's position in Bangladesh. *Jorimon* (ed. Yunus, 1984) gives a series of case studies of poor women facing overwhelming odds who achieve economic success and personal fulfilment after receiving loans from the Grameen Bank.[1] Abdullah and Zeidenstein present the experience of the Intensive Rural Development Programme Women's Project as the second part of their study of 'Village Women of Bangladesh'. Chen (1985) describes as 'a quiet revolution' the establishment of small businesses amongst women through the programme of BRAC,[2] one of the largest Bangladeshi NGOs.

This advocacy of small business for women apparently offers a key instance of gender constituting a contested image in the context of aid dependence. In working to increase women's market involvement (through, for example, a USAID micro-enterprise project) the aid community is directly opposing one of the strictest conventions of the purdah culture: the exclusion of women from marketing activity. In practice, however, it appears that both of these positions are somewhat overdrawn. The purdah culture is much more flexible than it appears in its notions of space and the varieties of activity it can accommodate; the aid community is not initiating something new, but highlighting and extending what is already going on.

The strength of these studies is the way that they challenge the separate spheres paradigm with its man–market associations. Their weakness, however, lies in the emphasis they place on external programme interventions in bringing women out. During my time in Kumirpur I observed that women were extensively involved in market transactions. There was, however, no development agency promoting small businesses, nor bank which was providing loans to the poor. Rather, it was evident that the notions of 'outside' (*bahire*) and 'inside' (*bhitore*) are figurative, not simply literal terms; their content is not set, but variable. Manipulation of these terms is a central part of the negotiation of gender identities. In channelling new resources to women, development programmes may extend women's options. It is a mistake, however, to see these as breaking down a monolithic local culture, or to underestimate the flexibility that already exists.

This chapter begins by discussing the growth of small business in Kumirpur. I give particular attention to rice businesses, as they bring out most clearly the interrelation of different aspects of the rural economy and of women's and men's work. This leads into broader discussion of women's market involvement and particularly markets between women for care of animals, smaller scale loans and female labour. This is followed by a more general discussion of the nature of relationships between women as neighbours and friends. The chapter concludes with a comparison of the major and minor markets, reflecting on points of difference and similarity, and the significance of their division.

This chapter is, then, not narrowly concerned with small businesses in themselves, but more broadly with the involvement of women in activities outside their own homesteads. It is this that epitomizes the enterprise culture of Bangladesh: the skilful management by women of scarce resources in a restrictive cultural environment, working in and with the rules and turning them to their own use.

Small businesses in Kumirpur

Changes in agrarian relations have perhaps received disproportionate attention in studies of development in Bangladesh. Alongside these and in direct relation to them, in Kumirpur at least, the growth of business enterprise is striking. While the form it took varied by class and gender, there was a general trend towards a culture of business visible throughout village society. Most households were still in some way involved in agricultural cultivation, but it was increasingly common for households also to pursue a business. Diversification into a number of economic activities to give two-legged expansion was particularly evident amongst the upwardly mobile of all classes: business was a prime aspect of household advancement.

The trend towards small business is attributed by the villagers themselves to an overall increase of pressure on resources with the declining ratio of land to people. All available resources need to be maximized if the household is to survive and (hopefully) advance. A number of people explicitly commented that this has meant in particular a new role for household women: both as labour, and as the brains (*budhi*) behind enterprises. At the same time, however, it is clear that households do not take up businesses at times when they are under particular pressure: there needs to be some surplus to act as starting capital. More positively then, the growth of businesses is also evidence of overall expansion in the rural economy: more goods are available for more of the time than in the past, and there is clearly the local demand to support this.

The new culture of business is interesting in view of the traditional picture given by BRAC (1983:171) that high social value inheres in landowning, salaried employment, education and ritual service/crafts, whereas: "Businessmen are caricatured as rapacious, exploiting the predicaments of others." My own observations suggest both that business is becoming more respectable as it becomes more necessary, and that some of the old paradigms still hold: people believe that there is now a new degree of self-interest and that the old community values have been lost. Perhaps people feel this at all times and in all places.

The increase in business enterprise has many more substantial implications. First, it indicates growing penetration of the market and the cash economy. The village ideal to be self-sufficient 'in all but salt' is now very far from the reality: poorer households do not have enough land to provide their basic needs; richer households have consumption tastes that cannot be satisfied by village produce alone. McCarthy (1981) notes that households' dependence on the market for traded goods declines with rise in socio-economic category, while the range of participation increases. This is supported by other studies (BRAC; Westergaard, 1982) and is consistent with the position in Kumirpur. Wealthier households therefore enter the market for traded goods on more advantageous terms. To give one example: richer households husk their own rice, and store paddy (unhusked rice) for sale when prices rise, thus realizing considerable profits; poorer people, on the other hand, often buy (more expensive) rice rather than paddy, because it can be purchased and eaten the same day, and is available in smaller amounts.

Second, the trend towards business affects cross-class relations. For poorer households, it may provide some independence of village patronage, in giving an alternative to agricultural labour as a source of income. This independence, however, is far from complete: businesses are typically supplementary to other economic activities, profits may be marginal and are subject to severe seasonal fluctuations. Also, the more profitable businesses of richer households consolidate both their wealth and political dominance through strengthening their links with the town and local officials. Third, the trend towards small business clearly has knock-on effects for the composition of gender identities. While women's work has always been of economic importance, its primary location within the homestead and close association with consumption (processing crops for use as food, for example) has allowed this to be masked. As more women become involved in small business, their work results more directly in income generation and is more easily recognized as economically significant. Alternatively, when men move into business on a more full-time basis, the household division of labour may shift, with women taking on a more open role in supervising field production while their husbands are away.

The presence of non-agricultural occupations is not new in Kumirpur. The Hindu groups have a history of hereditary occupations; aside from the Mahisyos, the Hindus of Kumirpur are all artisans by tradition. In other parts of Tanore the Boisnobs are sweet makers, but in Kumirpur they mainly produce snacks, *chanachur* (Bombay mix), poppadoms and so on. In the latter case, the whole household is involved in making the dough, rolling it out and otherwise preparing it to be taken by the husband/father and fried in the bazaar. With the shift to Muslim dominance observance of Hindu festivals has declined, and with it demand for these products. For most of the Boisnobs, therefore, snack-making is now at most a subsidiary occupation, pursued alongside agricultural labour and/or one of the newer businesses. The village blacksmiths are also Boisnobs, and one household produces small clay figures and decorative items for religious and ceremonial use. Men of the lower Hindu castes do metal-working (three households), shoe-making (four households) and their women midwifery (five households).

The man–market bias has meant that women's business involvement has received comparatively little attention: women's options tend to be regarded as limited to one of two alternatives – either work within the household, transforming basic resources, or employment by others. In fact, however, women's labour is involved in many small businesses. Thus in a (l/s ML) spice-trading household, it is the men who take goods to market, but by grinding 5 kg turmeric weekly the household women contribute Tk 100 in value added. The contribution of women to the business of many artisan households (such as weavers) is crucial to production. The weekly market, *hat*, is the main focus for marketing in the village, and is a pre-eminently male space. No woman goes there without very good reason, and usually not even with one. There is no doubt that women's options are constrained by their exclusion from the hat. Many none the less favour the possibilities of self-reliance and profit in business over dwindling opportunities for employment with little financial reward.

There is of course a tradition of female business enterprise in midwifery. 'Traditional birth attendants' (*dais*) have been 'discovered' in Bangladesh recently, as potential media for the dissemination of contraceptives and 'motivation' to sterilization. They have probably always been abortionists.[3] Muslim women may deliver their babies themselves, or with the help of a female relative, but some also call on a midwife, and Hindu women generally do. Payment for delivery varies according to the dai's skill and the woman's household's means, but the minimum is Tk 5 and 2.5 kg of rice for a girl, Tk 10 and 5 kg of rice for a boy (Kumirpur prices, 1986). When the girl is married, it is customary to send the midwife a new sari. In practice payments may be more generous but are also often delayed. With the abortionist side of the trade included, there is therefore some profit to be made through midwifery, though it is a very low status occupation and, at least among Hindus, tends to remain one limited to those born to the appropriate caste.

Without an extensive time–use survey, it is not easy to get reliable figures on seasonal businesses, as people tend to report only what they are engaged in at the time of asking, and may anyway filter their replies by what they consider worth mentioning (*bolar moto*). The figures given here therefore certainly underrepresent the degree of small business involvement in Kumirpur. There are also, of course, many businesses that fail but remain at the back of people's minds as a possibility for the future. Non-agricultural occupations clearly divide by status into those of salaried posts and services, and straightforward businesses. School teaching carries the most positive connotations: the five school masters in Kumirpur all belong to upper/strong households. Next are village doctors/pharmacists (four); and clerks in the land registry office (four). Members of these occupations belong to middle-income households (u/v or l/s). Businesses pursued by people in these categories have no particular status connotation, though they strengthen their links as individuals and their potential for giving favours. Examples of these occupations are tailoring (three); and salt or paddy trading (19).

Lower status businesses are such as: oil seed pressing (three); rice making (17); *murri* (puffed rice) making (six); (illicit) date/palm wine trading (eight); *gur* (molasses) making (four); onions, spices and potato trading (three); and curd[4] making (two). Households may signal social mobility by shifting the type of business they pursue. Hasan Mullah[5] is a case in point. He has been strikingly upwardly mobile, owning now forty bighas when he inherited only four. He used to have an oil seed press but let it fall into disrepair as he has worked to establish his new-found upper status. After some years one of his sons has learnt to use a sewing machine and is establishing a tailoring business. The oil press has been removed but people still talk of it to remind each other of Hasan Mullah's humble origins when they feel he is putting on airs.

The developments in agriculture over the past generation clearly underlie the expansion of business enterprise in Kumirpur. For paddy cultivation, fertilizers and pesticides have been in use since the 1960s, and most farmers do not grow even the amon crop without them. Reliance on inputs produced in the village is no longer viable and articulation within wider markets is a necessity, rather than an option. Sons of the richest households have therefore stepped in to manage the linkages between the local and wider markets. Aside from the sale of water itself, in four of the ten most prosperous households in the village, sons have businesses predicated directly on irrigation – fertilizer, spare parts and machine oil dealerships. Three of them own rice mills. The joint structure of these households means that such businesses may be pursued without neglect of agriculture. As they reach beyond the village area which is relatively 'safe' for women, these businesses are exclusively male. In discussion, however, women in wealthier households are more concerned with the new opportunities for household advancement that these businesses represent, than with their own exclusion from direct participation.

Poorer households have developed other kinds of business linked to the new technology. The men of two l/s households are professional STW mechanics and have a number of contracts for the irri/boro season at a set amount for maintenance. In each case the business was begun after dividing from a formerly more wealthy parent household and built on some initial capital (gained through dowry or inheritance) realized at the division. Two other men of the same class have become contractors for boring STWs and engage their brothers as labourers.

Women have been largely excluded from studies of new technology and agrarian change in Bangladesh. The case of rice mills is, however, an exception. Until recently, rice husking constituted the prime opportunity for employment for poor women in Bangladesh. The displacement of their labour by machine milling is widely cited as an example of the detrimental effect of development on women.[6] There is no doubt that this loss of employment has taken place. I believe, however, that the exclusive focus on this aspect leads to a misrepresentation of the impact that the rice mills have had in the village economy and in particular their implications for women.

Traditionally rice in the Kumirpur area is husked by *dheki*, in which women stand at one end of a heavy wooden beam supported on a pivot, working the beam up and down with their feet in order to pound grain with the other end. In place of this, rice is now husked by diesel- or electricity-driven rice hullers which are highly capital intensive and almost exclusively in male hands.[7] Only the simplest hullers are available in Kumirpur. In other areas, however, some employment is generated for women in mills that have on-site facilities for parboiling and drying the rice before husking.

It is impossible to gauge accurately what proportion of rice is now husked in mills since few of the rice hullers are registered, and they may not operate at full capacity as demand fluctuates and breakdowns occur. There is, however, no doubt that the number of mills is increasing rapidly: while I was in Kumirpur two new hullers were opened in a nearby village. At first it is primarily the richest households that use the hullers – those who used to employ poorer neighbours to husk their rice.[8] Over time, however, households of all classes gradually shift over to using the mill. Cost is the most common reason given for not husking paddy in the mill: it costs Tk5 per maund of paddy. Some of this can be covered, however, by selling for animal feed the powdered bran that the mill produces.[9] Another problem could be transporting paddy to the mill. In Kumirpur, however, women of lower-class households (Hindu and Muslim) are increasingly going to the mill themselves, and others can usually manage to arrange transport somehow.

The implications of rice mills for women are not, of course, class neutral. For richer women their prime result may be the removal of responsibility for engaging a poorer woman to husk their rice, and so the loss of an opportunity to bestow patronage. For women in middle income and poorer households who used to husk their own rice, the mills alleviate the heaviest part of their crop-processing work. For the poorest, the mills have meant loss of income for some, and have pushed others to shift from husking as employment into other work, including taking up rice businesses. In contrast to the negative way that rice mills are presented in the gender and development literature, there is no doubt that overall the women of Kumirpur regard the rice mills as a positive change. Women frequently and cheerfully remark how they used to spend hours at the dheki husking great volumes of paddy without thinking anything of it, whereas now even a small amount seems a great effort.

The separate spheres of academic debate tend to mean that discussions of new technologies in production and processing take place independently. In fact, however, the spread of, for example, mechanized irrigation and rice-husking equipment are linked at several levels. Increased production has resulted in increased consumption, although not at the same rate. Increased income is spent on food grains only in poorer households; when income has risen to a certain level, further increases are spent on other kinds of goods. In addition, it is the most prosperous farmers (those who were already consuming as much rice as they wanted) who have made the largest increases in production. Most of the surplus is thus sold as paddy, rather than processed to rice locally.

Even so, the consumption of rice has increased overall, both because of the growing population, and through a rise in the days of agricultural labour worked, and so total wages paid.[10] Rice is also used by many as the staple for financing week-by-week hat purchases, as well as directly by women in buying from door-to-door traders. The new cropping system thus predisposes towards rice mills from both the demand and supply side: on the one hand there is increased demand for paddy husking, and on the other there is new capital available for investment, from the richest farmers' profits from expanded production. The rice mills in turn are newly possible through the increased accessibility of modern technology (parts, mechanics, etc.). Thus there are clear links between the spread of rice mills and irrigation technologies. To give a very simple example: two of the three rice hullers owned by Kumirpur villagers are run by STW engines.

In line with the general trend towards small business in Kumirpur, rice husking businesses are becoming increasingly common. Rice businesses involve purchasing paddy and processing it to husked rice for re-sale. Profits vary greatly depending on marketing skill and season, but may be up to Tk30 per maund (approximately 25 per cent) in peak periods. I recorded 17 households in Kumirpur with established rice businesses; other households husk rice for re-sale on a less regular basis.

Eleven of the 17 households with regular rice businesses were in the poorest class, and all but one of the others lower/strong. All had separate or single internal structures.[11] Four were headed by widows which is particularly interesting in view of women's exclusion from the formal markets. A case study showing how one of these women manages this is given in the conclusion to this chapter.

The rice mills have undoubtedly been an important factor in the formation of these businesses, with elements of both push and pull. Negatively, the displacement of husking employment has undoubtedly been a push factor for many into starting their own business. A very high proportion of the women who now run rice businesses either themselves used to husk paddy for others, or have mothers-in-law who did. More positively, the availability of the rice mill for husking paddy means that business women can have a far larger turn over of grain than before. Parboti, a lower/strong Boisnob woman,[12] for example, says that she began processing weekly 1 maund of paddy; now she handles up to 7 maunds at peak times.

There are further pull factors which demonstrate the interrelation of activities in different sectors of the village economy. The seasonal migrants who come to harvest the irri/boro crop provide a captive market for local rice merchants. The extent to which traders are able to take advantage of this depends to some degree on their own liquidity. Parboti and her husband, Kitish, can afford to buy grain in bulk, process it in greater volumes on sunny days, and then store it to sell in rainy periods, when other less solvent households are unable to compete. Most households are not as single-minded as Kitish and Parboti. Many take up and drop the business as the seasons and their moods change. For some, the business is a way of halting or slowing decline. For others, like Kitish and Parboti, it is part of a deliberate and successful strategy for economic improvement.

Kitish is the eldest of four brothers, and he is the only one who has moved from the lower/vulnerable to the lower/strong class group. He and Parboti have achieved this through using to the full all of their human, material and social resources. Kitish was a boy worker in Dhiren's[13] household. Parboti brought with her a dowry of Tk1200. They gave it to Dhiren for safekeeping, because they were afraid that if they had it in the house it would just get frittered away. Dhiren lent it out for them over a number of years, and when the money had doubled, they bought a sewing machine with it. Kitish now works as an agricultural labourer, does tailoring in his midday break and on market days sells the rice that Parboti has husked and buys more paddy for her to work on over the following days. They are reinvesting profits from their businesses in the most enduring resource: land (mortgaged from Parboti's aunt). They are both committed to education for their children, though neither of them went to school themselves. They have fostered and used to their advantage strong cluster links, both with Dhiren and more recently with Sajjur[14] for whom Kitish works now. Summing up her own experience, it is Parboti who says of Kumirpur now: the rich may be getting richer but the poor are also getting on, by using their brains and hard work.

It is important not to assume automatic shifts in gender relations because of women's open involvement in economic activity. There is no doubt that the women who successfully run businesses do gain recognition for this in both their own households and the community more widely. It is difficult to distinguish cause and effect in this: it could be that more enterprising women take up businesses, and their centrality in the households derives more from their personalities than their business activities as such. The truth is probably that it is both more enterprising women who undertake such work and that they grow in confidence and recognition as their activities prove successful. It is however very important to be aware of the kinds of power that businesswomen may enjoy: they are still firmly tied to the household, rather than to their personal interest.

Thus in material terms, women may gain no new personal resources through their business activities. The type of personal rewards has not changed. Since the days of dheki husking, the ground bran by-product has been a perk for women. This can be sold as feed for ducks and cattle. Women continue to get this perk when they do rice businesses. It replaces the income that a woman could have made for herself by rearing animals, which because of the business she has no time to do. The rules for this income are the same as if she kept livestock: it is hers, as long as it doesn't amount to too much. The say that women have in the household depends at least as much on the quality of their relationships as on what they do. Thus Bindi,[15] a poor Boisnob woman, has for years covered their day-to-day running costs by her murri and rice businesses, while her husband spent their money on drink and other women. If she protested as he gradually sold off their land, he retorted simply: "I'm not selling your father's land but mine. So what is it to you?" On the other hand, in a good relationship, respect may grow as women show themselves able to make a major contribution to household advancement. This is quite evident in the case of Kitish and Parboti.

Women in the market

The ideal of purdah is for women to be fully occupied with their household work, and to do all this within their own homestead: the homestead is the area of fullest safety for women. The market-place (hat), on the other hand, is one of the most strictly male areas in rural Bangladesh. As noted in chapter 2, the apparent close fit between this situation and the separate spheres paradigm can lead to confusion between the analytical assumptions of the model and empirical observations. By a sleight of hand, the social 'household' is thus identified with the physical unit 'homestead'; the abstract 'market' is conflated to the physical 'market-place'. Then it is claimed, for example, that Bangladeshi women do not go out. This obscures cross-class relations between women and their participation in wider community affairs.

As already noted, it is simply not true that Bangladeshi women do not go out, but rather notions of 'inside' and 'outside' are open to complex manipulation. In Kumirpur, even those who observe the strictest purdah have to go outside the house for the performance of some household tasks. Washing dishes and clothes, bathing, fetching water, borrowing a bucket, borrowing the use of a dheki,[16] going to the mill, going to the doctor. All these and many more duties involve going outside. Muslim women tend to be more restricted than Hindu, and girls below puberty and older women are freer in their movements. As a general rule, poorer women have to go out more and further. Asked about purdah norms, poorer women say: "How could we run our households if we couldn't go out?!" One group of women laughed at the idea of men collecting fuel so the women could observe purdah: "There'd be nothing to eat!" Another said the men would beat them if there was no fuel in the house, not because they'd gone outside to collect it.

When they go out women meet and interact with one another, and these relationships are significant both for them personally and for their households as a whole. This gives a very different picture from the common stress on Bangladeshi women's isolation in their own homes. It might clearly be that Kumirpur is atypical of Bangladesh in this respect. Kumirpur is certainly in a part of Bangladesh where purdah restrictions are not particularly stringent[17] and my observations clearly reflect that. Comparable studies suggest, however, that the situation in Kumirpur is not unrepresentative. Maher (1976:72) remarks of her fieldwork in Morocco: 'I learnt that categorical statements like "women never go to market" cover a range of actual practice.' C. Young (1985:90) notes of Pakistan how women gathering to look at a pedlar's wares becomes a social event. Mayoux (1983:184) remarks that in the two villages in West Bengal she studied, women's collecting and gathering activities were an important opportunity for the exchange of information. Nath (1986:202) writing of a village in Rajshahi district, remarks how in the course of their daily work, women of different households meet and exchange news: 'Thus it is not true that village women who are secluded, do not know much about their surroundings.' While women may not commonly appear in the market-place, this does not mean that they do not participate in markets: their activities often underlie transactions in the hat, and there are extensive female networks for the exchange of goods within villages. Even beyond the bounds of the village, women play a central part in extending social resources: through marriage they form points of contact between households in different areas, and put a great deal of energy into celebrating and strengthening these links.

Before going further, it is important to point out what this does not show. In the first place, it is not the case that women can move about freely: there is no woman whose movements are not limited in some way. Second, going out of their homesteads does not signify women's independence of their households, nor is it necessarily an index of women's power within them. It is important not to reproduce assumptions that, for example, women's participation in activities outside the homestead is evidence of women's autonomy in/from the household. In fact, most activities outside the homestead serve to further the household interest. Even paid employment can be taken by women in fulfilment of their family roles, not in tension with them (Sharma, 1980a).

The most evident market for traded goods is the bi-weekly hat. On hat days a long crocodile of men can be seen making its way across the narrow field paths, on the way to market. Except for a very few Santals and some elderly Bengali widows, women keep well away. While women may be seen out shopping in towns, even widowed women who may move quite freely within the village still do not venture to the hat. This both ensures and expresses male dominance. On the one hand it identifies with men the basic power to use money as they choose, as even the labourers are temporarily flush with the pay they have just received.[18] On the other, it shows men also as the social and political representatives of their households as they gossip, bargain, make matches, lobby and so on, as the buying and selling goes on.

Their exclusion from the point of transaction does not however mean that women are uninvolved in the market. They may produce goods for sale and they often detail what should be bought or sold. They are eager to see and comment on (including abusively) the quality and price of goods their men have exchanged. In addition, women also buy and sell livestock in the hat through a male intermediary (usually a husband or servant). These are interesting cases which reverse the usual pattern: male activity on female instructions, with women taking, as it were, an executive role. Of course, this also makes women vulnerable as men may take commission on the sale, or even keep the whole profit themselves. This aspect should not, however, be emphasized to the exclusion of all others: women are intimately concerned with and knowledgeable about the market transactions on which the management of their households relies.

While the hat is the main focus for buying and selling, it is not the only one. People also buy from itinerant traders, or from one of the stores or another person in the village. The picture is not one of a single market, but rather of many different ones, each with different characteristics, in which people (including women) participate to different degrees. Table 5.1 shows a range of goods that are available within Kumirpur.

Table 5.1   Sales within the village

1 Regular stores
a) General stores (2): soap, cotton, rice, flour, lentils, spices, oil, biscuits, spiced nuts, molasses, tea, sugar, dried milk, potatoes, onions, cigarettes, biris,[19] matches, kerosene.

b) Hat traders who live in the village:
   Spices/potatoes, onions (2)
   Molasses (2)
   Medicine (2)
   Snacks (4)

2 Sales between households in the village:
a) Frequent: Food: eggs, milk, rice; Fodder: paddy husk; Fuel: charcoal, dung sticks, wood, paddy and wheat straw.
b) Occasional: Crop sale: mustard seeds, paddy, vegetables; Animals; Household items: mats, storage jars, fans, fishing nets.

3 Door-to-door traders
a) Year round: cloth, saris, lungis, bangles, jewellery; pots/pans, glassware, baskets, winnowing trays, brooms, fuel; fish, snacks, sweets.

b) Seasonally: Winter: sweet potato, gur, vegetables, lentils (bulk); Hot dry season (from the east): vegetables, yogurt; Rainy Season (from the west): mangoes, guava.

4 Services available from village households
Metal work (tools, knives, etc. – yearly contract), melding (metal jugs, plates, etc. – cash), lock repair; STW/cycle mechanics; Shoe repair; Midwifery; Medical.

Table 5.1 is not an exhaustive catalogue of goods and services available in the village but it clearly overturns the identification of the hat as *the* local market. The male bias of this emphasis on the hat is evident when it is considered that markets within the village are particularly important to women, and for households that have no adult men, or whose men are unwell, or poor at discerning quality or bargaining. It is these households also that make fullest use of the travelling pedlars – the range of goods, prices and often quality are generally better in the hat, so purchase in the village tends to be second best. Women also engage in secret purchases as part of their day-to-day household management (see chapter 7). The 'female' nature of these markets is reflected in their currency: for smaller transactions it is often rice, rather than cash. Rice is something that most women have relatively easy access to, cash they do not.

Personal links are important in these markets as in others. Larger items (such as saris) are commonly bought on credit – the same traders tour the villages every couple of months, and pick up payment when they return. Credit in fact is the basis for a very large number of transactions, including purchases at village stores and husking at the mill (both of which may be done by women). Further credit is refused for non-payment. Also, terms of payment are flexible for people of different classes and in different relations to (for example) the mill owner.

Women may choose to sell crops and animals in the village because that way they can keep direct control. This aside, sale within the village can clearly be convenient for both buyer and seller, saving on the time and effort of transport. This sometimes becomes a regular arrangement, often as part of a wider cluster relationship. Paddy, for example, is often sold by wealthier households to finance their weekly hat purchases. Poorer households with rice husking businesses need to buy paddy. The richer household may thus sell directly to the poorer, circumventing the hat. This lessens demands on the poorer household's liquidity[20] and has the added advantage that the poorer household may be able to use its own scales – rice made from a maund of hat-bought paddy can fall 2–3 kg short of that made from paddy bought at home.

Running parallel to the major markets for land, labour and loans, women engage in markets for minor resources: animals, female labour and smaller scale loans. As many examples already given show, relations between female and male members of two households are often interrelated. Thus BRAC (p. 45) record the 'daily labour of wife' as one of the 'gratis' items a regular worker may give his patron! As in the previous chapter, therefore, the concern here is to see what kinds of relations these markets involve and the ways that interaction expresses solidarity and contradiction. This highlights differences between the two sets of markets, as well as demonstrating interconnections and similarities between them.

Where share contracts between men concern land, those between women concern animals. In Kumirpur, goats, sheep and chickens are most frequently share-tended. Share-tending of cattle is found in other areas but it is rare in Kumirpur. The typical arrangement is for a richer woman to give an animal to a poorer woman to tend. The owner thus provides the capital and the tender the labour: animals are usually taken out to forage rather than fed in the home with fodder that would have to be produced or purchased. Profits are divided on an equal share basis – owner and tender take alternate kids/lambs/chicks, or divide the income from sale. Share contracts thus provide a means for richer women to generate some private income without withdrawing any labour from the household, and for poorer women to transform their labour into material assets.

Share-tending also has an important social aspect. While formally contracts only need to last for a single season, they often extend beyond this – the goat may produce only a single kid, or the mother be shared out again to the same tender. Even when they are not part of wider cluster links, such relationships may be very long-standing: when I asked one poor Hindu woman how she had come to take a goat for share-tending from an Exchange Muslim household in a different neighbourhood, she explained that she had share-tended another of their goats, 15 years before. In most cases particular contracts represent the activation of already existing but possibly dormant links. Alongside their economic value, therefore, share-tending contracts are given as a sign of favour from a richer patron and an expression of the good relationship between the two parties.

Mechanisms for the arrangement of share-tending contracts are *ad hoc*, but none the less fall into discernible patterns. As poorer women are less constrained by purdah norms they may be able to arrange contracts directly. In joint households this is usually possible only for the mother-in-law. Daughters-in-law thus generally have to refer to their mothers-in-law if they want to give or take an animal for share-tending. For richer women, however, there is less likely to be opposition than if they plan to buy an animal to keep themselves, since sharing out involves no diversion of their labour. They may also arrange it through their husbands. Workers, male or female, may be asked if they know of someone who would like to tend the animal, or may see it and ask for it themselves. A poorer woman may ask for an animal to share-tend, and so encourage a richer woman to purchase, either then or later on. Poorer women may sell an animal in time of hardship, and receive it back to share-tend. Information is also passed at social visits and by children.

There is a further aspect to share-tending. As it physically removes the asset from the owner's own household, it gives women a chance of greater autonomy than other forms of saving which are open to plunder from the family. Like loans between women, therefore, share-tending can represent a way in which co-operation between women acts to keep assets in female hands. Thus married women commonly share-tend out in their natal village to retain some independence of their husband's household. In less wealthy families, the animals may be tended by younger brothers or sisters; in other cases they may be given to a poorer woman in the household cluster. Both an asset is shared and a relationship is affirmed. Nath (pp. 235–6) notes also that this is a way that sub-units in joint households may covertly prepare for division. It is not only women who remove assets from the household to evade plunder. In Kumirpur I also came across cases of labouring sons keeping their wages with their employers, to save up for some larger purchase.

While animals are usually held by women in their own right, some women may give loans of household resources. On their own authority, women may formally lend only small amounts of rice – usually without interest, and often effectively as charity. While the amounts involved are small, so is the scale of the income on which those who need such loans have to manage, so this represents an instance for women of richer households to express power. This is reflected in the fact that the right to give such loans is an important expression of authority differentials between women in the household. There are tensions if, for example, a daughter-in-law gives such a loan without her mother-in-law's permission. This is seen as a bid for headship, and may unite other sisters-in-law with the mother-in-law against her. Such differentials in authority are an important means by which individuals are reconciled to their place in the household hierarchy – and so to the reproduction of their overall subordinate position within it. As Sharma (1978:274) remarks: 'There is no better means of social control than the devolution of internal control onto the group that is to be subordinate.'

Women also lend money of their own and this is probably the quickest way for them to build up savings for their personal use or for their sub-unit within the joint household. Borthwick (1984:20) in her study of middle-class Bengali women in the second half of the nineteenth century, notes some instances of women running money-lending enterprises. Abdullah and Zeidenstein (p. 46) remark that some women loan to small businessmen, such as weavers. BRAC record wealthier women loaning at a monthly interest rate of 8–12 per cent, slightly less than that taken by men. Loans between women are clearly exploitative and yet also contain elements of gender solidarity. They are often given – and taken – secretly, part of a subterfuge in inequality between women against men. They are part of the web of clandestine activity in which women are engaged (see chapter 7).

As part of their religious duties women give to the beggars who knock at their doors. Men may beg for a specific purpose, such as a dowry for their daughter, otherwise male beggars in the Kumirpur area are either religious mendicants or people who are mentally disturbed. Most beggars are impoverished women, who live in one of the neighbouring villages, and regularly tour the area in pairs or with a child. As they are exempt from the usual restrictions on female mobility, these beggars are an important channel by which information is passed between women over relatively large distances.

It is in employment relations between women that the character of the minor markets is most clearly shown. Employment is typically part of a clustering of links. R. Rahman (1986:68) states that of the 80 working women she interviewed, 30 had taken loans from their employer in the previous year. While the average amounts are small, a gift or loan can be of great importance in a sudden crisis. She judges that these ties are an important part of the reason that poorer women enter employment, and likens them to a social insurance system. Employment relations are thus built on contradiction. On the one hand a particular contract is important for its expression of a social relationship (and so appears to show solidarity). On the other hand, the transaction is deeply unequal, and serves to reproduce the inequalities between the two parties. The most complete example of this is domestic service, where a woman worker is incorporated as a 'family' member, but barely earns enough to cover her essential needs. These two contradictory aspects indicate key dimensions of the gender/class complex of inequality.

Female employment also provides a key instance for making local comparisons of the situations of different women, and so avoiding the dangers of distortion in analysis which is drawn from other contexts. In the exchange of labour, supervision and patronage, female employment expresses the key characteristics of class relations and thus shows how deeply the interests of women are divided. Looked at differently, the employment of women is like a mirror image of the situation of household women themselves. Live-in domestic servants again provide the pre-eminent example of this. They work very long hours, for no wages except their keep, and this is legitimated by use of 'family' terminology. They are open to physical beating and their sexual abuse is very common. The onus on them is to please, and they face expulsion if they fail to do this. The similarity between the position of these two groups of women might well be used to demonstrate a radical point about the oppression of Bangladeshi women. Sympathy between them can, indeed, lead to expressions of solidarity, especially in relation to sexual abuse by household men. Reflection on the differences in their circumstances, however, points up some factors of significance to power relations in the household, and to class dynamics.

In Bangladesh as a whole, the increasing numbers of women seeking employment is one of the most widespread trends. In the past women working outside the household has carried negative associations for social status. This seems gradually to be changing as at one end of the spectrum élite and middle-class women are choosing to seek salaried employment, and at the other a growing number of women are being forced by poverty to seek waged work. Traditional barriers are breaking down, both in the kinds of work that are done and in who is doing it (now often young married women, not only as previously, older widows). These changes act as key foci in the literature on women and work, because of beliefs that going out to work will raise female status.

Whatever the shifts in views of fit work for women, women's employment opportunities are still severely limited. Ideally women work only within their own gusti, as this does not have the harmful status implications of work for others, though in practice this is often ignored, or got around by referring to employers using kin terms. As far as possible, therefore, female employment shadows the work done by women in their own households: it is done amongst kin, involves accepted 'female' tasks, is done in mainly female company, and usually involves payment in kind. Many writers contrast the conditions of women's employment with the relatively 'free' market for male labour. Thus R. Rahman compares the 'attached-cum-casual' work of women, with the 'customary wage' at a fixed market rate, for men. Abdullah and Zeidenstein (p.

43) take a similar line, as they describe women's employment relations as 'feudal'. These studies underestimate the part that personal links play in the male employment market. None the less, it is probably true that personal factors are even more important in women's than men's employment. While the pay of male workers approximates to a market rate, payment of female workers is haphazard.

Even so, as in the male employment market, female labour relations in Kumirpur are now freer than they used to be. Unlike the male case, however, this reflects a fall in demand for female labour, chiefly because of the mechanization of rice husking. It is quite difficult to put figures to the extent of labour displacement, partly because of lack of information about the mills, as noted above. In Kumirpur, however, many of the women who used to have regular husking contracts are now too old to want them, or their sons have taken share-crop land which covers the short-fall, or they have married away into another village. The young women of poorer households now look to other means of income generation – such as through business. They thus take advantage of the new opportunities which mechanization affords, rather than looking backwards to what has been lost. It is not the case, as some reports imply, that the women who used to do husking work are now sitting idle and wishing those days back.[21]

There is no doubt, however, that the loss of rice husking employment has depressed wage rates for female labour. These differ greatly by area, and in the same region over time. In Kumirpur, there used to be a 'share-husking'[22] system, whereby 1 maund of paddy was husked for a payment of 4 seers of paddy, a ratio of 10 parts husked to 1 part unhusked. This has not been practised for many years. Now, women are paid the mill rate – Tk4–5 per maund. This is equivalent to about 1.5 seers, or a ratio of 27:1. This acute decline needs no emphasis.

Those who used to husk rice typically stay within the richer household's cluster, and do whatever work comes up. Before paddy is husked in the mill it has to be parboiled and dried, and some women take up a seasonal contract to do this.[23] At peak times, women may have a daily turnover of 2–3 maunds. The set rate is 10 seers paddy for every 20 maunds parboiled, a ratio of 80:1, in addition to meals. There may be four months' regular work parboiling paddy in a year in Kumirpur – three months after the amon harvest and one after the irri/boro paddy is cut. Wages for this work amount to approximately one-quarter of the male agricultural wage for the same period.[24] The longest term female contract at present in Kumirpur involves clearing out the cattle and making the dung into a usable form for fuel.[25] A yearly contract involving 1–2 hours work each day brings in 4 maunds of paddy. Women also get paid for a range of goods that they make to order. Large mud jars for storing paddy may sell for Tk80, smaller chicken coops for Tk20. Women who are particularly good at sewing may receive orders for a quilt. The materials are supplied, and payment is by size – Tk100 for a quilt would not be unusual, for work done over 2–3 months. As in other forms of employment, the payment depends on the relationship – a friend may do it for free.

For all but the richest households, the most common way to gain extra female labour is to call on someone to 'help out'. This phrasing clearly de-emphasizes the extent of labour involved. Women may hire other women in this way for odd jobs without reference to men, but would not arrange for a woman to come on a regular basis without consulting with other household members. Payment for helping out varies widely, and is often not spelt out beforehand. The exchange of labour is an affirmation of the relationship between women (or households) and this may mean the worker accepts working for minimal pay or (occasionally) is treated more generously. The rules of payment are better understood if particular pieces of employment are seen as expressions of a relationship between women, rather than as isolated transactions. Thus Gita, a very poor Boisnob widow,[26] husked paddy for murri for one of the dominant households in her cluster, Mannan's.[27] She worked the dheki alone, though it is usually done by two women together, as the beam was split so would only bear the weight of one. For this work she received no payment, as Mannan's wife put it: 'She only put her foot a little.' Gita felt abused, but that she had to go: she feared their anger if she refused and more general social criticism as lazy if she rejected a call to work. As a widow, she is particularly dependent on the goodwill of her neighbours and this requires she demonstrate herself to be one of the 'deserving' poor. The demands of the particular relationship are thus reinforced by wider community pressures.

Even for the same task, different women may receive different rates. Dhiren's wife, Sukhi,[28] employed three women – her second cousin and two in close cluster relation to her – to resurface the rough new inner walls of their two-storey house. It took five days, on and off, for which the women received their food and Tk20, Tk25, and Tk10, respectively. She told each of them not to tell the others, and believed they would not, justifying the differences in pay by the quality of the work: 'Everyone is not equal, there is more and there is less.' Sukhi was in fact employing them on a self-regulated unofficial piece-work basis, reckoned in the quality of their work and nature of their ties with herself.

A fuller relationship can work in favour of the poorer party also. Some households may thus invite poor women of their cluster in to sort through the paddy straw after threshing: the grain gathered in this way is regarded as a 'woman's perk'. One woman reckoned she had gained half a maund of paddy in this way over 5–6 days and a quarter maund of wheat for 3 days' winnowing wheat in the same household.

This section on the minor markets ends with consideration of the weakest case: women employed as domestic workers in other people's households. All except one (Kangali Serkar's[29]) of the upper/strong households employed a regular female worker, several upper/vulnerable households either 'borrowed' the worker of their wealthier kin or had in the past kept a domestic worker themselves, and hoped to in the future. Domestic workers were in short supply. This perhaps reflects some alleviation of poverty with the new opportunities for business or agricultural employment and share-cropping. It certainly is also due to the exploitative terms which domestic workers face. Only those women who have neither social nor material resources to call on would go as a domestic worker to another's house. The sharpness of the vulnerabilities such women face highlights a nexus of class and gender subordination.

A local Muslim girl, Khusi, was divorced because her father was unable to pay the full dowry he had promised. Her home is next door to Akhbar's, so she went there as a domestic worker, and lived with them fairly happily for a number of years, only going home to sleep. Finally she left, extremely upset, because of the misuse she had suffered at the hands of the junior daughter-in-law.[30] Asha and I saw her soon after, and I quote here what she said, as it captures much of the sense of double-bind, of being in the household but not of the household, of multiple vulnerabilities:

"She always used to be getting after me, picking quarrels. I put up with it for so long, but in the end I couldn't bear it any more. I mean, you have all the work to cope with, and then that on top of it. Who could bear it? Then sometimes I'd maybe answer back and that they don't want to hear, quarrels all the time. After all, it is their home, and I'm an outsider. I know that if you work somewhere then you have to do what they say, but all the time! Sometimes I couldn't even eat, I was so upset.

"The others weren't like that. They treated me like one of their own. They gave me my clothes – they never gave any to the girls who worked there before me. Even now – you saw – I can go and visit. They say all the time, why don't I come round any more. But somehow I don't feel like it.

"She used to complain about me getting clothes. But what could I do? I couldn't work for nothing. I had somehow to get clothes for my back. Just all the time, she got on at me. In the end she said, Go, go on home. So I did. Without even having my meal I left.

"How will I live now? If people call me, here or there, I'll go and work a morning or so and then eat lunch. No one has anything. My mother's alone, my brother's alone, they can't feed me. And then I came home at the very leanest time of the year. It was very hard, very hard that month.

"If I'd stayed at home, kept a goat or two, some chickens . . . but not even that. I've nothing. I'll have to try and share-tend some, but who'll give them to me? No one will. Then try a bit of business. Somehow I'll just have to try and make ends meet. Actually my luck is just bad. What your fate is, that's what will be. My luck's just bad."

This brought a furious reaction from Asha:

"Do you see? This is what it's like. Why do you think the rich say they can't find anyone to work? You've seen the state of things, how things are. Does anyone say they're well off? No one. In want, everyone. So why can't they get people to work?

"This is how it was for me too. I worked two years in Sajjur's house, and all the time his mother was getting at me. Then in Tozimember's, and his wife was just the same. When I left I came home and said, just like Khusi, I may die from want of food, but I'll never work in someone's house again.

"Take the Mondols. They get these little girls to work for them, and then if one doesn't understand . . . I mean, really little. There was one little girl from another village. They so got at her that she just took off one day and walked back home. Then Jori's sister.[31] Came home this morning crying because Sajjur's ma had been getting at her, just as she used to at me. But what can she do. The poor! In a day or two she'll have to slink back like a dog and ask to work there again.

"You've seen it. You understand this. And then rich people say they can't find anyone to work. There's a reason for that! If in the home there's just a little bit, who would send their daughter out to undergo this?"

Dependence is a key element in the cultural constitution of female identity in Bangladesh. This means that their relationships constitute their chief resources. This is true of both women in wealthier households and those who work for them. The women who oppress draw on the security of their social position in their husband's household. The women who are oppressed are vulnerable specifically in this: they are working in the households of others because they lack adequate social, not only material resources. It is not the employment relationship as such that underlies their vulnerability, but their lack of the sources of human support, which law and custom makes necessary to them.

These women occupy the lowest point of the social pyramid, where subordination by class and gender converge. They have access neither to goods or property by which to assert independence, nor a male guardian on whom they can depend. Their dependence is thus transferred to a household in which they have no stake, and their entry is on terms which ensure they receive only the minimum necessary to subsistence in return. Young girls have some hope, that they will marry and one day have their own home to work in. Women who are set to remain single are uniquely vulnerable. Domestic service is an extreme case of a relationship that can serve only to produce inequalities.[32] There is little within it that disposes its transformation – little, that is, but the intolerable nature of the terms of exchange, which may eventually force exit, to an uncertain alternative.

Friends and neighbours

The interweaving of personal and formal elements in market transactions makes it difficult to draw a strict line between 'social' and 'economic' relationships. Mutual help relationships between female neighbours therefore have much in common with the more supportive elements in the minor markets. While male household members have the formal responsibility for supporting the family, in practice this informal co-operation between women is crucial to the day-to-day running of the household. Sharma (1980a:193) describes a 'local team of friends, neighbours, and female kin who assist a woman (not without conflict at times) in fulfilling her obligations as a wife.' It is important to note, however, that these relationships sustain women in doing their own work: they do not represent sharing work in common (see Jeffery et al., 1989:48). As with market relationships, these forms of co-operation express both alliances and divisions between women and households of different classes.

Informal co-operation between sisters-in-law may persist long after the household is formally divided. This calls into question the popular myth that conflicts between women are responsible for the breakup of joint households. In fact, many writers interpret this as a culturally acceptable fiction, where brotherly love is strongly prescribed. Rohim's and Karim's[33] households occupy adjoining rooms facing a narrow covered passage which comprises the women's workspace. While working separately, their wives are effectively together all day long, and take turns for example, one to watch the paddy as it dries outside and make sure the birds don't eat it, while the other is cooking or doing some other work. If either runs short of something, she always borrows it from the other, or from a third sister-in-law who lives round the corner. This kind of co-operation is very common, and not only between kin. A Hindu woman dries her paddy in a Muslim neighbour's yard, as there is no sunlight or space in her own; a poorer woman borrows a bucket and fetches water from a richer friend's HTW – and her son makes secret sales and purchases for the friend in return.

As these examples show, the needs that are fulfilled by this web of mutual support vary according to class. Poorer women most frequently borrow small amounts of (particularly) food, as they are most likely to run short and often lack funds to buy in. Patterns of borrowing differ. One household in Kumirpur is notorious for carrying on virtually all its business on the basis of pawning objects (such as brass dishes) for rice, then redeeming them on the strength of having pawned them again elsewhere. Such households that are frequently in want may have to search over a wide area before they find someone willing to help them out. More commonly, however, items are borrowed on a reciprocal basis, particularly between kin, or households of similar economic standing. As one l/v woman remarked: 'The poor are more feeling towards the plight of the poor.'[34]

Mutual help is central to women's everyday management of the household. Relationships between women are thus a crucial part of a household's social resources. They are clearly also a personal network of support for women as individuals. In view of this it is surprising that McCarthy (1967) writes that half the women she interviewed said they had no friends. This varied according to education – friends are formed in class – and reflected the fact that friendships tend to be something for the natal, not marital village. The supportive relationships noted above are, however, between married women. There is clearly thus some kind of paradox here. Part of this may reflect the specialized nature of the Bengali term for friend, *bondhu* (f. *bandhobi*). While this can be used in a general way, it is often used for a very close and formalized relationship, amounting virtually to fictive kinship. This is clearly very different from the English understanding of the term, 'friend'.

Sharma (1980a) believes the dominant use of kinship terms means that women's relationships among themselves are defined as belonging to the domestic and family sphere. A similar ambiguity is of course present also in the West, with the rediscovery and celebration of 'sisterhood' in the women's movement. In Bangladesh, kinship is the idiom for a wide range of relationships. Thus employers may be called *Caca* or *Kaka* (uncle, Muslim and Hindu respectively); schoolmistresses *Apa* or *Didi* (sister, Muslim and Hindu) or a senior male colleague *Dada* (elder brother). Also, people 'adopt' one another formally as fictive kin and this is taken very seriously, sometimes meaning more dependable ties than blood relationships (Nath, p. 123). In such circumstances, the lines between 'friendship' and 'kinship' are far from clear.

Women's relationships – whether construed as 'friendships' or 'kin-relations' – are often presented in caricature: women are either 'sisters' or locked in jealous combat. Pastner (1974:412) reports that in Pakistani Baluchistan women are 'forced' to rely on each other by the norms of sexual segregation and so each has a set of linkages with other women defined as their *wati* (own). Vatuk (1971:190) similarly stresses the bonds between women as she notes in a village in Uttar Pradesh how one woman acted as 'banker' to a group of friends, enabling them to retain control of their money by depositing it outside their own household. This is quite common, she says, and is: 'an expression of her long-established relations among a close-knit in-group of women friends within her neighbourhood.'

By contrast, for the Hindu community she studied in Pakistan, C. Young states that the overall group identity of being female, and of a particular caste, was extremely important, but particular friendships between women were short-term alliances formed for a specific (usually economic) purpose. It is, as Sharma (1980a:178) remarks, a hazardous thing to try and judge the quality of other people's lives and relationships. There is in particular the danger of implicit criticism that friendships are not more disinterested. At the simplest level, the discrepancy in the views noted above might derive from the use of two different time scales – with Young taking minor ruptures more seriously, while the other studies take a longer view. More substantially than this, however, I think that reflecting on women's construction as dependent on their relationships can make sense of aspects of mutuality and the elements of contradiction and instrumentality in their dealings with one another.

Women's friendships need to be considered in the context of interconnecting 'market' linkages and 'personal' ties. This is expressed very well by Maher (1976) in discussion of another Islamic society, Morocco. In Morocco, Maher (p. 53) states, co-operation between women is an institution, like kinship or marriage, and in a situation of declining landholdings: 'the woman network acts as a buffer against the vicissitudes of the market, and in a minor way it channels the means of subsistence from the richer to the poorer members of kinship-based communities' (ibid.:55). She links women's lack of economic and political autonomy with a drive to establish security through ties of personal indebtedness resulting in: 'a mode of relationship in which women combine sentiment and instrumentality' (ibid.:68). Maher's crucial insight here is the importance of personal relationships, of social capital to women. The fact that women in Bangladesh are constructed as dependent is repeatedly made. What fails to be noted is that this may become the centre of their power, as well as a site of vulnerability.

Women's dependence on social resources has a dual aspect. On the one hand it fosters careful adherence to gender and communal norms. These set women against one another. First, they encourage harsh, and damaging, criticism of other women's 'misbehaviour' in 'gossip'. Second, they lead to distance – and distrust – between women of different communities. These are both very evident in Kumirpur and noted widely elsewhere. Liddle and Joshi (1986:234) refer to: 'the gender specific notion of respectability' which is crucial to caste maintenance in India. Cohen (1978) remarks how mutual help between women on a middle-class British housing estate and in a Creole community in Sierra Leone, serve to reinforce class difference. One of the most common refrains in women's conversations during my time in Kumirpur was the phrase: 'People will talk badly . . .'. It was a very effective deterrent to any nonconformist action. On the other hand, women's lack of rights in material assets makes their relationships of overriding significance. While social linkages are important even in more formal market settings, this is still more striking in areas of women's activity, in both family and market. Few women can fulfil their household responsibilities without calling on the network: for labour, for loans, for help with child-care or marketing. In defence of their own interests too, women need to be adept politicians, fostering good relations with their neighbours and in the family, both immediate and extended, to build up their social capital.

Women's relationships with each other are a key part of their social resources: they are an important means through which they negotiate their own, and their households' advancement. It is thus not surprising that these linkages show contradictory, as well as solidary, aspects. It is their social capital, the relationships which 'combine sentiment and instrumentality' (Maher), that constitutes the prime means of female power in Bangladeshi society.

Conclusion

Looking at women in business enterprise and transacting labour and goods overturns the common view of women isolated within their own households. Rather, it is as though there is a wide-reaching skein of relationships binding women to one another, persisting over time. These relationships may cross class, and are articulated with the household's class position, just as are those between men. To a large extent, the male network and the female skein overshadow one another and they interconnect at key points. Even aside from this, activity in one sphere is vitally predicated on that in the other. Women's networks extend over a wide geographical area, taking in the woman's natal family. Because of the norms regarding women's activity, the skein remains half-hidden, but is none the less strong. Rather than dealing directly with one another, women may interact by pulling on the threads by which they are linked.

Women's interaction through the minor markets in many ways mirrors exchanges between men in the major markets. Both have been significantly affected by new technology; in both, the terms on which people participate are clearly differentiated by class and class relations are in turn reproduced or transformed through them; both show a high degree of interlinkage; in both social and economic factors are closely interwoven; both show contradictory and solidary aspects. The great difference between them is of course in the scale of resources: the gender segregation of markets clearly prefigures male dominance. It also has implications for relations within the two sets of markets. As the scale of material resources that women exchange is smaller, so the social element in any transaction is relatively larger. This intensifies their contradictory character: often it means a particular transaction between women shows even more severe exploitation than one between men; sometimes it can mean greater solidarity or charity.

Relations between women are both important for mutual support and may serve as a means of personal and household advancement. Their links beyond the household, however, do not indicate women's independence. Rather, women's social and economic activities are in fulfilment of their family roles: providing for the reproduction of the household unit. Even for single women running businesses, their economic activities complement their relationship network, they do not provide an alternative source of support.

The example of Gita[35] shows this very clearly. Gita was widowed ten years ago. Before that, she and her husband used to run a small business selling murri-based sweets.[36] Their daughters learnt marketing from their father. Since his death, Gita has run a rice business, mainly relying on her daughters to sell the rice in the hat. Her oldest daughter was the best businesswoman, and Gita still regrets her loss: at puberty she had to give up going to hat and has since married away. Gita's son now does their marketing, but he can manage only 1 maund at a time, while her daughter used to sell 2 maunds at each hat. The household income is further augmented by keeping goats and her son's wages – he now does agricultural work on a regular basis.

While Gita has managed in this way to run an independent household, she has still needed to foster close cluster relationships. Her daughters sold rice in the hat under the protection of their 'uncles': their neighbours or the men of Sajjur's kin group, to whose cluster she belongs. Gita often buys paddy from Sajjur's kin group, and supplies some rice on a regular basis to (generally single) households in the village that have difficulty in going to the hat. Gita also takes work in the households of others in her cluster – thereby cementing relationships as well as earning a little extra income (as in husking for Mannan's wife, noted above). In this way she has kept the household solvent, even marrying her eldest daughter (with a dowry of Tk3300 and gold) without going into debt. In March 1986 Gita's second daughter was married, however, and this time she had to take loans of Tk4000 from her brothers. Again, the material significance of social relationships is very clear: loaning to a Bangladeshi landless widow is not a good investment proposition.

The social and juridical laws of Bangladesh which construct female dependence without doubt place great constraints on women's options. What is however most striking, is the way that women have taken these constraints as resources, and turned them to their own use. The strong structural discouragements to female independence thus foster women's concentration on their networks and relationships for social capital, and these come to represent the crucial locus of female power, in a society of which networking is the central underlying principle.

Notes

1. The Grameen Bank was formed in 1976 with the aim of providing credit to poor village people. From being a project of the Bangladesh Bank and a quasi-NGO, it became registered as a fully fledged bank in its own right in 1983.

2. Bangladesh Rural Advancement Committee.

3. Despite the strong ideology of sexual morality, unwanted pregnancy, both within and outside of marriage, is common in rural Bangladesh. Both local doctors and midwives regularly perform abortions, by various methods. See in addition Blanchet (1984); S. Islam (1986); Jorgensen (1983).

4. This is sold as a basis for sweets.

5. 6.1 ME u/v j.

6. See Nelson (1979).

7. There are three main types of rice mill: rice hullers, which are the commonest form in villages and husk rice primarily for domestic use; major or commercial mills, which are quite common within easy reach of villages in better connected areas and have on site parboiling and drying facilities; and automatic rice mills, huge plants used primarily by large business or government interests.

8. Greeley (1985:271), for example, states that 75 per cent of those who used the mill in the first year that it was introduced in the village he studied in Tangail district were in this category.

9. Dheki husking also produces this gure, but in much smaller amounts.

10. Wages are paid partly in cash, partly in kind (meals, rice or paddy).

11. Wealth and household structure are, of course, related.

12. 2.5 HB l/s s.

13. 1.1 HM u/v s.

14. 2.1 ME u/s j.

15. 5.3 HB l/v j.

16. Many richer households no longer have a dheki as they husk all their paddy in the mill, but there are some items for which dheki husked rice is preferred (such as rice flour for fried cakes). In this case, richer women may go to a poorer homestead to use its dheki.

17. A woman in a burqa would be seen only on the bus to Rajshahi, and then only one or two in a full bus.

18. Employers often pay daily workers at the hat.

19. Local cigarettes.

20. If they are going to buy and sell in the same hat, the traders have to buy paddy first – and therefore have cash to cover the full amount with them – and then take whatever time necessary to sell their rice.

21. This clearly assumes that some other opportunities become available. Kumirpur is in a period of expansion, so this is perhaps more the case there than it would be elsewhere. But on the other hand, the spread of rice mills is itself a part of that expansion: the same process which removes some kinds of opportunity itself generates others.

22. By analogy with share-cropping, share-cutting and share-tending.

23. For details of this process see Martius Von Harder (1981) or Abdullah and Zeidenstein (1982).

24. This is calculated on the rate of Tk120/maund of paddy which is an average figure for markets in the Kumirpur area.

  For four months' work:
  Male wage: Tk1000 + 8 maunds paddy @ Tk120 = Tk1960
  Female wage: 120 days parboiling @ 3 maunds paddy = 360 maunds
      Worker's share @ 80:1 ratio = 4.5 maunds
      4.5 maunds paddy @ Tk120 = Tk540

Thus the ratio of male wage: female wage (Tk1960/Tk540) is approximately 4:1.

25. There are three main forms of this: squeezing dung around sticks, slapping dung cakes against the house wall to dry; or letting it dry in small loose balls. In the rainy season, the dung is usually used for manure.

26. 2.7 HB1/v si.

27. 2.2 ME u/v j.

28. 1.1 HM u/v s.

29. 5.1 HM u/s j.

30. Who has problems of her own, with a poor marital relationship, see chapter 6.

31. 6.2 ME l/v s.

32. Perhaps the main factor that mitigates this is that the 'adoption' of a girl worker into the 'family' may mean that her employer acquires a responsibility (as *Mama* (maternal uncle) or *Dada* (elder brother) to find her a husband when it is time for her to marry. This by no means always takes place: it depends on the quality of their relationships and the employer's susceptibility to the pressure of social norms.

33. 3.2a ML e; 3.2b ML s.

34. In Bengali: '*gorib goribder maya besi bujhe*' the translation provided is a free one – these are the exact words used.

35. 2.7 HB l/v si.

36. Murri and similar rice products are coated with a mixture of flour and gur (molasses).

6.   Links in a Chain

Introduction

While I was staying in Kumirpur, I used sometimes to visit Sufira Begum in her home in a neighbouring village. She was a striking woman, one of the first in the upazila to take an office job, who had faced out the opposition of her family and somaj and gradually won wide respect in the local area. As we sat together one afternoon, she described to me her experience:

"Sister, listen. Listen to what I say. Let me tell you what I went through, how many different things I had to hear, when I first took this job. If you hear you will be amazed.

"I was married when I was still quite young. The marriage took place suddenly, they came from here to see me, and all we heard about them was good, that their economic position was good, that the boy's character was good. And he is good. That I'll never say. It was not him, but the others, who caused me so much trouble. Remember, a household is not just one person, it's twenty. And among those are good and bad.

"I said to my father afterwards, You have married myself and my elder sister this way, that is enough. You don't know how much I had to hear, how many bad things, because of how quickly I was married. Everyone said that there must be some fault, must be some reason, that without even coming to look at the boy's house my father married me. What could I say? I just had to listen to this, and weep before God at night.

"It was not just that. The customs of everywhere are not the same. In my home, we were brought up to be free. It was town, and we were encouraged to go out to study, to learn music. There was only one rule, that we must be home by nightfall.

"Then I came here. And suddenly there was no electricity, no fans. All the women did all day was cook, and I couldn't cook, at home my mother did all that and our cooking was different anyway. I hadn't had a thought in my head to marry. But my father said, we have arranged it all, it will be disrespect if you don't agree. So what could I do?

"You can't imagine how they used to get at me. Always saying, this must be done, that must be done. I wasn't used to living like that. That's why I took the job. In the end I thought, I must do something, I must stand on my own feet. I'll take a job so that I can support myself, so I don't any more have to take anything from them.

"So then I heard that they were looking for people for this job. I'd been married three years then, and my daughter was about three months old. So I said that I wanted to try for a job. Again, all sorts of things I had to hear! They were all against it, even my husband sometimes said yes, sometimes said no. My father-in-law wasn't like that. While he lived it was better. He loved me. He always said to me, study, take a job, do as well as you can for yourself. But after he died there was no one.

"But, I wouldn't listen. I thought, if I can't get a job I will die. So I went to the interview. . . .

"Then my supervisor was very pleased with me. He said I deserved promotion and sent me on a training, 27 months long. O, the things they said at home about that! They wouldn't send one penny to support me. It was the other daughters-in-law, one particularly, who was the worst of all. She was so jealous. But in the end they paid my salary just as if I'd been at work, so I was able to go. My daughter stayed with my mother-in-law. Even so, while I was away, they divided off our household, in spite at me. Though it's better for me now – like if we weren't separate I couldn't have sat like this so long with you – but it hurt me very much at the time. . . .

"So here I am, still in this job. . . . But I haven't the same spirit I had at first. I've had to fight it all so long. And even though I fight, I'm still restricted, still blocked. If my husband were a bit stronger, then I could have done much more, but he himself has to hear all these things people say, and he doesn't like it, so he too says I must conform. O sister, it has been so hard for me.

"So I said to my father, You give in marriage, but it's we who have to live in the families. Keep the younger girls at home. Let them study, let them do as well as they can for themselves. And then let them look themselves and see where they want to marry. And that's what has happened. My younger sisters have been to university, found a boy themselves, told my parents and they gave them in marriage. For them there is still hope. But I, sister, am so weary sometimes, so weary of it all."

In Bangladesh as elsewhere, marriage is central to an understanding of gender relations. Sufira's statement brings out a number of important elements in this. First, there is the sense of radical change. At marriage women move from the home and setting where they are known and all is familiar, to a household in which they have a very different role and very different expectations to fulfil. In Sufira's case this rupture was particularly severe: not only did she move to an unknown family in a different district, but also she also moved from an urban to a rural environment, where the way of life was very different. Of course, not all marriages involve such an extreme constrast. Amongst Muslims in particular, marriages between close kin are common, and this may mean that the sense of dislocation is much less severe. In general, however, marriage does represent a very significant break. Popular culture dramatizes the trauma for a girl of leaving her father's house and having to 'adjust' to her new place amongst strangers. It is fully expected that the first months or even years of marriage may be very unhappy ones. Thus Maloti[1] said of her daughter, married a few months earlier: 'Won't she find it hard there? Another's house has to be made your own.'

The way Sufira's marriage was arranged by others and her lack of any alternative, despite having formally to give her consent, shows clearly the social construction of passivity and dependence in female gender identity. Marriage arrangements are typically surrounded by tension, with complex negotiations both within the bride's family and between them and the groom's. This atmosphere does not make it easy for a girl to intervene, or to disagree when something is decided. She is also hampered by restricted mobility and ideals of female deference, heightened by convention which considers it indelicate for a girl to show any open interest in her own marriage.

As a new bride, also, women occupy a structurally weak position. While marriage marks the transition from childhood to womanhood, it also involves the loss of what she has known and 'rebirth' into a new life. She becomes the household's most junior member, whose chief virtue is submission, learning how to do what will please the family and proving her worth through obedience, hard work, good temper and modest behaviour. Most women in rural Bangladesh start their married lives within a joint household structure. This means it is not just her husband that a woman has to please, but the whole family. She will spend most of her time with the other female members of the household, and it is they who may be most sharply critical. This clearly undermines any picture of a single gender identity which gives all women automatic common interests.

Sufira's statement also brings out the centrality of work to marriage and the way this can be used to enforce women's subordination. The need for more female labour is in fact one of the commonest reasons given for marriage. This is also the central consideration in the timing of wives' visits to their natal homes. Women talk of their father-in-law's house as *porer bari* (another's house), the same term that is used of the house of an employer. The wealthy Hindu, Kangali Serkar,[2] who has five married sons, reflects this as he refuses to employ a woman worker: 'With all these daughters-in-law what need is there for *more* women!'

Sufira used another kind of work – her office job – to free herself from the tyranny of her husband's family. In this she clearly had more options than most of the women in Kumirpur. Even so, her opportunities were limited first by the kinds of work available to women, and second, by her lack of education – only up to Matriculation. This was largely due to her marrying so young. She felt this strongly herself, remarking how women came to her clinic rather than approach the male doctor, and her frustration at having less skill and commanding a much lower salary than if she had been able to study for higher qualifications. In response, Sufira is fiercely educating her own daughter, who in 1986 won a scholarship as one of the top school students in Tanore.

The final point that Sufira highlights is the way that the wider community enforces subordination within the household/family. The disapproval and opposition of key members of their somaj made Sufira's defiance difficult for the whole household, whatever their personal feelings about what she was doing. The social cost for Sufira has been very high. Ironically, however, this has perhaps also meant that the impact of what she had done has been very wide-reaching. Following her a number of other women have taken salaried jobs in the area; her small clinic opens doors to women who are hesitant to go to a male doctor; and she is a symbol of women's admission into public life. Now widely respected, Sufira was, for example, appointed as an official to oversee women's voting in the 1986 parliamentary elections. Through her struggles, Sufira has become a catalyst for change. What makes her exceptional is the way she took on directly some of the conflict inherent in the institution of marriage and the family which other women are either lucky enough to avoid or lack the means to confront.

Critically then, marriage is about difference. It is the turning point in a woman's life, the major rite of passge, on which all of her fortunes depend. From this may follow other key moments: the birth of her children, the marriage of her children, the end of her marriage through widowhood or divorce. At each of these points, a woman experiences radical change in her situation and options. Marriage also constructs difference between women: the divide between married and non-married is, particularly in the villages, probably the single most crucial one. Beyond this, through marriage new hierarchical relations are formed between women: if the immediate result of her own marriage is a woman's subordination, the marriage of her sons typically gives a woman the strongest chance for an overt expression of power. Marriage also confirms communal difference, since weddings are very much community events and choice of marriage partners is strictly confined within communal lines. Again, marriage is articulated with class as well as gender relations: marriage is a key way in which the household gains access to labour, and forms an alliance between families which may serve wider social, economic and political use.

This chapter follows up these themes. Looking at the constitution of difference within gender identities is an important corrective to the predominant stress on male–female as the key axis of difference. In the case of the building of the madrassa in chapter 3, I emphasized how it is important to consider together the structural differences between people and the space they have for manoeuvring within these. Sufira's case bears this out: family structures and marriage practices are fundamentally inscribed with power relations; within these there is none the less some room for redefining an individual identity. This duality continually recurs. Marriage is essentially contradictory: it is both a prime means of female subordination and also the basis of women's fulfilment and advancement. Its association with sex makes aspects of it shameful, but it is also a matter of pride and celebration. While it is hoped to bring love and affection, marriage also has a clear economic dimension. New wives are new workers, whose labour, sexuality and fertility belong to their husband and his family.

The chapter begins by looking at how marriages are arranged and this leads into the question of marriage payments. This is followed by a discussion of household structure and wider kin-based links, noting how these have both personal and structural significance. Finally, I present a negative case, where a woman's 'misbehaviour' according to established gender norms led to a downward shift in her household's class relations. The discussion here is complemented in chapter 7 by a fuller exploration of relations within the family household as shown through women's work and use of assets.

Marriage arrangement

In Islam marriage is an obligation and a contract; Hindus conceive of marriage as a sacrament. The practical politics of marriage arrangement, however, are reminiscent of any other form of transaction. The different parties manoeuvre and fight their own corners, aiming to achieve the best bargain they can. There are many different levels in this process. Most clearly, there is the skilful dance of the bride's and groom's parties as they meet, fête one another, withdraw, discuss in lowered voices, dispute, and finally agree. Steps in the Hindu version of this dance are more elaborate, but the essential patterns are similar. The ideal is for the groom's party to seek out the girl's, but in practice the girl's party may take a more active part, especially as she gets older. Male kin or friends of the groom, and increasingly often the groom himself, come to 'view the bride' as part of this bargaining and decision-making process. In and behind this is the work of the matchmaker who puts the parties in touch with each other and negotiates between them. Quite often, each party has such a representative, rather as a person who goes to the cattle hat takes a second with him to negotiate. The many interests involved in the making of a marriage undoubtedly colour the evidence given. Mismatches thus occur not only through lack of information, but also through deliberate deception. As one man, who virtually makes his living as matchmaker for Sajjur's somaj, remarked: 'In the making of marriages, some lies have to be told.' Who is named as matchmaker can also be a political question: weddings may be used to affirm existing links as well as to make new ones. The person named may thus be a prominent person of the somaj, while many of the practical arrangements are managed less formally by others.

Asha gives an example of this. One of her sisters had been cheeky and argumentative with their patron, Sajjur, and as a result he refused to help them with her marriage. Her father then went to ask the Hajis for help, and they said the girl could join the wedding for two others that they were holding in their house. Asha's family refused: it would have alienated them from their economic and social community. Instead they asked for 10 seer of paddy from each of the richer Muslim exchange households, and managed to put a meal together. Their main fear was that the simplicity of the occasion would reflect badly on Sajjur for having refused to sponsor the wedding, but in the event it went off without problems.

In another case, Sukhi[3] arranged the marriage of her husband's youngest sister to one of her own cousins. She named a person from a nearby village as matchmaker because, she says: 'It doesn't do to say all things oneself.' None the less, Sukhi takes her role in the marriage very seriously, fêting the man as son-in-law (*jamai*) and helping frequently with child-minding. Behind the set-piece occasions of the negotiation process, there is thus a web of other less formal manoeuvres. Information is passed primarily among kin, but social or business visits of neighbours also prove important channels. These do not necessarily follow communal lines: it is quite common for a Hindu to be the matchmaker for a Muslim marriage, and vice versa. For wealthier households, classmates at school or college may provide suitable contacts. While the ceremonial celebrates relations between men, in practice in a purdah society much of the exploration of possible matches relies heavily on women, and the activation of female networks.

Hara (1967) and others note that women try to arrange the marriages of their kin to become their sisters-in-law, or their neighbour's wives and this was also evident in Kumirpur. Women have several interests in making such matches. First, they may hope thereby to gain an ally in the marital village. Second, finding an acceptable bride may enhance their own standing in their husband's household, and give them some extra leverage as patron to the new woman. In the third place, as they share a corporate sense of honour and common fortunes, women have at least as great an interest as men in finding a suitable match for the household in class terms. In this women contribute crucially to the reproduction of class relations (Jeffery, 1979).

But it is not only between the two parties that complex negotiations take place. To avoid giving offence, the matter must be discussed with a wide circle of kin. The potential for internal disputes within each side is quite considerable, as is the possibility of the marriage becoming the vehicle for expressing longer standing alliances and divisions. At the time of Suresh's and Maloti's[4] eldest daughter's marriage, Maloti's brothers favoured a groom in Kumirpur, but Suresh said the dowry demanded was too high, and married her further away. When it came time for their second daughter to be married, there was no discussion with Maloti's brothers, and they were only invited informally, not given a written invitation. Some came, some did not. Maloti, still upset over the earlier experience, refused to get involved: 'It is his daughter, let him marry her where he will!'.

There may also be disputes within the household itself. While girls are supposed to remain ignorant of and detached from the forthcoming marriage, there is no such pressure on boys. They frequently object to the timing or terms of the match and may refuse to agree to it, or at least put up a struggle. In one Exchange Muslim household, the father gave a motorcycle to reconcile one son to the marriage he had arranged, and threatened to disinherit the other, who was carrying on an affair with a low caste Hindu woman. When the son agreed not to marry her the woman committed suicide by poison rather than marry someone else. The man is now married to someone of his father's choice. Matters are not necessarily settled even when the marriage takes place.

Akhbar's youngest brother was forced to go through with the marriage that his father had arranged for him. Subsequently he beat his wife so badly that he had to be publicly reprimanded, but she alienated the rest of the household by favouring him (ironically) and not paying sufficient attention to the other household members. After demanding another marriage many times, after six years he finally arranged one for himself. He returned with his new wife after a month away and the marriage was accepted as a *fait accompli*. The pressure was then on his first wife, whose fitness to remain was made conditional on her behaviour.

In polygamous cases such as this uncertainty in reckoning the odds for a successful marriage are clearly that much greater: not only is there the husband and his family, but also the other wife to worry about. Two of the five (three Hindu and two Muslim) polygamous marriages in Kumirpur represented an extreme example of how marriage may be arranged through the gamble that pays off. They came out of affairs between the daughters of a very poor (Hindu) woman and two middle income married men.[5] These were countenanced by their mother, apparently as a calculated risk: how could she hope to raise the money to get her daughters married otherwise? While this is a particularly extreme example of a high risk strategy, all the cases in different ways show a calculation of costs against benefits on the woman's side, reflecting an initial position of considerable disadvantage.

Joia[6] lives next door to Dhiren and Sukhi and is one of Sukhi's closest friends. Her daughter was married in January 1986 to the son of a middle income household in an adjacent neighbourhood of the village. This case expresses very well how the vulnerability inherent in female gender constructions can set women against each other, rather than give them common interests. It was a court marriage, Dhiren took the girl to Rajshahi and they met the groom and had a civil ceremony there. The reason for this was that the groom had already been married, less than a year before. He had decided they were not suited, apparently because of sexual problems and his wife's failure to ingratiate herself either with him or the family. His family first opposed the second marriage, but then accepted it and a low key religious ceremony was finally held. This all took place while his first wife was away at her parent's home, having their first child. On Joia's part there was a clear trade off between the wealth of the household, the potential tensions there, and the fact that they could get away with paying a slightly smaller dowry. They still had to give more than Tk3000, plus 0.75 bigha as a marriage payment. Joia talks grimly of what may happen in the future. In the meantime, relations appear quite friendly, and the first wife frequently brings her son to visit Joia, leaving the new bride to get on with the work at home.

The current ideal of an arranged marriage is to make a fully suitable match, in terms of class, community, education, temperament and personality: the fusion of the individual and the household interest. Of course this sometimes happens, but in practice the marriage market is far from perfect, and choice is strictly limited. In particular in Bangladesh at present rising demands for dowry payments weight marriage negotiations very heavily against the bride's household. Within the constraints of an appropriate match, therefore, attention in Kumirpur is often focused primarily on the wealth of the household, and the amount of dowry which is demanded or offered. Women who have worked in others' households are particularly vulnerable, as they are likely to be subjected to sexual harassment by their employers and even if they resist their reputations suffer. This does not mean they cannot marry, but it does not make it any easier. While marriage may serve household advancement through the links it forges, for many poorer parents of girls, it represents primarily a terrible pressure to get them off their hands at the lowest cost, as the chances of a half-way decent match recede for ever further as the years tick by.

In cases like Sufira's, households can be matched economically but not culturally, and this can mean considerable hardship. This is particularly likely when women from a wealthier home are married into a newly rich household, which maintains the strong ethic of self-exploitation which has helped it towards upward mobility. In Kumirpur Hasan Mullah's household[7] is a case in point: the resentment that his daughters-in-law feel at the way they have to work is related in chapter 7. A similar case is Kangali Serkar's household:[8] as one of his daughters-in-law explains, her party looked at the boy, and he was educated and good, and looked at the wealth of the household, but they did not look at the character of the household, and its 'lower-class' outlook.

Marriage payments

The practice of dowry significantly shifts the terms of exchange at marriage in favour of the groom's party. This reflects a change over the last two generations in Bangladesh and parts of North India, where bride price (payment by the groom's family) used to be the norm. Dowry (payment by the bride's family) was given predominantly between high caste Hindus, lower castes gave bride price. Amongst Muslims the *mehr* was payable at marriage by the groom's family, as security for the bride in case of marriage breakdown. In Bangladesh, this was typically given only in the case of divorce, if then (R. Ahmed, 1987: 24–5). Dowry is now common amongst virtually all groups, and the amounts payable have risen dramatically. The earlier Hindu ideal saw dowry as 'gift' – the most auspicious form of marriage in Hindu culture, *kanya dan*, means literally 'gift of a virgin'. The present practice of dowry is very far from this: in village Bangladesh, it is often called by the English term 'demand'. This accurately reflects the way that dowries are perceived – a dowry is the demand of the groom, to which the bride's family unwillingly accedes.

No one really knows why this change has taken place. The most common theory relies on the idea of female status which is indexed by women's 'productive' work. This is termed by Sharma (1980a) the 'economic compensation theory'. According to this view, bride price is given where women do 'productive' work, to compensate the natal household for the loss of an economically active member, and the resources that have gone into raising her. Dowry, on the other hand, arises in situations where women do no 'productive' labour, and so represent a future 'cost' for which their husband's household must be compensated. At present however, rapid inflation of dowry is taking place alongside an expansion of extra-household employment of women. In view of this, Sharma (1980a:68) suggests a new twist to the theory: that changes in marriage payments may reflect shifts in the proportion of household income earned by male and female members. Shifts in marriage payments (the decline of bride price and the spread and inflation of dowry) thus reflect relations of economic dependence between men and women rather than absolute amounts of work performed or cash earned.

As I dispute the equation of women's work and status, I am doubtful of this theory's validity. It reflects an academic context that favours economic explanations, rather than being derived from links observed in empirical cases. Bardhan (1986), for example, points out that the economic costs and benefits of women's work are not the main determinant of differences in actual marriage payments or the treatment of young wives. In fact the theory's economic phrasing obscures its social content: ideas of work being 'productive' or of 'value' are social constructs, not a reflection of the real value (in economic or any other terms) of the contributions different members make to the household. The argument is thus circular: at most it says that the higher value given to men's work is reflected in marriage payments, but this leaves open the question of why particular kinds of activity should be culturally valued while others are not.

Other approaches emphasize women's social construction as dependent and their lack of alternatives to marriage. Kishwar (1986:10) states that gifting from her parents constantly affirms the bride's inferiority to her husband. She states: 'Dowry is given, not for the daughter's happiness, as is often claimed, but to increase her dependency.' (Ibid.:9) The phrasing of this statement in terms of purpose clearly makes it controversial. It does, however, help to underline Kishwar's assertion that by giving more to a son-in-law who mistreats his bride, her parents only strengthen his power over her. She states that they should rather give her the means of an independent income. This is a much more satisfactory approach, siting dowry payments in the overall context of women's disadvantage through lack of access to material resources, the threat of violence and social criticism.

Whatever the reason for marriage payments, they come to have wide-reaching consequences for gender relations. Van Schendel (p. 109) in his study of household mobility in Bangladesh states:

> A household with many daughters was sure to experience economic deterioration as a result of their marriages. As it was out of the question to leave a girl unmarried, girls were viewed as liabilities to parental households, while boys were viewed as assets.

Once begun, dowry inflation sparks off a cycle of spiralling disadvantage for young women. They are open to mistreatment if their parents cannot pay the whole sum at once in full, and new, or even recurrent, demands may be made even several years after marriage. One son-in-law of Kumirpur threatened to 'take the difference in beating', and this attitude, and practice, is far from uncommon. In extreme cases this leads to 'dowry deaths', when women are either pushed to suicide or directly murdered by their husbands' families. Even when the dowry is paid on time and in full, it does not represent female property. The bride's subordinate position in her marital household means she may have no say in how it is used. Sharma (1984:70) states:

> Contrary to the dominant ideology and the terminology of traditional Hindu law, dowry property is not women's wealth, but wealth that goes *with* women. Women are the vehicles by which it is transmitted, rather than its owners.

The fact that dowries are not female property is reflected in the type of goods that are given. Personal gifts to the groom are very common, typically a watch, cycle, or radio, or even a motorbike amongst the wealthy. The significance of these is not only in gender relations: they clearly express the increasing penetration of the international market, and a preference for foreign-produced goods. Lindenbaum (1981) similarly links the new forms of marriage payments with growing urbanization and commercialization plus increasing dependence on foreign imports. She points out that this is predominantly male-centred, while feminine ideals remain largely traditional.

In Kumirpur as elsewhere, the shift to dowry and inflation of payments is striking. There are still some special cases in which dowries need not be paid. The most common of these are: 1) when there is a kin relationship between the two parties; 2) where there are religious objections to dowries (Muslims); 3) when one or more of the parties has been married before; 4) *ghor jamai* marriages in which a man is brought into his wife's household, usually because she has no brothers; and 5) marriages where a brother and sister in one family marry a sister and brother in another. Aside from these, dowry is almost universally assumed. When I visited Tanore in February 1989, Biren, the younger son of a wealthy Hindu family of long standing in a village near Kumirpur, was getting married. Seeing dowry as a social evil, Biren stated that he would accept what his future father-in-law chose to give him, but would make no demand. Some thought him a fool – he could have commanded a very high price – but many of the women praised him. Most of the other young (and not so young) men simply disbelieved it – there must be some secret arrangement.

While people are highly conscious of the trend towards dowries, it is not easy to put precise figures to it. In the first place, men may deny they took a dowry: women give much more honest answers. Secondly, general inflation makes it difficult to assess the relative values of cash sums. Also, gifting at marriage is regarded in different ways: a watch (for example) may be in one case part of the groom's 'demand' and in another a free 'gift' from the bride's father. The weight of gifting may thus be with the bride's father, without it being conceived as a dowry as such. Similarly, when bride price was the norm it was a matter of pride not to take the cash element, while it was an honour for the new daughter-in-law to receive gold from her husand's family.[9] In view of this, figure 6 shows the direction of payment at marriage in Kumirpur, and does not limit this to exchanges which were formally regarded as 'bride price' or 'dowry'.

Whatever the problems in precise calculation, the overall trend towards increasingly large dowry demands is unmistakable. Some examples of weddings in Kumirpur in 1986 indicate the amounts then being paid. Aynuddin Mondol's niece (Muslim Exchange upper/strong) married with a dowry of a motorcycle, a watch and gold worth Tk25,000. Her family also gave a feast for 700–800 people. Suresh and Maloti[10] gave with their daughter a dowry of Tk32,000 (Tk15,000, a bicycle and gold). Even the poor widow, Gita,[11] had to find Tk3,000, bangles, ear-rings, a ring and all the expenses, for the wedding of her daughter. In all three cases when the girls' mothers were married the major expenses were borne by the groom's side. Figure 6.1 shows the shift in direction of marriage payments over time, amongst households in Kumirpur. The four sections illustrate differences by clan and religious group. Within these, each column shows what percentage of marriages contracted at each time period had the bias of gifting towards the bride's or groom's party, and the proportion of marriages in which costs were borne equally by both sides.

While figure 6 shows a clear overall shift to dowry from bride price, there are marked differences between classes and communities. Amongst Hindus, dowry dates from the British period and is now universal: only 7 per cent of marriages in the early Independence period (1971–81) took place without payment of dowry, and none in the last five years. By contrast, bride price was paid in more than 90 per cent of Muslim marriages in the British period, and dowry in none. Amongst Muslims dowry has been significant only since Independence, and only in the upper class up to the last five years. In the years 1982–86 there was an almost equal balance between dowry and non-dowry marriages amongst Kumirpur Muslims. Comparing households of the same class in different communities, the volume as well as the number of dowries is significantly greater amongst Hindus than Muslims.

While the bride and her mother may contribute some part of the marriage gifts (usually jewellery) through their personal income generation, the main part of the dowry is held to be a household (male) responsibility. Despite a tradition to plant a tree on the birth of a daughter to grow and cover the costs of her wedding, most dowries are raised by asset stripping at the time of the wedding, rather than saved gradually. Richer households may be able to raise dowries through business profits or crop sale. Others with fewer alternatives may have to turn to the last resort and sell land. Poorer households with good cluster links may call on patrons or wealthier relatives to help. Those who can be claimed as Mama (maternal uncle) are of particular use, since a mama has special responsibilities for helping in a marriage. Others may have to resort to begging.

Increasingly, though, people are trying to save in advance against the need to give dowries. Dhiren and Sukhi[12] have already saved Tk20,000 towards a dowry of their seven-year-old daughter – though they say that much more than

Figure 6.1
Changes in marriage payments

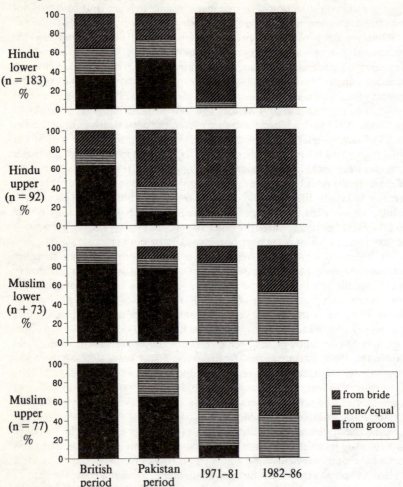

this will be needed. People in most poorer households say that they have not the spare resources to put aside, but there are cases of forward planning none the less. In a couple of cases, money-lending within the village is explained by the future need for an infant daughter's dowry, in another tin was bought to reroof the house now to allay the need of rethatching later when there will be the need to give dowries. In each of these cases, of course, preparing for dowries may only be a part of the reason. Some do not save for fear of tempting fate: where infant mortality is high, it can seem unwise to presume on a future.

Marriage law and practices are intertwined with legal and social norms which give men privileged rights in property and employment and these reinforce one another. On the one hand these assume female dependence and on the other they construct it. It is assumed that women are supported by men and that therefore there is not the same need for them to have direct access to income or property in their own right. Women remain always statutory minors: they exchange dependence as daughters for dependence as wives, and eventually as mothers. The laws construct female dependence in as much as their inferior access to income and property means that they have little choice but to look to men for support. Then again, their dependence on their relationships makes it harder for women to assert the formal rights to material resources they do have (so, for example, they forego their inheritance to keep good relations with their brothers). The legal framework for their relationships again enshrines male privilege, and women's overwhelming material dependence on their relationships further weakens their *de facto* position.

Household structure and kin celebration

As noted above, the norm in Bangladesh is for a woman to join her father-in-law's household at marriage. In the first few years she may still spend a good deal of time in her own home, but gradually these visits become less frequent and she comes to be based permanently with her parents-in-law. Alternatively, the young couple may set up their own household within a year or two of marriage, this is very common especially amongst poorer households. Much less common are ghor jamai marriages, in which a man joins his father-in-law's household, usually because it has no sons of its own. Men tend to dislike ghor jamai marriages as they have less authority in their father-in-law's house. Perhaps for this reason the arrangement seems often to break down within a few years of marriage, and the young couple set up separately or return to the husband's natal village. In Kumirpur four households involved ghor jamai marriages, and four more sons of Kumirpur are living as ghor jamai in other villages. There are seven further households who married as ghor jamai but have since set up independently.

Karve (1957) sees the North Indian practice of marrying women into an unknown and often distant household as signifying greater gender inequality than in Southern India, where women are generally married close by their own natal families. I am uneasy with this kind of wide-ranging comparison, as it is in danger of reducing actual relations to cultural practices and abstracting a few factors as significant while eliding many other points of difference.[13] There is, I think, no doubt that the system of distant virilocal marriage does tend to support age and gender hierarchies. On the other hand, distance of marriage cannot be used as an index of gender inequality in particular cases: there are clear differences in choice of marriage location between the communities of Kumirpur, which reflect other factors not directly related to gender. None the less, it is evident in Kumirpur as elsewhere that wives who are also daughters of the village on the whole enjoy considerably greater freedom than those who marry in.

Overall, 16 per cent of wives in Kumirpur are also daughters of the village. Hindus generally marry within their caste. For the smaller caste groups, this means they may have to go some distance to find a suitable marriage partner. For the Mahisyo, on the other hand, Kumirpur provides a concentration of potentially eligible families, while continuing migration to India gradually reduces the populations elsewhere. It is thus not surprising that the Mahisyo have the highest proportion of in-village marriages (21 per cent). Exchange and Local Muslims have tended not to intermarry, though this is changing. Exchange Muslims still tend to arrange marriages through links that date from before they migrated. This means they marry at greater distance than the Local Muslims, over 85 per cent of whom marry within Tanore upazila. There are two cases of cross-caste and one Hindu–Muslim marriage.[14] There are also seven cases of 'love' marriages in Kumirpur, which followed a relationship between the bride and groom. These were initially frowned on, but were accepted in time.

Marriage exchanges centre on particular areas. It is almost exclusively the Local Muslims, for example, who have marriage links to the west with the (mainly Muslim and Santal) Borind Tract. Perceptions of distance also depend on social links. Villages with which there is frequent contact and multiple links seem 'nearer' than those which are unfamiliar. A newly married woman visiting her natal family said to me of her husband's home: 'I am alone there'. She lived in a large joint family: what she meant was that there was no one from Kumirpur married nearby. Sharma (1980a) notes that the concept of the 'village as basic unit' reflects a male perception of space: to women the kin network can be more significant than the boundaries of a particular village.

Marriage links show a strong clustering tendency just as do economic and social links. The most striking example of this is in Sajjur's somaj. As noted in chapter 3, this somaj spreads across three neighbouring villages, as it did in India. There is a similar small group of villages in the upazila to the north-east of Tanore, with members of the same original somaj. Since coming from India, ten of the Kumirpur marriages of Sajjur's somaj have been made in that area, involving both rich and poor families. There is thus a dense network between the two areas, with criss-crossing links of economic exchanges and women given and taken in marriage.

While the tendency of distant marriages may be to reinforce brides' subordination, this does not mean that women prefer to marry within their natal village.[15] In practice, many women favour more distant marriages because they can then get properly away when they go home for a visit, get special treatment which they lose if they see their families more often, and minimize the risk of spoiling relations by being drawn into petty disputes. Parents of daughters may also feel that it is better to have the girls married away so that they will not hear if they are unhappy. This does not mean they do not care what happens to their daughters, but shows recognition that once they are married the best thing for them is to adjust as best they can to their husbands' household, and use home as an escape hatch at times. Except in cases of extreme abuse, women who stay married are better off than those whose marriages break down. While a woman's own family remain an important back-up, after marriage it is her husband's family that represents her prime social resource.

It is as new brides that women in Bangladesh come closest to the feminine ideal of subordination and dependence. Unless a double wedding takes place, with two sons married at the same time, a new bride can be very isolated. She has often to work very hard, taking over many of the heavier tasks under the guidance of her mother-in-law, and may not make any 'management' decisions herself. She is also strictly watched to ensure her behaviour brings the family no dishonour. She has contact only with members of her husband's household or at most their social group; if she has a problem she has to go to people in authority over her. Not surprisingly, this significantly reduces the number of problems her husband's family has to hear about. While these restrictions are probably at their tightest in richer Muslim households, the subordination of new brides is broadly similar across community and class. In talking about it, women intermix moral or ideal statements about how a new bride should be with very practical arguments: deference as a strategy to ingratiate oneself in a situation with few options.

For the new bride, hierarchies between women in the family household are often more keenly felt than those between women and men. Daughters-in-law are ranked according to the seniority of their husbands, but the sharpest difference is between women and their mothers-in-law. Many of the contradictions of management–labour relations inhere in this relationship, with the added ingredient of restrictive gender norms. The elements of contradiction and solidarity in relationships between women in different households are thus also present between women within the same household. In their work, mothers and daughters-in-law are crucially interdependent and this gives them a great deal of common experience and some degree of common interest. In addition, they represent a key aspect of each other's social resources: in the early years at least, the nature of her mother-in-law is at least as important as the character of a woman's husband. This is well expressed by Purnima,[16] a middle-income Hindu woman, as she reflects on her own experience as a daughter-in-law and her expectations of her relationship with her son's new bride:[17]

At first when I was married, my brother-in-law used to test my honesty, leaving the business money somewhere for me to find. But I always gave it back to my mother-in-law. We were very close. If I slept five nights with my husband I slept ten nights with her. And I shall teach my daughter-in-law like this. If I buy two soaps I will use one, little by little, for a month, and keep one saved. I'm always like that, thinking about the next day. I've said to her, if you do like this, you'll do well, and if not, you'll starve. Well, my own daughter-in-law, isn't it my duty to teach her?

While there are undoubtedly many tensions inherent in the relationship, Purnima looks to her new daughter-in-law for company and love, a new daughter, to replace her eldest girl who had died two years previously.

At the same time, however, gender subordination makes mothers and daughters-in-law dependent on the same social resource: their relationships with the son/husband. It is these conflicts that are usually stressed, with the mother-in-law a common evil figure, analogous to the stepmother in European folk tradition.[18] In my own field work, I certainly found the mother-in-law to be the most significant constraint when I tried to talk with daughters-in-law – much more so, for example, than the women's husbands. It is in relation to their daughters-in-law that women gain a rare opportunity to exercise overt power.

Even in this case, however, a woman does not enjoy authority in her own right, but through her relationship to the significant men in the family. Over time, therefore, the balance shifts as the daughter-in-law becomes a mother and her husband replaces his father at the head of the household. Ironically, a very strong mother-in-law may set a pattern of female centrality in family affairs, which finally works against her as in most cases the husband/wife relationship gradually pre-empts the mother/son, and the older woman is increasingly marginalized. Often, also, the young couple splits away to set up a separate household and the mother/daughter-in-law dynamic becomes less significant. While this typically gives the younger woman greater centrality, it also deprives her of a lot of back-up and support. In particular, it makes it difficult for her ever to get away for a break, as there is nobody at home to substitute for her labour. While the joint household structure is clearly based in hierarchy and power differentials, therefore, it is important not simply to assume that a separate household represents in all ways a more positive option for young women.

A further key moment of difference in female gender constructions occurs with motherhood. In rural Bangladesh, infertility is a disaster, and is almost invariably blamed on the woman. It is a common reason for divorce or for the husband marrying again. Also, it is important to have sons. Male bias in the culture means that there is a general preference for sons, which also has some practical aspects. Sons secure the transfer of property into the next generation. They have also better prospects as wage-earners, while daughters have far fewer opportunities for employment and will anyway marry and so leave. Giving dowries at daughters' marriages drains family resources, while sons bring funds into the household on their marriage. The gender composition of households is a very significant factor in their class mobility.

While motherhood is essential to adult womanhood, it is also contradictory. As one of Dhiren's sisters put it: 'When women have children, they lose everything'.[19] This is at first sight a surprising statement, since it is in mothering that female gender identity is most highly celebrated in Bengali culture. What she meant, I think, was the experience common to women in diverse settings, that having children involves a loss of the sense of self and one's personal boundaries. In Bangladesh this is particularly clear, as women typically lose their own names after childbirth and become known as their children's *Ma*. The culture of female dependence heightens the contradictory character of motherhood, since women who survive their husbands usually have to look to their sons for support. This ties women's material interests as well as emotions to those of their children, and particularly sons, and locates their nurturing role in weakness, as well as strength. Motherhood thus represents a key area where women are engaged in relationships which 'combine sentiment and instrumentality' (Maher, p. 68; see chapter 5).

It is not coincidental that when their children get married, women are generally discussed as mothers-in-law, that is, as mothers of sons. They can, however, also play a vital role in supporting their married daughters. Two examples make clear how extensive this can be.

Joia[20] still stays with her husband, Narayan, but they lead quite separate lives. He used to buy her clothes, but now she says she 'eats rice' of his house, nothing more. In June 1986 he beat her severely for 'stealing' Tk7 from the household funds to buy soap at the village shop. For the first year of their marriage he lived with Joia in her widowed mother's house, but then moved back to his parents, since he was having an affair with someone else. Joia's ma then managed by sharing out her land, sometimes mortgaging it out, and gradually selling off her wedding gold. Finally Joia's ma exchanged her house land for agricultural land and moved back to her brother's house. A community hearing ruled that Narayan must support Joia, so she went to live with him. It is the support of her mother that has made it possible for Joia to continue. At both of Joia's daughters' marriages, her mother sold land to help with the dowry. The major trouble now is her 16-year-old son, whom Narayan insists should leave school and start work. Joia resists this, and supports her son herself, through sharing out 0.5 bigha of land that she bought with her mother's help, and sharing in a cow and some sheep from her mother. Her mother was in the process of buying house land nearby, because Narayan refused to keep his son in the house any more.

Bindi,[21] a poorer Hindu Boisnob, has been similarly important in sustaining her daughter's marriage. The girl was married into a landless family, and ever since her first son was born her husband beat her severely. She became very ill, and Bindi took her to Rajshahi, paying for the medical treatment she needed through her savings from the sale of milk and proceeds from rice husking. The family came and stayed in Kumirpur, since there was more work available for the son-in-law there than in his own village, and for two years they lived as a joint family. They hoped he would stay and build on a separate house, and the head of their cluster group, Kangali Serkar,[22] even offered to let them build it on his land. But the son-in-law wasn't happy, and took his wife and younger son home in mid-1986. The older grandson (about seven years old) decided to stay with his grandparents. The daughter and her husband still return for short periods around harvest time.

It is significant that in both these cases the mother was effectively running her own household – in Joia's ma's case because she was a widow with no sons, and in Bindi's because her husband just squandered their resources, and then became unwell. Conventionally, a woman looks to her father or brothers if her marriage gets into difficulty. They go and try to reason it out, or if necessary represent her if the case should come to a community hearing. The extent to which a woman can look to her natal family for help varies to some extent by class: if her family is poor, she may not feel able to ask and they may be able to mobilize little social pressure on her behalf. Almost all of the current cases that I heard of in Kumirpur were the woman's family trying to persuade her husband to keep her, behave better towards her, or have her back. This may, of course, just be coincidence. It may, however, reflect the strong bias in gender constructions, which make a woman's family try whatever possible to sustain her in the relationship, rather than precipitate marriage breakdown, in which almost invariably she – and they – would come off worst.

Jane Pryer's (1989) study demonstrates the centrality of a healthy male head to the household's well-being as she shows what happens 'when the bread-winners fall ill'. This points up the radical uncertainty that faces the poor in rural Bangladesh: alongside the vulnerability to the weather of an agricultural economy, people critically depend on their own good health and that of those on whom they rely. The gender dimensions of this are independent to a certain extent of class: widowhood, divorce, or abandonment propel women into severe crisis. This can again be a key point of difference in a woman's life. First, there is clearly the loss of a central emotional support. Second, women alone also take on an ambivalent social status. Years on from her childhood divorce, Asha still feels self-conscious about her ambivalent social position, and hesitates to visit beyond her immediate neighbours for fear of their questioning.

Third, the end of a marriage can mean economic collapse. Older women whose sons have all set up separate households may find themselves left alone with no option but to beg. Young women with small children, even if their husbands had some land, may have to return to their parental home where they may bring shame and often an economic burden. Of course, sometimes wealth provides a buttress against decline, especially if the woman and her family is older. The wealthy widow of one of the Haji brothers has been able to secure her substantial landowning through her own resourcefulness, good support from her brothers-in-law and their gusti, and the commitment of her sons. Even in this case, however, it is important to note that good social resources were as important as her personal qualities. While to some degree this is true for all households, it is especially the case for those with female heads: the gender division of labour means that autonomy is not a realistic option except in abject poverty. In having to rely more heavily on mediation by male kin or neighbours, female-headed households are particularly vulnerable to sharp practice or fraud.

For men, the disruption of marriage breakup tends to be much less severe. Their economic security is not threatened in the same way, and it is much easier for them to get remarried. As one old and impoverished Hindu woman somewhat tartly put it: 'If girls are married as children and their husband dies their whole life is ruined. If a man's wife dies he marries again the next day.'

While in general widow remarriage was frowned on amongst the Hindus, there were two cases of young Hindu widows in Kumirpur who have remarried. One of these became the second wife of a man with whom she had an affair. In 1986 she was living in Kumirpur with her mother, since her co-wife refused to let her come to live with them. In the second case, the only son died soon after his marriage, and his mother arranged a second (ghor jamai) marriage for her daughter-in-law, in order to bring male labour into the household. Remarriage does not bear the same stigma amongst Muslim women and may be relatively easily arranged, particularly if they have no children and are ready to go to an older man who is already married or has been widowed or divorced.

Divorce and abandonment are increasingly common.[23] The Bangladesh Fertility Survey of 1975 found that one in five first marriages end in divorce (Miranda, 1980). Because there is still a certain shame attached to it, people do not always state that they have been divorced. I came across 21 cases of divorce amongst Kumirpur Muslims (82 households), all but one of which were in the lower status group. This is consistent with the impression given in other studies, but more detailed research on class variables in divorce is needed before any kind of explanation could be offered. There is a tendency for divorce to run in families: in one case the father has been married five times, and each of the four sons has at least one divorce to his name. I heard of only five cases of divorce or abandonment amongst the Hindus (141 households), though there were several cases of longstanding marital disputes, during which the women had returned to their father's house.

Amongst Muslims, there are three forms of divorce: by mutual consent; by wife's petition through the court; by husband's will. The weighting of this towards the husband needs no emphasis. As noted above, in Muslim marriages a sum should be set for payment to the woman on divorce, but in practice this is rarely given. A wife loses her rights to maintenance if the marriage dissolves. While divorce is not formally recognized among Hindus, separation and abandonment none the less occur. Accurate reasons for the breakdown of marriages are extremely difficult to discover in Bangladesh as elsewhere. In Kumirpur it is usually the woman who is blamed, and this is most often phrased in terms of inability to work, madness or sexual misconduct. Other women are often very quick to make such accusations, perhaps feeling they can make their own position safer by emphasizing their commitment to social norms. If men are criticized it tends to be either for greed (wanting more dowry) or excessive lust. Interestingly, the Bengali word for these, *lobh*, is the same.

Women's lack of access to land and opportunities for income generation, combined with their high risk of being subjected to sexual harassment and social criticism tend to make them acutely vulnerable to the dissolution of relationships with the men on whom they rely. In marriage male and female roles are clearly complementary, and have a certain equality in their interdependence. When the marriage breaks down, however, the radical disjuncture in the constitution of gender identities becomes clear. While it is still a minority of women who suffer divorce or desertion, the proportion is increasing. As Abdullah and Zeidenstein (p. 86) remark, enough women experience these desperate life crises for them to influence the behaviour of all.

Women's interest in fostering their relationships shows in the work they put into maintaining and celebrating kin links. In part, women's celebration of these links is clearly a personal matter. Bonds of a married woman with her natal kin may be a crucial lifeline to her in the difficult early years of marriage, before she has established herself in her marital household. Her visits home are the only holidays a woman gets, and welcome opportunities to escape some of the stresses of her husband's home. Even if a woman has good relations with her marital household, she may draw on her natal kin for special purchases, when they will buy better quality or she wants to keep it secret. This may then serve a double purpose – Vatuk (1971) notes that women may buy themselves gifts for their brothers to give them, thereby at once enhancing the status of their natal household, and conveniently disguising their own saving. Women who have married into wealthier households may try to help poorer kin in more material ways, but this is hazardous: 'stealing' household grain is grounds for a divorce. These links are thus not only one-way: they form channels for the transfer of material resources, as well as emotional support.

None the less, it is a mistake to see the links which women foster between different families as primarily personal. They are also important to the household as a whole. The form this takes differs by class. Households that are poor in resources or people may be chronically dependent on kinship links for basic survival. Where possible, links are reciprocal – Asha's brother-in-law goes to *hat* to look for a bullock for them, and she goes to 'help out' her sister, when there is extra work after harvesting. The support of kin can be particularly important at crisis times. Thus when Kangali Serkar's school teacher son was very ill with heart trouble, he spent a month having medical treatment in Dhaka, being given free care by doctors who were his wife's kin. Here again social links have quite direct economic implications.

The term, 'household service work', is introduced by Sharma (1985a), reflecting on Papanek's (1979) term, 'family status production work'. Interestingly, Di Leonardo (1987) introduces a very similar concept in the totally different context of Italian Americans in North California: she terms it 'kin work'. 'Household service work' brings together many activities which have conventionally been seen as individual matters – religious observance; celebration of kin relationships – and shows how their performance is in fact a central part of a household role. Such work is not necessarily done by women, but very often tends to be. Women appear very widely in the literature as being more religious, and almost every study that discusses female expenditure, notes 'gifts' as a major item. While not conceived as 'work', this activity is none the less crucial to the social reproduction of a household's position in society. Thus N. Ahmed (1968) notes the importance of the ability to visit and exchange gifts in cementing the 'denser and closer' kin networks of the upper class in the village he studied.

The argument for seeing such social activites as work is strengthened by the fact that generally there is a sense that they are not simply a matter of choice, but things that ought to be done. This may be felt either as a moral or more straightforward social pressure. Thus Asha explained the expense her family could barely afford in fêting one of her brothers-in-law: when he got home he would be asked what he had been given to eat, and it would reflect badly on them if they hadn't fed him well. These obligations can be quite wide-reaching. Raising the sums involved may mean significant effort, and some concealment. Purnima relates a striking example of this.

Purnima's eldest daughter died two years ago. Her husband remarried, and had a new baby in November 1986. Purnima felt it would not reflect well on them not to show respect. As her husband showed no interest, she went herself to a trader in the nearby hat village and asked for a brass dish and beaker, the main necessities. Together they were worth Tk310. It was the pre-harvest lean season, there was nothing in the house. She bargained hard, and got the trader to agree to wait for payment. When the price of paddy peaked, she sold 2 maunds. Part was kept for the household, part went to repay the trader. By keeping the change left after the hat each week, Purnima gradually made up the rest of the sum. She is proud of this, that she not only fulfilled a household obligation, but did it in such a way that no one noticed.

Women's celebration of particular events is clearly not simply a calculated act of self-interest. It is also a sign of personal affection between women, who know how much such gifts can mean. Ties strengthened in this way may of course subsequently serve household advancement. These statements are not self-contradictory, but express the essence that Maher observed, of ties which combine sentiment and instrumentality. This is recognized also by Di Leonardo (p. 446) as she states: 'Kin work, then, takes place in an arena characterized simultaneously by co-operation and competition, by guilt and gratification.'

A negative case

Up to this point my claims that women's and men's activities are interrelated in and with class and gender relations have been made through generally positive examples, where fulfilment of gender roles have contributed positively to class position. Sharma (1985:190), however, notes that:

> to claim any explanatory value . . . we should need at the very least to be able to show that if these practices did not exist the consequences might be different.

The experience of Samad and Jori[24] offers such a case. It shows clearly how Jori's refusal to abide by gender norms and fulfil her given role had profoundly negative consequences for her household's social and economic status. As an example of things going wrong it is a forceful refutation of any claim that class and gender relations can be considered in isolation from each other.

Samad and Jori are brother and sister who live with their parents, two younger brothers and two younger sisters. Two older brothers have moved away and cut links with them. They are very poor. All of them except the very smallest boy work in other households, all but Jori in houses of the Haji gusti. Samad has saved his earnings, and managed gradually to buy two bullocks, so they now have their own plough. On the strength of this and of his good relationship with his patron, in 1986 Samad took from her some irri/boro land to share-crop, and had plans to take 1 bigha amon land also for the first time. The decline of their household was thus halted, and just on the upward turn.

Jori, her mother and her next youngest sister are all said to sleep with men for money. They are unusually free in the number of households where they will accept work and are generally seen about the village far more widely than any other women. Jori is contemptuous of prevalent norms. Her (unwell) father has been reprimanded and even publicly humiliated in his somaj because of Jori's behaviour, but she takes no notice. While Samad is the main economic support to the household, he leaves such matters to his father. This then is the background: the following is a series of edited extracts from my field diary.

Diary: 25 November – 9 December 1986

Over the past months Jori has much thinned about the face. People are saying she is pregnant. Several people have asked her but she has denied it.

25 November: Asha comes round. Jori has told a (Hindu) neighbour that she is seven months' pregnant. The girl spoke to another neighbour and she to her husband. He said it to another man, out in the fields in front of everyone. Samad heard it in the fields and went home to beat Jori. She fled to her aunt's house.
Asha: Whose name will she call? The last one maybe.

26 November: Jori stays at her aunt's overnight. A number of the richer women of their community go to her at dusk to ask whose child it was. She names Hakim's son [the nephew of Sajjur, one of the richest men in the village]. Women neighbours (Exchange Muslims) fetch Jori home in the early morning. Coming through the village she says angrily to Asha her brother owes her Tk20, she needs the money now.

27 November: Late morning, the major figures of the Exchange Muslim community are in Jori's house attacking her father for not controlling her better. This is one of many such times. The whole village is talking about it, the men's voices loud with blame and quarrelling, the women in lowered tones full of a sense of scandal.

Jori claims that at two months she went to Hakim's son wishing to abort the child. That he said no, it is mine, I will take it. They had an affair before and Hakim arranged a marriage for the boy to put an end to it. People seem to be accepting that Hakim's son is the father. They are saying that he will have to marry her.

Evening: Community hearing Night. A mat on the ground in an open area near to Jori's house. A hurricane lamp, and Akhbar sitting before it, pressing together his fingers in deliberation. An inner group of the village big men, around them a muffled crowd of village men and on the very outer circle, hidden by the darkness, one or two silent women.

The hearing is haphazard. Jori gives evidence (angrily) but her word counts for little. Her poor reputation is constantly alluded to: her father is blamed. The one witness she cites denies her story: he is a close dependent in Sajjur's cluster. How will they make a decision – the boy's word against hers? There is no cross-examination. People call for a blood test. Akhbar nominates a small group of the dominant men to make a judgement, one declines so all refuse. Some people get up to go. The Hajis announce: Jori's household will be expelled from their somaj. There will be no eating together, speaking together, or employment. The meeting disperses.

1 December: Hakim is offering (via the younger Hajis) Tk500 to Jori to abort the child.

3 December: Jori asked me for Tk500 to file a case against Hakim's son. I said I doubted it would do any good, and asked if there were anyone on their side whose advice I could ask. There is no one, she said, showing emotion for the first time.

4 December: Jori's father and fictive uncle have been to the Upazila Chairman but he said to wait for a blood test. People say that Hakim and Sajjur have sworn that whatever it costs they will keep Jori out of their family. I told Jori I would not give her the money – a court case would achieve nothing, only consume all their hard-won assets.

8 December: They took their bullocks to market to sell to finance the court case. They did not get the price they wanted so returned. But will go back to sell another day.

9 December: To Jori's house at night. Samad is taking the family decisions now. The youngest girl will not take part in the savings co-operative Asha is setting up. It is part of their withdrawal of the women from all outside involvement. They do not discuss their chances in a court case. Samad speaks: what is fate will be.

1987 February: Asha writes that Jori has had a baby girl, and seems set to keep her. There is no more talk of a blood test.

1989 February: Jori was married to a much older man, and left him after a few weeks. She has taken her daughter and gone from the village. People say she has a job in one of the commercial rice mills.

Samad's and Jori's case is a disastrous example of things going wrong. Their vulnerabilities by class and gender compounded each other. They lacked both material and social resources. In a paternity case, the odds are always stacked against the woman whose 'guilt' is clear. Had Jori been a rich man's daughter, however, she might have been presented as the victim rather than the guilty party. As it was, their class made them more vulnerable to gender rules – no one had an interest in supporting them. Not only was Jori poor, but also the man she cited was the nephew of one of the richest men in the village. It is very difficult for a poor family to win a case against a rich one – villagers frequently comment that community hearings represent 'justice for the rich'. Even outside the village, an 'independent' blood test can very easily be bought.

Lacking the material resources to fight the case and win, Samad's and Jori's only hope was to enlist another wealthy family on their side. But Samad's personal good links with the Hajis could not outweigh the harm of Jori's behaviour, which was 'shameless' in the strict sense – she remained throughout, at least publicly, scornful and hostile. As a result they were left isolated. Their expulsion from the somaj cut all the links on which they depend – for employment, loans and share-cropping land. The reversal in their circumstances was exemplified in the sale of their productive assets, the bullocks for which Samad had worked so hard. There could hardly be a clearer example of the crucial interdependence of gender and class relations.

Notes

1. 5.4 HM u/v s.
2. 5.1 HM u/s j.
3. 1.1 HM u/v s. Kumirpur is Sukhi's natal home. Dhiren's family are elsewhere. He came to Kumirpur to set up his medical practice.
4. 5.4 HM u/v s.
5. One of these women was a widow, her case is referred to again later in the chapter.
6. 1.2 HM u/s s.
7. 6.1 ME u/v j.
8. 5.1 HM u/s j.
9. The precise nature of marriage payments amongst Hindus and Muslims in theory and in practice is a very complex matter. For more details, see Mayoux (1983); R. Ahmed and Naher (1987); Sharma (1984a).
10. 5.4 HM u/v s.
11. 2.5 HB l/v si.
12. 1.1 HM u/v s.
13. Boserup (1965) and Goody (1976) make similar arguments concerning farming systems and inheritance practices respectively. These are usefully discussed by V. Das (1976) and Whitehead (1977).
14. This, like all those I heard of, involved a Hindu woman married to a Muslim man.

15. For very similar evidence from a village in Uttar Pradesh, see Jeffery et al. (1989:34–39).

16. 4.2 HM u/v j.

17. The new bride was Suresh's and Maloti's daughter, the arrangements for whose wedding are described in chapter 4.

18. See, for example, the ironically named 'nectar-mouthed mother-in-law' of Day's (1909) *Bengal Peasant Life.*

19. *Meyeder chelemeye hole kichu thake na.*

20. 1.2 HM l/s s.

21. 5.3 HB l/v s/j.

22. 5.1 HM u/s j.

23. This is often attributed to increasing poverty, with general agreement that divorce is more common amongst the poor. Unfortunately I know of no study that has carried out a rigorous analysis of this important issue.

24. 6.2 ME l/v s.

7. You Can't Get Ghee Out with a Straight Finger

Introduction

The family household marks the crux of both class and gender relations. It is the basic unit to which people belong, and through which they enter into society. In this it is essentially contradictory: it gives people a common identity and common interests, but also divides them into specific roles and places in the hierarchy. This dual aspect of the family household tends to polarize studies of class and gender. Mainstream studies of class generally treat the household as a simple unity, they ignore internal differences and collapse its identity into that of its (typically male) head. By contrast, gender-focused studies tend to stress the divisions between members, they treat men and women as individuals or in gender groups with distinct interests (which may differ by class), and underplay their common household membership. Within development discourse, the emphasis is firmly on the 'household' rather than 'family': the basic unit is above all an economic one. In this chapter I question this premise, showing that even the economic choices that people make are heavily inlaid with notions of the family.

This chapter looks at relations in the family household as shown through women's rights and responsibilities in the work they do and the assets they may hold. These should not be seen in isolation, but against the background of the wider relationships with other households and kin that are described in earlier chapters. In practice, there is interaction between all these dimensions: relations in wider society both reflect and reshape those within the family household unit. This chapter thus explores further the themes already introduced: the implications of economic activities to gender identities; how these relate to ownership and use of assets; how power is articulated in relationships; and whether this is helpfully thought of in terms of autonomy in action. Through looking in detail at what happens in the home and what this shows of gender roles I come back to the fundamental questions raised at the beginning of this study: how women conceive of their own interests and how notions of gender figure in interpersonal negotiations of power.

To talk of the 'family household' itself begs a lot of questions. The 'household' is not, of course, equivalent to the 'family': it may include non-family members such as resident workers, and the family stretches far beyond the household, which is defined in chapter 3 as the unit that shares rice. At the same time, the household in rural Bangladesh is founded on the family links between members, and this is central to the distribution of different roles and responsibilities within it. This chapter stands in the tension between these two notions. For the sake of continuity with earlier chapters I therefore refer generally to the 'household', but talk also of 'family' when it is these associations that seem predominant.

Managing the household

In chapter 2 I note how the literature assumes a close association between the low status of women's work in Bangladesh and that of women themselves. As a result, discussion of women's work in the household has mainly focused on asserting that it is 'productive', resisting its dismissal as 'just domestic' and stressing its economic significance. Looking at women's market involvement clearly supports this, and in general I think this is now well established.[1] From a theoretical point of view, there seems no obvious justification for considering one kind of work – field production – as more fundamental than another – crop processing – when both are necessary for consumption. Unfortunately, this preoccupation has tended to focus attention on the tasks that are done, rather than their context. Arens and Van Beurden (p. 34), for example, suggest that women's work is not recognized because it seen as 'supplementary'. Without using the terminology, this clearly echoes the 'productive' versus 'domestic' debate.

Of course, it is possible to regard male activities as 'primary' and female as 'secondary'. Thus men grow the rice, women process it; men build the houses, women maintain them; men purchase food and women cook it. Some local cultural images support this: conception, for example, is often described as the male seed falling into the fecund, but ultimately passive, soil of the woman's body. On the other hand, in Bangladesh women's work is quite openly recognized as fundamental to the household and is quite consciously calculated between women themselves. Thus one daughter-in-law of the wealthy Hindu, Kangali Serkar,[2] has a sewing machine which she may use to mend other household members' clothes during the day, but for her own business only when all the household work is done. The sense that one member is not doing her share of the work is a common source of arguments. At the same time, of course, it is often said women don't work, just as it is of housewives in the West. Interestingly, this can apply also to men. Thus, asked what her husband does, a woman may say 'nothing', when she means that he just works in their own fields.

This suggests that the direction of influence is in fact the opposite to that which much of the literature assumes: tasks do not themselves have some innate character which implies dominance or subordination. Rather, the way work is conceived depends not on what is done, but on the person who does it and the context in which it is done and is being talked about. Central to this is the notion of 'family' and the roles that this prescribes.

Two examples from Kumirpur make this clear. Women's participation in field cultivation has been widely recorded in other regions in Bangladesh, and is often taken to show the breakdown of the 'traditional' gender division of labour. In Kumirpur, I saw only two cases of this, and heard of only a couple more. Since field work is culturally unacceptable for women, people tend to deny it. It was thus almost certainly more common than I was able to record, though not widespread (I looked hard for it). The first case involved Maloti, Suresh's wife,[3] and a poor widow neighbour of hers. The second, Minu,[4] a young married Local Muslim woman of the lower/strong class. In these cases, any negative associations for household and personal status were avoided by the work being conceived as fulfilment of their family obligations. As Maloti put it: 'It is our homework (*barir kaj*) so how can it be shame?'

For five years Maloti has planted and harvested potatoes in the fields, and in 1986 for the first time picked mustard. She also has a small plot near the house on which she grows chillis, aubergines, tomatoes, turmeric, etc. The reason given for her work in the fields is that there was at that time a shortage of male labour available, as it was the period of irri/boro transplanting. Picking the mustard gave an intriguing instance of four people doing exactly the same work but each having a quite different conception of it. First there was Maloti, who was fulfilling her role as female head of household, playing her part in the efficient management of resources. Beside her was their regular male worker. He was doing agricultural labour, for which he is paid Tk250 a month plus food and clothes. Third, there was Maloti's widow neighbour. She was doing domestic labour in another's household, for which she received only her day's food. Finally there was a researcher, in pursuit of data through 'participant observation'.[5]

In this example the work was very clearly defined not by what was done in itself but by the people that did it and their gendered roles as 'mother', as 'domestic' worker, or as 'agricultural' labourer. This also indicates how gendering of tasks is significant to class relations. Here, it served the economic interest of the dominant household which substituted unpaid female domestic service and household labour for paid male labour; and it secured a full day's work from a non-household woman giving her no return beyond the food she ate.

In the second case, Minu has planted many different fruit trees within their homestead compound. She also grows mustard, potatoes, onions and garlic, on 0.5 bighas, while her husband has the responsibility for the paddy on their remaining 2.5 bighas. The plot is near their house, so she can work on it without being criticized for immodesty. Like Maloti, she regards her family responsibilities as primary. Towards purdah norms, she takes a robust attitude: 'I'll talk politely to everyone, I'll not say anything I shouldn't, but in the end, they're humans and we're humans too!' These manipulations of definitions of work are not just random, but reflect contradictions in the constitution of female identity within Bangladeshi culture. As in these cases, this is often clearest where the ideal that women 'don't go out' is in conflict with their need to do just that to fulfil their family duties. On the one hand there is the nominal responsibility of the male head of household to support all his dependents and to keep his women in purdah. On the other, prudent and skilful management of household resources is very much a part of local ideals of woman as wife and mother. In popular imagery, this is expressed in the figure of Lokkhi (Laxmi), the benevolent goddess who bestows wealth, children and prosperity. She belongs to a common Bengali heritage and is revered among Muslims as well as Hindus (Blanchet 1984:42–3). Resolving the tension to some degree, Lokkhi is always conceived as wife, her powers harnessed to devotion to her husband, never threateningly dominant and alone like the darker image of feminine power, the goddess Kali (Liddle and Joshi, 1986:55).

Recognizing this contradiction helps to explain another of the recurring themes in the literature on women's work in Bangladesh: its invisibility. This is partly because it is done behind the homestead walls, but also because it involves activity which culturally 'does not happen'.[6] Asked if she did outside work, Maloti would thus answer, quite honestly, that she didn't. As noted in chapter 5, the notions 'inside' and 'outside' do not refer to set locations. Rather, their meanings are clearly adjusted to resolve the tensions between differing cultural prescriptions. Thus, at one level, women are openly recognized as central to the day-by-day running of the family household. It is typically women who process and store crops, help tend livestock and vegetables, gather fuel and water, look after the house and family, watch that stocks don't run down; and so on. In many homes it is the women who keep the money, though men may have more scope to determine how it is used.

At the same time, women are presented as relying wholly on male provision. This leads them to conceal aspects of their work, either, like Minu and Maloti, by representing what they do in culturally acceptable ways, or by actual secrecy. In the day-to-day management of their households women thus engage in a mesh of activities which underlies and interweaves with what is done openly. This leads them to count as illicit and exceptional, strategies that are essential to getting their business done. These appear *ad hoc*, and women tend not to formulate them even to themselves, but they may none the less be quite systematic. I rarely learnt of them by asking directly, but usually simply stumbled across them. A range of examples can indicate what I mean.

The amount of molasses that Dhiren[7] buys at the hat always runs short. Rather than tell him – she thinks he would accuse her of being extravagant – his wife, Sukhi, buys small amounts of molasses secretly at the village shop. She finances this by selling rice via the son of her close friend and neighbour, with whom she has a supportive cluster relationship. By 'stealing' one household resource, she makes up the shortfall in another. In a slightly different example, Parboti[8] says that if things run short, she will buy secretly out of her own money, understanding that the money was not enough for purchases in the hat, and wanting to spare her husband shame. As in her business ventures, Parboti frequently stresses the importance of planning and ingenuity in running the household. She sees women's work as crucial to household advancement, and stresses its diversity: 'Using our five wits we do five kinds of work.'[9]

Purnima[10] describes her own experience of managing household resources. She is admittedly exceptional, but represents only the logical extension of tendencies which are present in women's management of household resources more generally.

Look, I'll tell you what I do. I say to him, I need new clothes, we'll have to sell some paddy. So he sells it. Then I take the money and give it to someone else to buy the cloth. But maybe the sari doesn't cost so much. So what's left, I keep separately in the house. He never asks anything about it, how much it cost or what happened to the rest of the money, give it to me – you know how so many are. He was never like that. He doesn't understand such things.

'Sometimes, I would even do this. I would say my sari was torn, I needed another, then take the money and keep wearing the old one. Gradually the money increased and I used to give loans and take interest. So it got to a lot. How would I explain it?! So I fixed it with my friend. I said we needed money and should put some of the land out on mortgage to her! So he agreed. Then she came to him and said she'd give it back to him to share-crop. So he is share-cropping his own land! Then when the harvest comes, his half is in our store and mine lying in a sack. My friend comes and takes it, and we sell it! . . . When the mortgage ran out, I told him about it all, and he said, then you run things. And since then I have!

'Have I done bad? If I had been stealing things and buying things I fancy for myself, then that would be something else. But this way I've saved us, in three girls' weddings, from having to sell any more land. Am I like an educated person? Think what I could have done if I could read and write!

While Purnima is unusually resourceful and bold, the sense of illicit activity, even though she is acting in the household's best interest, and the lingering self-doubt which this enjoins, makes her experience characteristic of women's management activities.

When men are away – particularly as migrant workers – women may take on more openly areas of responsibility generally considered male. Kumirpur is not in an area from which many migrate, but business enterprises are increasingly taking men away from the village, so that they cannot fulfil the male role of going to the hat or overseeing cultivation. Responsibility for this work does not automatically shift to women – there may be other male relatives nearby who can step in. In some cases, however, it undoubtedly does prefigure shifts in the gender division of labour. Minu's husband has a business boring shallow tube-wells, and she describes how this has affected them:

Listen, this is how it was. At first he used to run everything, and I just sometimes said some things. Then he went to Rajshahi one year, to work as a building contractor. While he was away, I had to manage everything here. I managed 1 bigha myself – his brothers next door used to work it for me – and

I share-cropped the other one and a half out. He wanted to stay on in Rajshahi, but I said to him, what profit is there in it? He was getting Tk600 a month – he can earn that here and work our land. So he didn't go back. Since then I've managed everything. He tends to let things go, so I have to take things on a bit more.

Rather than concealing her activity, Minu is proud of it, and the confidence of her success gives her added weight not only within her own household, but also in her immediate female (cluster) group. It would not, however, be true to see Minu's undoubted power and centrality simply as the result of her economic activities: she tells gladly how her husband has adored her from the first, and this gave her initial confidence, as well as being in turn strengthened by her achievements.

Purnima and Minu are unusual in being so open about what they do. In general women are much more ambiguous, finding on the one hand fulfilment in their centrality, and on the other continuing to disguise aspects of what they do with a complex web of conventions and petty deceits. Paradoxically, these activities typically serve the household interest, but appear illicit because they are concealed. Sharma (1980a:113) suggests that the household can more easily substitute for female labour than for male, and that this is a factor promoting women's dependence on men. Recognition of the management role that women fulfil, suggests that this is less the case than it appears when, for example, women's cooking is compared with men's marketing. But it is clear that women themselves, by concealing what they do, actively collude in allowing men a disproportionate degree of credit for the economic support of the household and so in devaluing their own contribution.

The first part of the explanation for this lies in the strength of the ideology noted above, that enjoins women's dependence: it is a matter of shame if a husband cannot support his wife in full. In the interests of good relationships in the family – and social status in the community – women have on the one hand to be adept domestic managers and on the other to conceal the extent of their activities so they present no challenge to the formal authority of their men. Women may be managers, but men are the owners of the key assets. In the second place, by secrecy women retain some control. In this way, women's management of their households is similar to their arrangements for share-tending animals or taking loans. Where women have few formal rights, concealment allows them some autonomy in action and represents a tactic of resistance to male domination.

The third dimension lies again in reflecting on the context in which work is done. The key issue is not that women's work is not valued, or even recognized, but that it is subsumed within family roles. In terms of the activity these will accommodate, these roles are extremely elastic, but in the relations they express they are extremely resilient. In the family, women are defined primarily by their relationships to (male) others, particularly as mothers. This at once makes them central – as givers and nurturers of life – and identifies them as dependent: they rarely stand by themselves.

It is therefore clear that the gender division of labour, which is widely remarked to be unusually strict in Bangladesh, is in practice amenable to considerable variation. This is, of course, not peculiar to Bangladesh: the gender division of labour is typically characterized by some cross-over of activity, it is the responsibility for what gets done (who gets blamed when it isn't) that constitutes the crucial factor (Oakley 1974). Women's work is affected by wider patterns of change in economy and society. As long as women's family membership remains their key resource, however, changes in tasks are unlikely in themselves to result in fundamental shifts in male–female power relations.

Women's 'personal' assets and income

If women are primarily dependent on social capital, do they then have any assets which they can call their own? There are two parts to the answer to this question. At the simplest level, the answer is, yes: ownership in Bangladesh is highly individuated and women, like men, may hold animals, trees, goods, gold and land in their own names. This is not, however, a full answer. The kinds of rights that nominal ownership confers can themselves differ by context. Here, I therefore look specifically at how 'personal rights' in assets and income vary first by gender and second by class.

Reflecting the divisions between major and minor markets in wider society, within the household women have control over smaller, less prestigious assets and rights over marginal income. Women thus may set aside a *mushti chal* (handful of rice) at cooking for their personal or their children's use, or for religious celebrations or alms giving. This seems to be on the decline, but is still quite common. Women may sell the charcoal from wood fires (now declining with the shortage of wood) and the bran from husked rice. They may keep the grain they glean from among threshed paddy straw. In theory, women should also keep the money given to them by those who come to view them as new brides, but in practice this may be taken by other household members.

These patterns appear again in access to different forms of livestock. Larger, more dependable, more prestigious animals are mainly found in wealthier households, and are generally owned by males. Thus the buffaloes and bullocks used for draught power in Kumirpur are mainly held by men: the stronger and more expensive buffaloes are found exclusively in richer households. Cows may be owned by men or women. Smaller, lower status animals – goats, sheep and geese – are found in poorer households and owned by women. Ducks and chickens are virtually exclusively the property of women and children. Ducks and chickens are thought beneath notice: to ask about numbers invariably draws a laugh. 'Foreign', improved species of birds are kept in a few of the richer households, and these are properly vaccinated. The vast majority of women, however, still keep the small 'local' birds, which never come within miles of the Fowl Vaccination Office in the upazila headquarters. They are chronically vulnerable to disease. None the less, they may constitute a significant resource: a prosperous household might keep 50–100 chickens.

People gain animals through gifts, purchase, share-tending, or breeding from existing stock. It has been a common practice for a cow to be given to a daughter on or after her mariage, and so to provide her with a minor source of independent income. Amongst Hindus in particular, the gift of a cow is extremely auspicious. With declining numbers of milch cattle and increasing dowry demands, however, this practice is becoming less common. Cows and other animals may also be bought for children, especially with the gifts given by relatives and neighbours who come to view the child in his or her first months. Gifts of smaller animals are also used to express fictive kin ties. It is often the child's mother who is responsible for looking after the animals acquired in these ways.

While the normal place for the purchase of livestock is the hat, in practice information may be passed and transactions carried out through personal links within the village. In general, the larger the animal, the more likely it is to be bought in the hat: there are special hats for the purchase of cattle and buffaloes. Ducks and chickens are most often bought in the village, and sheep and goats are also commonly exchanged directly, without going to the hat. There is, however, no doubt that women's exclusion from the hat does lessen their independence in rearing livestock. The Santal labourer, Bolai, expressed this neatly. When I asked whether he gave his wife the full price of her goats which he had sold, Bolai (who has never been to Rajshahi) laughed and said: 'If I ask you to bring something from Rajshahi and it cost Tk30 and you say it cost Tk50, then won't I believe you?!'

Amongst the case study households there were clear differences by class in terms of the degree of tension focused on marketing. Women in the upper/strong class did not seem to consider it an issue. Most women of this class share-tend out animals and so can conceal their assets and protect them from plunder. They can then reinvest the cash they gain in usurious loans and realize substantial profits. Some women ask their mothers-in-law or servants to buy or sell animals for them, but most sell their goats or sheep through their husbands, confident that they will not be cheated. In the wealthiest households chickens, eggs and milk are typically consumed within the household, though women may make a little income for themselves through informal sale. Men of this class would be laughed at if they took a chicken for sale in the hat, so if at all, this is done by servants. Status considerations thus constrain men's actions, as well as women's. Norms also vary by community. In Sajjur's somaj a woman's ownership rights are strictly observed: she is paid the market price if one of her animals is eaten by guests other than her own natal kin.

In contrast to this, women in the upper/vulnerable case study households felt considerable tension over marketing livestock. The consensus seemed to be that the person (husband or wife) who sells the animal keeps the money. Where possible, women thus sell their animals directly in the village, or through intermediaries other than their husbands. Control depends also on the amount of money that is involved: the larger the sum, the more likely that the men will take it. Daughters are better able than wives to keep control of their income: in four of the six case study households of this class, daughters had bought jewellery for their weddings with income gained through rearing livestock.

In the lower status households the picture is similar to this, but women are less likely to expect personal assets. The overall scarcity means that all resources tend to be mobilized in the household's immediate interest. In times of stress women have to subsidize what are formally male responsibilities. Livestock are particularly central to single households, where they may represent the major source of income. They can also be kept as risk insurance: sale of a goat (for example) in the lean period before harvest may save a household from having to take a loan at exorbitant interest rates. With this and vulnerability to disease, there may therefore be quite rapid turnover of stock. Asha[11] took a goat to share-tend from her employer. From this she reared two kids, which themselves produced five more, of these:

a) two goats were sold to buy medicine when her mother was ill. Her father was also unwell so unable to go to hat, so Asha had to sell in the village to Rashida, the wife of their 'patron', Sajjur, at little more than half the market price;

b) one was seen eating paddy, by one of the wealthy landowners. He beat it so severely that the goat went crazy and had to be sold for meat – at half of what it would have fetched live;[12]

c) one was sold for lack of someone to tend it, when Asha began a regular job as domestic servant;

d) two were sold and the money taken by her father for cultivation. After harvest, he gave her 3 maunds of paddy. Asha stored it, and sold it later for Tk450. At *Eid*[13] she sold another goat for Tk425. Her father took from her the Tk900 for cultivation expenses, and did not return it.

The fate of these goats clearly shows the vulnerability of the poor, the articulation of activities in the major and minor markets, and the limits of talking of individual ownership in a situation of scarce resources. It is important not to over-idealize the sharing of resources in poorer households: it is due to severe shortage and is often founded in inequality, it does not simply reflect a stronger sense of unity, nor always free choice.

In households of every class, women keep animals at the discretion of their husbands. Even though the work, and often the capital, is the woman's, her husband has the right of veto, and may decide on whether her animals are sold, eaten or kept. If she makes the decision, it is because he allows her to. In all households of which the head is male, women keep secret the exact amount of income they make. It is known that women keep some separate funds, but they are overlooked as long as they are discreet. Like the ambivalence over women's management activities, this is contradictory. On the one hand construing women's earning as illicit eases the dominant picture of total female dependence on male provision, allowing women some private funds. On the other hand it sustains the ideology of full male support, while still allowing the household to benefit from women's activities. This kind of practice is not limited to Bangladesh. In Britain a close analogy to this is noted by Whitehead (1984a). She reports Hunt's (1977)[14] findings in a north Midlands mining village that wives' earnings are used for 'extras' while husbands finance 'necessary expenditure'. Such divisions in categories of consumption similarly reinforce gender stereotypes while still allowing households to benefit from the wives' income.

While the sample is small, the case study material throws doubt on the common assertions that gender relations are more unequal in the richest households (see chpater 2), at least in terms of the room for manoeuvre women have. There are four aspects to this. In the first place, the overall wealth of richer households means that all household members have a better chance of some personal property (though women clearly have less than men). Thus women in richer households are more likely to have gold, larger numbers of animals, and even land, than women in poorer households. Secondly, in comparison with household income as a whole, the sums women make themselves seem comparatively small in wealthier households, so they are more likely to keep control of them.

In the third place, wealthier households are more likely to have a joint internal structure, which allows a greater degree of internal differentiation. This allows more autonomy to women, though there is clearly subordination between them. In less wealthy households there is greater pressure on resources and concentration of activities, which results in far more male plunder of nominally female assets. In the fourth place, women in (typically poorer) separate households, who have no sister-in-law or mother-in-law to substitute for them, may find it very hard ever to find a time when they can go away for a break to their natal families. The fact that they perceive this themselves rather than have someone else insist that they stay, does not necessarily ease the burden of incessant hard work.

None the less, it is important to note that even in the wealthiest households, women's resources are 'personal' only in line with cultural constructions of gender identity. Thus women 'choose' to spend their own money largely on gifts, to their children or wider kin, which ultimately serve the household advancement. While the form it takes differs, in all classes of household the income which women generate is ultimately used in the service of the household as a whole.

Land and property

Women's marginalized access to the major resources is clearest to see in the obstacles that face their acquisition of land. Thus amongst the Hindu and Muslim case study women, 23 out of 40 (58 per cent) have no land property, nor any prospects of it. Only 4 out of 40 (10 per cent) presently hold any land by inheritance. Amongst the Santals, women do not normally inherit land, and none of the case study women had any prospects of doing so. This is a matter of some resentment: it was the one point in the group session which I held with the Santals on which women forcefully spoke out. Potentially, Muslim women have some advantage: three Muslim women have gained some land, and eleven more are legally entitled to some, while only one of the Hindu women has inherited and one more has prospects of inheriting any. Not surprisingly, women in the upper status have significantly better prospects of owning property (70 per cent) than those in the lower (20 per cent). In practice these differences will be evened out to some degree: formal entitlement to land does not mean that women in fact gain possession, women's legal disadvantage in land rights is forcefully backed up by social practice which is to a large extent constant across class and community.

In practice, then, strong normative sanctions and practical family politics mean that women commonly give up their rights to land divided after their fathers' death. Of the case study women, only Rashida (Sajjur's wife) has all the land that was due to her, and even she share-crops out the land to her brothers, taking only half of the main paddy crop, and leaving them fully free to use the land as they like in the rest of the year. In only two other cases have Muslim women taken any land from their natal family – one half and one quarter of their formal entitlement. Both have kept the land rather than sell it and buy nearer by and they share-crop it out to male relatives. In three more cases, Muslim women have been offered land which is less than their fair share, and they are set to accept it, rather than involve themselves in struggle to gain the full amount. Some of the hazards for women in claiming their rights are clear in the case of Sajjur's sisters, who might be thought to have a better than average chance, living as they do within the same village and somaj as their brothers and parents.[15]

It is said that Sajjur took the transfer from India as an opportunity to register much of the land in his own name, rather than keeping it in his father's name, for division after his death. With some reason therefore, his sisters are anxious about their inheritance, and are agitating to receive their share now. This has brought a negative reaction from Sajjur's Ma: 'What sort of daughters are they, wanting their father's property before he is even buried?'

The weakness of the women's position is evident here – their lack of direct access to the land – though they do have the right – means they can only try to gain access in ways which may be considered unacceptable and so reinforce their exclusion. In this case, their mother is alienated by their claims so allies with their brother against them.

Sukhi is the only Hindu woman who has inherited any land. The story of her inheritance is salutary. Before they were married, Dhiren was a lodger in Sukhi's father's house. Her mother had died long before, leaving 5 bighas in Sukhi's name. Before Sukhi's wedding to him was talked of, Sukhi's father went to Dhiren and discussed with him this plan. Her father would go to court and swear he had no daughter, so that he could register all his dead wife's land in her son's name. Dhiren countenanced the idea, and it was done. Then, after they were married, Dhiren became angry about it. Her father said that for the meantime they could take half the land and work it. Dhiren went ahead and formally registered 2.5 bighas in her name, not taking the full amount for the sake of goodwill in the family. At the time, Sukhi saw no need to take any of the land. Since then family relations have worsened. Both now regret that they did not claim the full amount, though they will not undertake the court case that would be necessary for its recovery.

While Dhiren is a little embarrassed about his part in this story, Sukhi loves to tell it, laughing with glee at the way Dhiren's perfidy rounded on himself. It is, however, indicative of how lightly women's rights in property are taken, that her own father and an upright young man lodging in her house could conspire to defraud her. If Sukhi had not happened to marry Dhiren, who knew the story, she would never have recovered even part of what was hers. Sukhi herself appears to have played little part either in the loss of the land or its partial recovery. She has, however, refused Dhiren's repeated suggestions that she should register it in his or one of their sons' name. In this way she guarantees some support for herself in her old age, and some security for her daughter so that she will not be totally dependent on her (future) husband's family.

The reason most commonly given for women giving up their rights to inherited land is that the land represents a kind of ransom to the natal family, to keep relations sweet there and so ensure continued visiting and support as needed: a straight trade-off, in other words, between material and social capital. It may also demonstrate the identity that women continue to feel with their natal family. The strongest sanctions are against women taking immediate possession of their inheritance. On the one hand this may clearly strengthen the claims of brothers over sisters. On the other hand, however, the years before possession is ultimately decided allow women to keep some material stake in their natal family without souring relations there, and so mediate their dependence on their husband's families. Simiarly, if women share-crop out to their brothers, they have more chance of retaining a personal income than if the land is sold and then more bought in the marital village, and so added to the stock of joint household resources. This is the equivalent of married women keeping animals and perhaps savings in their natal home, as a way of preserving some autonomy.

It is important, however, not to ignore elements of conflict between brothers and sisters. As in the two cases outlined above, women do not always wish to give up their rights to inheritance. Women's exclusion from direct participation in cultivation and restricted mobility puts them at a structural disadvantage which their own relatives may well be prepared to exploit. This situation may be intensified with the inflation of dowry payments. While dowries are given with women, not to women, from the point of view of the natal home, dowries are a claim by daughters on common family resources. Explicit comparisons are often made between daughters' rights to dowry and sons' rights to inheritance. These are set in a situation of overall scarcity, where there is a fixed amount of the main resource, land, from which an ever growing population has to gain a living. The dowry is thus regarded as daughters' share in the inheritable property, and used as a further legitimation in excluding women from any share in what is divided after their parents' deaths.

Whose name is on the land title is of course only part of the story: further implications of marriage payments and inheritance practices hang on the question of control. What use is made of dowries after they enter the household? Did bride price mean that women had fuller control over the gifts exchanged than dowry does? How do women's rights over their inherited land differ from those in the wealth they bring at marriage? It is crucial to explore not only who has rights in what but also how property rights themselves differ according to whose they are.

Within the small sample of the case study households, these questions may only be very tentatively approached. In the two cases where gold given by her parents-in-law had been exchanged for land, it was registered in the woman's own name. By contrast, out of eight cases in which land or goods were bought with the proceeds of dowry, only three purchased assets in the woman's name (land). On the face of it, in this very small sample it thus appears that women were slightly better able to retain control of their bride price, though it must be recognized that nominal ownership of land does not automatically confer real control. There is a special term (*benami*) for the transfer of nominal ownership to avoid taxation or land ceiling legislation, which results in no shift of control. Women may be quite happy about this. Asked if she kept any separate accounts of the crops grown on land in her name, Aynuddin Mondol's wife[16] laughed and said: 'Why should I need to? As I am now, it is all mine!'

Registering land in a female name can also express the distinct interests of the sub-units within the joint household. In particular, registering land bought from a dowry in the daughter-in-law's name may serve to keep the property separate from that of the joint household as a whole. Registry of land in women's names may thus reflect the rights of males as husbands, rather than females as owners, though it must be recognized that women in joint households typically articulate their individual interests through those of their own sub-family. In many cases the dowry is seen as the property of the young couple (particularly the groom) but sometimes it is controlled by the older generation. The dowry given to a son may therefore be used immediately in the marriage of a daughter, with no recognition of his separate rights, or sometimes it may be seen as a loan, to be repaid later on.

It is important to note that women do not always object when their men take over assets that were formally theirs. Dhiren took Sukhi's dowry gold from her, and suggested that they share out her land to her father, and use the harvest to repay what she lost. She felt it was foolish for them as a household to lose income by sharing out land, so this was never done. Since then, Dhiren has gradually sold off all Sukhi's gold, buying land in his name, and only ever recompensing her with one pair of ear-rings. The profit from the final sale he lodged in a fixed deposit in their daughter's name, in preparation for her dowry. He only told Sukhi about this afterwards. She, however, agrees that the land should be in his name – otherwise what would the boys eat, while their daughter will be provided for at her marriage. This clearly undermines too strong assumptions about individual interests, or simple identity along gender lines. This is discussed in more detail in the following section, and the concluding chapter.

Amongst lower class households, wedding gifts from either party are most commonly sold in household need, even though selling wedding gold is a matter of shame. Women of the upper status case study households are divided equally between those who retain their jewellery and those who have sold it for land. There is also a smaller number of wealthy women who have made gifts of their jewellery within the family. There is no obvious distinction between bride price and dowry in any of these factors. Overall, time is perhaps the most significant factor. Westergaard (1983) states that on marriage the only personal possession of the women in the Comilla villages she surveyed was their jewellery. Only a small number retained even this (richest 38 per cent, landless 10 per cent) and very few of these were older women. Richer women gave their jewellery as wedding gifts to their daughters, or sometimes to their sons' brides. The jewellery of poorer women tends to go in distress sales. This is consistent with Mayoux's (p. 241) findings in two West Bengal villages. Like personal income, the ownership of an asset – as shown by rights over its usage – commonly changes over time. What begins as personal female property, almost invariably ends as a household resource in all but a few of the richest cases.

The use of resources is an important indicator of different forms of power and identity. In terms of land property, two women of the richest households, Rashida, wife of Sajjur,[17] and Nilufar, wife of Akhbar,[18] enjoy the greatest autonomy. Both keep the produce of their land separately and dispose of it at their own discretion. This is not to say, however, that they use it on themselves. In 1986, Nilufar helped buy her husband a motorycycle – an important status symbol as well as a convenience. Rashida has given the bulk of her profit to her eldest daughter, who was mismarried into a relatively poor family, to help her and her husband start a business. Rashida has plans to open a bank account in her name. This would mean travelling the four miles to the nearest bank branch. She laughed at my surprise: 'We are not absolutely in purdah, that we can't go out as we need to!'

What underlies these two women's relative autonomy in using their resources? First, both Nilufar and Rashida have good relationships with their husbands, and in spite of their fathers-in-law being alive, their husbands have assumed the effective headship of their households. Second, they belong to wealthy households in which the income from their own landholding is of relatively minor significance. These are the components that lie behind these women's rights. It is not the owning of property in itself, but these background factors, which allow them to enjoy this relative freedom. Nilufar's and Rashida's choices of how to use their money are also indicative: they serve the interests of the household, rather than the women's personal interests as such. To be more precise, they serve the interests of their own sub-family within the joint household.

At the close of this section, it is thus clear that richer women are much more likely to own land than poorer women, and have a far better chance of retaining their personal assets (such as gold or silver). Within these bounds, a woman is more likely to be able to dispose of the income from her land if she has good relationships with those in authority in the household. How far her choices are seen to advance the household's interests may also be a factor. A woman who share-crops out her land to relatives in her natal village, may enhance both her chances of control of her material assets, and affirm the social capital of her relationships with her natal kin. Even if a woman's land is farmed as part of the joint household stock, it represents some security against the day when her husband dies.

Property rights show the mark of the social context in which they arise. In Bangladesh, women have access to relatively small amounts of property and income and depend primarily on their relationships. This in turn affects women's rights in the assets they hold. There are two aspects to this. First, the quality of her social relationships determines the extent of control a woman has over assets that are nominally hers. Second, the choices women make in the use of their property show the priority they give to strengthening those relationships. This, and the wider social context, means that women's personal income or property do not in practice constitute a basis for women's independence of men. They may, however, serve crucially to strengthen the terms on which women negotiate their dependence.

The marriage ceremony for both Hindus and Muslims confers rights of support on wives. Women's (formal or customary) exclusion from property holding thus assumes that they will have a male provider on whom they can rely. Their own lack of material resources in turn reinforces this dependence. In Bangladesh at present the assumption that women are always secure in male protection is false. On the one hand divorce is becoming more common, on the other, widow women without their own resources are increasingly unlikely to be supported by married sons.[19] In Kumirpur there are at present seven women living as a separate unit in the same homestead as their married sons,[20] and several more wander for a few months at a time between their children's houses. A comparable number are living with their youngest unmarried son, and are likely to be made destitute when he marries. The majority of these women are beggars, hurt and bitter at being discarded by their sons.

Women in upper/vulnerable households who have typically neither land of their own, nor experience of landlessness, express considerable anxiety about the changing norms of family responsibility. Increasingly they urge their husbands to settle on them some land in their own names. Maloti[21] gave a prime example of this. When I asked her if she had any land of her own, she gestured roughly towards her husband, Suresh, beside her: 'Ask him!' Her own mother was not a happy example, shifting as she does for a few months in each of her children's houses, since none of her sons will support her full time. Maloti explained further:

'The husbands do wrong in not giving land to the wife, then how will the sons do right? Now it is possible to register land in the wife's name for her life, and to pass it on to sons when she dies. Even that he doesn't do!'

As within marriage, the point is not so much that land would give women like Maloti the chance of independence, but that it would provide better grounds to secure their customary rights to support. Family relationships alone are no longer enough: women are much less likely to be abandoned by their children if they own some land from which to draw their subsistence. In circumstances of declining family solidarity, increasing numbers of women may be caught in the scissor action of norms which largely preclude material independence through expectation of other (social) sources of support, and the actual failure of those forms of support to sustain them.

Approaching power

Looking at women's rights and responsibilities in the household brings into sharp focus the question that underlies this study as a whole: how is power articulated in class and gender identities? Here, as in the earlier chapters, it is shown how power inheres in the kinds of asset which different sets of people exchange and the terms on which exchange takes place. Divisions by class and gender cross-cut one another and interconnect. Social relationships are important in even the more formal market transactions, advantage in one area predisposes towards gain in another.

There is no doubt about the centrality of class and gender in structuring inequality. Wealth and social status are highly significant far beyond the economic sphere: the state does not aim to serve the interests of the poor, and anyway its weakness means that the state can have little levelling effect. Access to health care, education, government services or the law are heavily dependent on ability to pay and the social and political strength associated with that. Similarly, the male bias in the legal, social and economic framework acts like a fly-wheel in relations between actual men and women: it adds a vast amount of extra weight to the male side in any encounter. This is so strong that it prevents many potential conflicts of interest even being expressed – women accommodate themselves to men's wishes, or manoeuvre by indirect means against them.

At the same time it is clear that relations between rich and poor or men and women are not simply based on conflict but show complex negotiations of mutual gain and shared interest. Conversely, relations between members of the same class or gender group are often characterized by conflict. This contradiction appears distinctly in the family household, which is most strictly structured on gender oppositions, yet also fosters a common identity which undercuts them. This brings out the inadequacy of talking about who has more or less power. The point rather is that power is constitutive of identities which are in turn malleable and open to change, as are the rules and notions that define them. In this final section I therefore want to look again at the family household, what it shows of identity and divisions of interest, and the implications this has for understanding power.

Towards the end of my time in Kumirpur, I arranged a discussion between the women in each cluster group. This gave me an opportunity to discuss with them the impressions that I had received and at the same time see how they related to one another. We covered a wide variety of issues, which in each case included the question of power. There were two points on which everyone was united. First, everyone agreed that their room for manoeuvre crucially depended on the quality of their relationships, in the first place with their husbands, and then with their mothers-in-law. They explicitly compared women with close marital relationships with those whose husbands were indifferent or hostile, through a mixture of teasing and indignant commiseration. Time and again, in talks with individuals also, this point was made: women's fortunes depend primarily on the 'kindness' of their husbands.

In the second place, the women clearly recognized some relationship between economic activity and power relations in the household: work that gained income did result in greater centrality in household affairs. Here again there was a good deal of (often wry) humour. Older women were lightly mocked for having run the household for many years (through rice husking) and then having to cede power to their sons, and take whatever pennies they would spare. Women's ability to earn is certainly significant if their husbands are unwell, absent for long periods, or if the marriage breaks down. It was clear, however, that while women may enjoy considerable *de facto* power, particularly in alliance with their sons, this rarely translates to formal authority and is rarely sustained in the longer term.

The situation seems a little different in communities with strong traditions of female earning, such as the Robidas Hindus whose women are midwives, or the Santals. The relationship of the midwife, Nondo,[22] and Robi her husband did indeed seem strikingly egalitarian. Nondo, frustrated by my questions about who did what and who had authority, stated: 'Our work gets done by two people's agreement.' When I asked whether she had to ask Robi's permission to go and attend a birth, Nondo said that she just let him know she was going, and told him to look after the house and the children. The Santal group was very small and isolated, and cannot serve as any kind of basis for general patterns of relationships amongst Santals as a whole. Amongst the Kumirpur Santals, however, relationships between husbands and wives in stable households seemed to differ less than I expected from those amongst the Bengalis. Bolai's wife, for example, would ask him if she had an offer to work anywhere at any distance, while he would decide for himself. At the same time, women's ability to earn a living wage clearly gave them a stronger basis to set up on their own in cases of marital breakdown. This might be a partial explanation for the high rate of fragmented households among the Santal group, but this obviously primarily reflected their acute social marginality.

However economic activities may affect relations within the family, this cannot reverse the overall culture of male dominance. The crudest expression of this is the use of violence by relatively 'marginalized' men against their relatively 'central' wives. The case of Kaniz[23] exemplifies this: for years, Kaniz has been responsible for the major day-to-day running of their household, as her husband is somewhat simple, and disinclined to work. One day in June

1986, she came crying into Asha's house, badly swollen after her husband had beaten her with a stick across her back. The 'reason' was that she had protested at him having engaged two labourers (costing Tk40) to work on their house, rather doing part of the work himself.

Gender violence is common, particularly in the early years of marriage. It is better hidden amongst upper than lower status households. Thus, asked if her parents-in-law would intervene if her husband beat her, one of Kangali Serkar's[24] daughters-in-law replied: 'How would they know?' In extreme cases, violence may lead to a community hearing (*bichar*). Often, however, it is accepted (including by women) as a legitimate male response to female 'misbehaviour' – such as not returning at the agreed time from a visit to the natal home. Violence is also used as a simple expression of male dominance, with no question of a 'legitimate' cause, as in the case above.

It is important to reject the convention that Bangladeshi women have no power and to count in forms of power (such as personal influence and brokerage) that are excluded in more formal models. These are important in transactions between men as well as between women. It is, however, also necessary to be sensitive to the overall context, which may counterweight heavily the impact of any apparent reversal in the activities of household men and women. There are many coercive aspects short of overt physical violence in the social conditions in which women live in rural Bangladesh, as elsewhere. Their construction as legal minors, their exclusion from property rights, the distrust and policing of their sexuality, their isolation in an unfamiliar setting after marriage, their segregation into the least valued and least remunerative kinds of work – all these are a kind of violence which helps to enforce female submission. It is not for nothing that folk culture disproportionately represents women as weeping, as in sorrow, as undergoing loss and pain.

To view gender as a contested image, however, suggests that this motif of female submission expresses only a part of the story. While women may bow to the dominant culture, they also pursue strategies of resistance. Jori's[25] defiance of norms circumscribing women's movement (see chapter 6) is a clear example of the way this may explode into open revolt. James Scott (1985) in his study of peasant resistance, contrasts the formal deference of poor villagers to their 'off-stage' defiance, seeing as the peasantry's characteristic feature a smouldering resistance which occasionally erupts into open rebellion. In Kumirpur this is clearly evident in women's secrecy about their own money. It shows also in humour and the use of stinging irony. Thus Rufia, elder daughter-in-law of Hasan Mullah,[26] had to come one day to the house of a neighbour to husk rice in her dheki, since theirs was broken. A passer-by asked:

'What, isn't yours mended yet?'
Rufia answered: 'The work gets done this way, why should they mend it?'
Her mother-in-law, coming up behind, quickly rebuked her: 'Do you have to say such things before people?'.

On another occasion, I asked Rufia what they would do if a child got sick and there was no man at home. Her response was bitterly self-mocking: 'Even if the child dies, still we won't go out.' Her younger sister-in-law was similarly angry, but less able to externalize it. For months she kept wearing a torn old sari, refusing to point it out to her husband's family: 'Can't they see?!'

As in this case, there is a clear danger that women's restricted scope for resistance can make it self-destructive. This is particularly so if it goes on for any length of time and results in long-term damage to the relationships on which she relies. Suraiya Begum (1989:119) relates a more positive example. A woman in her research village in West Bengal offered her tea with milk and drank the same herself, while giving her husband and his friends only black tea. The reason, she explained, was that they should not think she had nothing better to do than make tea for them all day, and should be discouraged from returning.

Another strategy for resistance lies in hijacking aspects of cultural constructions of gender and redeploying them in women's own interests. This can be used also in defence of class interests. Thus while poorer women are usually relatively straightforward about how much land their households have, wealthier women almost invariably claim they know nothing about their households' landholding. This could, of course, show the greater centrality of women in poorer than richer households. But at least in part it also reflects the general reluctance of wealthier people to reveal what they have, and richer women's use of conventional gender roles to evade having to answer an unwelcome question. Countering the negative tone of the examples above, it was Rufia who gave me a very positive example of the way that women can take the constraints upon them and transform them into strengths. She tells how they used to have an open well in front of their house, but it dried up. After six months of fetching water from the hand-pump in front of a (Hindu) house some 150 metres away, the women petitioned the men for a HTW of their own:

'Bear in mind, we don't go out much, or see people. And then we were having to go out all the time and see people. We really didn't like it. We feel if we can stay in the house, *that* is good.'

In itself, this appears evidence of the full internalization of the norms of female seclusion. From her other remarks, however, I judge rather that Rufia objected to having to go so far every time to fetch water. The conventional phrasing made acceptable a request for expenditure to her economical but upwardly mobile father-in-law, appealing both to his concerns for social status and to his strict adherence to Islam. Rather than bowing to the ideology, she was making it work for her.

The notion of the family household as a simple unit clearly breaks down when it is looked at more closely. Thus necessary clothes may be purchased from the common budget but special ones bought from separate funds; cattle may be kept together but owned individually, so that if one son's cow dies it is remembered and he does not receive one when the household is eventually divided; salaries from office jobs may be kept individually or only a proportion given to the joint fund; and of course dowries may be invested in land which is kept separately from the common resources. Jansen (1986) points out that some degree of separate saving can in fact sustain the joint household by postponing withdrawal of more productive sub-units. This identification of separate interests is not always consensual, however. Kaniz[27] told me how she bought one third of a bigha of her father-in-law's land while they were still together. The purchase was never registered, as they thought they would save costs by registering it all together when the land was divided after his death. Some years later her father-in-law sold off the land to someone else. Their fury and sense of betrayal was a precipitate factor in making Khalek and Kaniz leave the household and set up independently.

Conversely, links also stretch well beyond the household boundaries. Ties within the homestead (bari) that has divided into separate household units are particularly strong. Links between brothers and their widowed sisters, or mothers and married daughters are noted above and may be the basis of substantial economic transfers. The autonomy of the household as the 'getting by unit' (Pahl, 1984) is obviated by the support, and demands, of wider kin.

External factors also have an effect on relations within the household unit. Before the crisis of Jori's pregnancy, Samad's and Jori's family was highly individuated, apparently sharing little more than a common living space. All but the youngest brother were earning their own incomes and bought their clothes and personal needs out of that. They were also each pretty much a law unto themselves: despite being subjected to discipline by his somaj, Jori's father was unable to get her to behave more conventionally. When the disaster came, however, they suddenly had to face it together. The whole family was excommunicated from the somaj, the girls all withdrawn from their jobs and the family began to look for husbands for them. Samad took control in place of his father, sacrificing his own assets to fight the paternity case and committed to persist until whatever fate determined.

The family household is thus clearly cross-cut by internal divisions and affected by outside links and pressures. This does not, however, undermine its significance either in terms of people's sense of themselves or their place in society. One way of conceiving of the household is as a common venture, which unites its members while not removing their individual interests. This can clearly account, for example, for the subdivisions within the joint household while recognizing the economic interests (two-legged strategies for advancement) and social benefits (prestige and fulfilment of cultural norms) that unite its members. This conception is limited, however, in its identification of the household in purely economic terms. In practice, the association of the household with the family is a crucial factor in holding it together. This also legitimates the inequality within it, since it helps to make the household appear a 'natural unit' and so bolsters the relations it expresses (Harris, 1984). In fact, however, kinship is itself not a matter only of links by blood and marriage, but has embedded in it a mesh of obligations and responsibilities. As seen above, family roles prescribe different types of work, not only sexual or biological relationships.

What is central, however, is that in the family people are essentially constituted in relationship, whether through ties of love, blood, or proximity. In this it specifies a strong interdependence, which is always founded in inequality. This is the key to understanding the relations that the family household expresses. It does not represent a collection of individuals held together by mutual interest or coercion, nor any straightforward unity. It rather engenders different perceptions of interests at different times and a moulding of persons in and through their relationship to each other.

If this analysis is correct, it clearly throws doubt on the notion of 'autonomy', as an indicator of degrees of power. Examples are quoted above of how women's work, even outside the homestead, is in fulfilment of family roles; of how property is significant to women largely as a basis for better negotiation of dependence; and how even women heading their own households rely on male kin and neighbours for practical and moral support. McCarthy (1967) in her classic study of women extension workers as 'mediators between tradition and development' suggests instead the notion of 'centrality'. As this focuses analysis on relationship, rather than assuming an essential individualism, it seems a more appropriate term than autonomy as a way of conceiving interpersonal power in the Bangladesh context, and indeed more generally.

Appreciating how power inheres in relationship helps to bring together economic relations and cultural constructions of gender identity. This is shown very clearly in a common indicator of power: choices about resource use. While women may be more central in poorer households, the element of choice for any member of a household struggling at the edge of subsistence is strictly limited. Similarly, choices in use of personal income vary greatly by gender. At a quite simple level, hierarchies of gender and age in the household structure resource access. As two daughters-in-law, one Hindu l/v and one Muslim u/s, independently remarked: 'Even if it is your own, what does that mean, you are still beneath your husband.'

This is not, however, simply a question of brute authority. Just as any work done by women can be subsumed within their gender roles so those roles prefigure even formally 'free' choices. This is recognized by Whitehead (1984a:112) in the term 'the ideology of maternal altruism'. Thus Sukhi says that she is glad that her husband keeps the money, because: 'Money doesn't stay in my hands!'

Women are defined by their relationships. They thus both lack individual rights in material resources, and also bear an ever present responsibility for the care of family members. This is found by Whitehead (1984b:185) in Ghana, where she remarks that while the men grow groundnuts as cash crops, the women grow them: 'For the children to chop (eat).'

Sharma (1980a:108) considers factors that limit women's control of cash, and notes two[28] of particular interest here: 1) the sense that it is 'not her own', and 2) that she is 'responsible to the rest of the household'. Categories of female expenditure are prescribed to serve the household interest even through female choice. Thus women's personal income may buy clothes, jewellery or cosmetics, for the woman herself or her children. Crucially, this personal saving also allows women to purchase gifts to take on visits. These gifts foster both good relations with other households and good personal relations between women. They thus represent both a household and a personal resource. Women thus fulfil their family roles even in their personal choices.

In practice, women themselves often do not distinguish the personal from the family household advantage. This is easiest to see in the poorest households, where women's whole effort may go directly into the generation of basic household resources, under threat of scarcity. In fact, while the form this takes varies, in every class female income, which is invested in female goods (such as gold) comes eventually to be used for the household good. It would be mistaken to see this as 'false consciousness'. In terms of economics, the exclusion of women from direct access to major material resources means that women's prime resource is their relationships, and in particular those in the household to which they belong. This means that, whatever the inequalities that remain within it, it is quite reasonable for women in Bangladesh to identify their own interests with the advancement of the household as a whole.

But this is only to go part of the way. The contradiction and solidarity in patron–client relations, the interpenetration of class and gender inequalities, the notion of difference within and between women, the negotiation of definitions of work and so of gender roles, the complex shifts of interests and identities in and through the family household, all point to the malleability of social relations and how individuals are constituted through their relationship to each other. This undermines the assumption that women have set interests as individuals or as a gender group. In practice, perceptions of interest are much more ambiguous. As Minu[29] remarks: 'What is his is mine and mine, his. Isn't that how it is in your country?'

Notes

1. See Abdullah and Zeidenstein (1982) or Nur Begum (1988) on Bangladesh; and Mackintosh (1984) on more general debates.
2. 5.1 HM u/s j.
3. 5.4 HM u/v s.
4. 3.3 ML l/s s.
5. The predominance of gender in determining payment was illustrated still further in this case: Maloti repeatedly pressed me to come and eat with them that day, clearly feeling that I should be recompensed for my work, in the way another woman would be.
6. In Bengali, *hoy na*. This has a much stronger sense than the English, 'does not happen', more like, '*is* not'. It is, however, used very commonly, and often has a connotation of moral prohibition.
7. 1.1. HM u/v s.
8. 2.5 HB l/s s.
9. '*Pac rokom budhi kore pac dike katchi*'. 'Five' here just indicates variety.
10. 4.2 HM u/v j.

11. 2.4 ME l/v s.

12. This case of a richer man's violence against poorer people's stock is by no means an isolated example.

13. *Eid Korbani*, one of the two great Muslim festivals, at which cattle and goats must be slaughtered as a sacrifice. At this time the price of animals peaks.

14. Hunt, P. (1977) *The Parlour and the Pit*, unpublished M.Sc. thesis, University of Keele (noted by Whitehead, 1984a).

15. Their husbands are Mannan 2.2 ME u/v j and Hakim 2.3 ME u/v j.

16. 4.1 ME u/s j.

17. 2.1 ME u/s j.

18. 3.1 ML u/s j.

19. Daughters risk destabilizing their own position in their marital households, if they take in their mothers, so this is less common, though not unknown.

20. They live, that is, in a separate room within the homestead. All these women at present in Kumirpur are Hindu, but there are many single Muslim women in the neighbouring villages.

21. 5.4 HM u/v s.

22. 6.3 HO l/v s.

23. 4.4 ME l/v s.

24. 5.1 HM u/s j.

25. 6.2 ME l/v s.

26. 6.1 ME u/v j.

27. 4.4 ME l/v s.

28. The others are illiteracy and purdah.

29. 3.2 ML l/s s.

8.   Tracing the Shadows

Introduction

Coming to write the conclusion, the image that arises is one of a series of Russian dolls, each of a similar shape and fitting within the other, but each also distinct from the next. This book began by setting the discussion of women's situation in Bangladesh in the context of the aid discourse through which the debates were produced. I have pointed out how images of women, even the category 'Bangladeshi women' itself, belonged to that discourse, and their content could not be understood without taking account of the family of meanings that the discourse assumed and the power relations it expressed.

My aim, therefore, was to set these images and the prominent debates in the literature, particularly on women's work, against the experience of actual Bangladeshi women, and how they see their lives. To do this, I have concentrated on particular examples from the village where I stayed, and quoted women's own words whenever possible. But it is a very partial achievement. Not only due to personal shortcomings (though there are those) but also because I have been writing within the discourse, and to a large extent have reproduced the very assumptions I set out to question. In the following section some of the alternative issues that need to be looked at are indicated, and also parts of peoples' lives that are in the shadows thrown by the aid discourse, and by my study in particular. In place of the customary conclusions, this chapter therefore exposes the essentially provisional character of the study as a whole: in raising further questions, the partiality of the picture that I have presented is indicated.

There is, though, a further dimension, and it is this that makes me think of the Russian dolls. When you peel off one layer of the aid discourse (for example) you don't have the kernel, the real essence; Bangladeshi women – or society – in themselves. Rather, you find there are yet more layers of conflicting definitions, legal rules, social practices, religious ways of life and political ideologies within Bangladesh society and articulated with outside perspectives, each of which construct and define men and women at times similarly, at times differently. Gender roles and relations are not tangible and static, but are matters of controversy and debate. Women do not exist as some essentially gendered, ahistorical group, but, like men, their identity is worked out in society, and is constantly under negotiation and review.

Having traced some of the shadows cast by my own study in the first section of this chapter, I therefore widen the discussion to consider the limitations of talking about women, and what a broader analysis of gender might look like. What is important, is to distinguish the fact that people in society are always gendered – male or female – from any assumption about what the significance of their gender might be. Thus, at some times and places ability to do the job may be what counts, though a bus driver, plumber, or child minder, for example, will still be either male or female. At other times and places, entry to employment may be restricted by gender, regardless of a person's capacity to do the work. Similarly, roles that are explicitly gendered, such as 'new bride', or 'mother-in-law', may imply very different experiences and relationships, actually dividing women, rather than uniting them. It is not something out there, but the discourse itself, that constructs women as a group with common features and interests more significant than those which divide them.

In view of this, I advocate a strategy of tracing the constitution of gender difference through points of disjuncture and conflict within and between the ideologies, cultural rules, practical situations, customs and ideals, that compete to define and shape people's experience. This follows the notion of gender as contested image. In its indeterminacy, this clearly makes problematic the use of gender as a basis for social and political action. This reflects a central dilemma in feminism: if feminist analysis deconstructs the category of women, does it thereby undercut its own basis for mobilization? What is the women's movement without women? In the aid context of Bangladesh, an additional form of this question arises: what is the implication for women's programmes? As Mohanty (1984:339) states: 'Sisterhood cannot be assumed on the basis of gender: it must be forged in concrete, historical and political practice and analysis.' In facing this I draw on some recent feminist writings on the nature of gender identity. Through these I suggest some possible approaches as to how writings on women in Bangladesh may develop an alternative discourse, more imaginative and resourceful, and so closer in character to the subjects for which they claim to speak.

Tracing the shadows

At the simplest level, the shadows cast by my study, like others in the women and development family to which it belongs, are the gaps, the areas of people's lives that I failed to address, or glanced at only briefly. More fundamentally, the categories used, both those I adopted and those I introduced, need themselves to be subjected to critical reflection. Some of the major gaps are discussed first, and then the categories of analysis are questioned. Of course this exercise is itself provisional: only a few of the problem areas are pointed out, and the shadows that I identify have further shadows of their own.

Politics

For a study that claims to be looking at the politics of gender, the first and most glaring of the gaps is the absence of women's political activity. This comes first, I believe, from the separate spheres model, which excludes women from the public sphere, and second from the development discourse, which fights shy of politics whenever possible. Stressing the economic (read, public) significance of women's work in the household challenges the separate spheres model to some degree. It does nothing, however, to draw in the political dimension, and may even make it more obscure.

Take for example decision-making: the key political indicator found in women and development studies, drawn originally from political science. The typical analysis compares 'decision-making power' with 'economic activity', and thereby implicitly reduces the political to the economic. Compounding this, almost invariably the focus is on who takes the decisions within the family, not on how negotiations are managed over dowries, labour contracts, business arrangements, votes, or judgement in disputes. This, first, reconfirms the association of gender with the domestic sphere. Second, it launders out the essentially complex and political character of decision-making as neat tables are produced to show who decides on this or that. The inaccessibility of the evidence contributes to this: to give detail on how choices are made one would need to be privy to the practical politics of the kitchen and the bed. This domestication of decision-making again reinforces the identification of women's issues as non-political. If decision-making is to be retained in analysing the significance of gender, it is vital that it be extended to take in bargaining beyond the family, with its focus shifted on to the practicalities of how negotiations are made.

The most recent Bangladesh study of women's political participation at the village level is Suraiya Begum's (1989) *Poschim Banglar Rajnoitik Ongshogrohone Gramin Nari – Ekti Somikkha* (Village Women of West Bengal's Political Participation – An Observation). Speaking for the Muslim village she studied in West Bengal, Begum states that women are largely excluded from public life and takes as her main focus 'household politics', with a wealth of detailed case studies of micro-politics largely within particular families. These show the negotiation and enforcement of gender conventions and illustrate clearly how women do not passively accept the rules but work to enlarge their own room for manoeuvre.

I think it is useful to extend the definition of 'politics' and to problematize the construction of the public/private sphere divisions by counting in this household dimension. At the same time, it is important not to concede all of politics as more conventionally defined to male-oriented analysis. The danger is of an ironic twist to the rallying cry of feminism: the reduction of the political to the personal. The attack needs to be mounted on two fronts. First, there needs to be much more thoroughgoing analysis of women's involvement in factions, political struggles and the community life of the village and the nation. Some inspiring studies exist, such as Custer's (1987) enthusiastic analysis of women's leadership in the Tebhaga peasant uprising, in Bengal in

1946–47, which shows poor women becoming centrally involved in radical political action.

More typically, women are primarily active behind the scenes. Thus in Jori's paternity case (chapter 6), for instance, it was the women of her somaj who went to try and get her to reveal who was the father of her child. The whole village was buzzing with the scandal, and there seems no reason to dismiss women's talk as just gossip, while men's is seen as social or political manoeuvring. This is not, however, something that I looked into in detail, and my observations of it are incidental and haphazard. Where women are in fact excluded, this should not be accepted as natural. Rather, it needs to be shown how this happens, when in general women so excel at covert activity and the application of pressure through relationships, which is the very stuff of politics.

Looking at women's involvement in community affairs is only part of the story, however. Also, there needs to be fuller exploration of how notions of gender are themselves politically created and refined. Tanika Sarkar's work on the politicization of feminine imagery in the nineteenth century nationalist movement, is noted in chapter 2. Strathern (1987:6) points out how the stress on gender difference can mask other kinds of inequality, by promoting an image of male community, which obscures the social and economic divisions between men. Conversely, controversy over gender roles may be the means of expressing other divisions, or shifts in gender definitions may be the unintended outcomes of other conflicts. The way that stated issues become the vehicle for other struggles both within and between communities is related through the story of building the madrassa in chapter 3. Statements are commonly encoded at many different levels. Thus Bindi,[1] who has spent her life struggling to keep her own household afloat and support her daughter in her marriage, complains: 'If this were India I'd have no problem. I'd go to the hat myself, but here! Even widows can't go to the hat.' At one level, this clearly shows a sense of the malleability of gender rules, but at another, it is also an expression of Hindu resentment of Muslim dominance.

In Kumirpur, community hearings (bichars) were held by the men, women attended only to give evidence, or listened in under cover of the darkness or nearby houses. Purnima,[2] however, showing her characteristic audacity, successfully got her daughter reinstated in her husband's house after going herself to the neighbouring upazila where her daughter had been married, and approaching the Union Council chairman there to call a community hearing to settle their dispute. At both the hearings I attended in Kumirpur it was women who brought the cases and both argued on their own account, though in other areas of Bangladesh men may substitute for female witnesses. One of these hearings was Jori's paternity suit. The other was a case of attempted rape, brought by a poorer Hindu girl against a wealthier Hindu boy.

The hearing began in the early afternoon and lasted until evening. Most of that time was spent not in hearing the case itself, but in the arguing that followed. The Exchange Muslims dominated the occasion. The girl spoke first, defiantly but near to tears. She was bringing the cattle home in the evening. The boy had grabbed her arm and said that if she called out he would kill her. She managed to shake him off and ran home and told her father. The boy claimed he stopped her because he thought she was stealing mangoes from their tree.

Murmurings followed: the two accounts did not match up. The boy, who had been joking earlier, began to look worried. His father was quiet, his face rigid with distaste. His mother was listening from the house just behind where the hearing was held. Some men were asked to speak. Others made general comments. Most felt the boy was guilty. The Muslims told the Hindus they must make the final decision. Four or five of the prominent Hindus ruled that the boy should be beaten 20 times and made to pay the court fee. The girl's side protested – they had thought he would have to marry her, which would be a good match for them. Taking the opposite view, one of the Hajis' sons said it should be explained why the boy should be punished at all, since the girl had come to no harm. General shouting and argument broke out. Tozimember and another of the Hajis' sons, friends of the boy's father who had tried to prevent the bichar happening at all, came in late and took advantage of the disarray to break the meeting up. It was left uncertain whether or not the judgement would be followed. Afterwards, no one I spoke to had any doubt about the boy's guilt. Mostly, however, they expressed disgust at how the meeting had gone: 'You see! There is no justice for the poor! Nothing will happen.'

As in Jori's case, the boy's party was also richer and had stronger political links. Whereas few had sympathy for Jori, here the majority of the villagers took the girl's side. Social, economic and political advantage, however, outweighed local perceptions of justice. The significance of wealth and social status in these cases cannot be overemphasized. In all three further cases I heard the details of – another paternity case, a withdrawal from a marriage that had long been arranged; and a ghor jamai who had deserted his wife – the final outcome, though not necessarily the formal judgement, was in the favour of the wealthier party.

People of all classes in Kumirpur hold that the authority of the somaj is in decline. The implications of this are contradictory. On the one hand it seems to reflect some shift in the terms of economic exchange in the favour of labourers against landowners. This may lessen the degree to which richer members of the community can enforce cultural conformity, for example in the kinds of work that women do. On the other hand, it may remove a safety net of social pressure, and so make poorer people more vulnerable to blatant exploitation by richer; younger women more liable to abuse and divorce by their husbands; and older widows more open to abandonment by their sons. Community hearings by their nature debate the boundaries of social and cultural life. Looking at who speaks and on what subjects, along with changes in their style, frequency and power to compel compliance, can indicate important elements in the constitution of gender and other forms of social inequality.

Religious and cultural practice
Alongside its judicial dimension, the somaj also has religious and cultural aspects. Suraiya Begum notes in her discussion of women's participation in community life that while the somaj is envisaged primarily in male terms,

women do take specific parts in certain occasions, such as the ceremony for blessing the bride before a wedding. Female relatives and neighbourhood women are invited to come and eat sweets and *pan*,[3] and oil and dress each others' hair (Begum 1989:108). In Kumirpur these were very joyful occasions. In Hindu wedding ceremonies themselves, and in the other rites which lead up to them, women also take a prominent part. Furthermore, while there are (puja) ceremonies from which women are excluded, there are also many in which women take the major role. An example is Swarsati puja, to the goddess of wisdom and learning. This captures the dual aspect of women's gender construction. On the one hand it is a fast, women mortify their bodies in the hopes of securing educational success for their children. In this way they assert the intimacy of the bonds that tie them to their families, such that even their bodies become not the minimal expression of separate identity, but the embodiment of family links and shared interests. On the other hand, as women come together bringing baskets of fruit for the Brahmin's blessing, they also express their common situation and so in some sense their shared identity as (Hindu) women.

The ritual, religious and ceremonial life of the village is a further important aspect cast into shadow by my study. I present a fairly strictly secularized view of social interaction. This again reflects the development world-view in which religion and ritual tend to appear, if at all, as traditional attitudes or beliefs that hinder the adoption of 'modern' practices. The secularity of my presentation leads to loss on two counts. First, it undercuts my stated aim to explore how people themselves experience their lives. Second, it means that I missed out on some of the most fecund imagery through which people assign meanings and describe their society and the place of gender within it.

Aside from the development bias, there was a second reason that I shied away from a stronger emphasis on religion. This is the tradition within feminist studies which traces male domination to the ideological construction of femininity in key religious texts.[4] I was uncomfortable with the tendency of this to emphasize formalized culture rather than actual behaviour, and so incline towards monolithic presentations of religions as ideology. Once in the village, my difficulties were if anything intensified: at some times and on some issues the Hindu/Muslim divide did seem the key factor of difference, but at other points the various somaj were aligned in other ways. The division between Sajjur's and the Hajis' somaj, for example, was expressed in religious terms (some different use of words and conventions at the mosque) as well as social ones. Muslim consciousness also appeared in very different forms. It was the Local Muslims who asked, repeatedly, did I share the food of the Hindu family I lived with, or did I cook separately myself? The Exchange Muslims, on the other hand, seemed much more likely to see their religion in political terms and had in fact fought (and won) an early battle with the Hindus that they should share common water sources. I did not find that within my small sample, differences in gender relations in particular, could be neatly grouped along communal lines.

To say this is not to claim that religion is an insignificant factor, but rather that one cannot simply read off particular relations from a given religious affiliation. Of course, there are clear differences in religious practices. Thus many Muslim women keep the Muslim rule to pray five times a day, and Hindu women perform small daily ceremonies of blessing. Rituals of birth, marriage and death were different, though there are elements in common due to the different traditions rubbing against one another and integrating with a common folk culture (see Blanchet). Ways of cooking and eating also differ, and women observe particularly strictly rules about only eating with people of their own religious group. There are no clear differences by dress (only three families owned burqas and they were never worn in the village) and it was difficult to categorize patterns of mobility, work, or access to key resources by religion. Overall I would say that the village shared a common culture, with particular shadings by community group, and that age, wealth and status were at least as important in generating differences in ways of life and world view.

There are two main strategies of attack on the thesis that religious ideologies reinforce male dominance. First, some apologists maintain the religious founders have been misunderstood, and were actually far more positive about women than they are usually presented. This formally traditionalist position may provide a platform for a programme of contemporary reform. Brijbhushan (1980) for example, rereads Islamic texts and tradition to support women's property rights, the end of polygamy and gender disparities in divorce laws and rethinking on child custody, plus revival of payments for women at marriage. Second, and very creatively, contemporary feminists have made significant moves towards drawing out the principles of female power and activity hidden in the dominant religious traditions.[5] This reclaiming of religion and culture is clearly an important part of the feminist movement. It demonstrates the multiplicity of possible readings and so the falsity of claiming a single 'traditional' view, of whatever complexion.

The diversity found in textual analysis is all the more clear when people's empirical practices and beliefs are taken into account. There is not one Islam – however much Fundamentalists would like to claim it – nor even one Bangladeshi Islam which specifies always and everywhere the same practices and beliefs. These are matters of controversy even within the village: the mullah may speak, but whether or not he is listened to depends on other social and political factors. There is need for great sensitivity in conveying the power of rites and rituals, the way they symbolize hopes, ideals, spiritual union and the sense of the sacred, while relating these to a grounded analysis of social practice. There is great richness here which the literature all but ignores, or at best treats in a one-dimensional way.

Although, then, I like others stress the importance of marriage in the subordination of Bangladeshi women, I give no close account of wedding rites, the meaning they hold for different participants and how these change through the ceremony and subsequently. Yet the power of Hindu wedding rituals in particular is almost palpable. Questions of Hindu/Muslim difference are clearly relevant here, where Hindus see marriage as a sacrament and Muslims view it as a contract. Even this is not straightforward, however. There are clearly contractual elements in Hindu views of marriage with a complex of rights and duties in feeding and clothing, sexual access, and so on. Also, a sense of sacramental irrevocability was clear in the way some Muslim divorcees talked about their marriage and their feelings that they would not get married again. The implications of this for practical relationships need to be followed up.

Another neglected aspect is death. This is perhaps not surprising in a literature dominated by concerns for development. Blanchet makes some glancing references to rituals at death, but nowhere have I seen a detailed study of who participates and how and the views they express of identity and what it is to be human. In my own study, as characteristically in the literature, death appears only in sanitized form as 'child or maternal mortality'. It is no coincidence that it is beliefs and rituals surrounding pregnancy, childbirth and women's health that receive greatest attention, given the dominance of state and donor concerns with population control.

Within these studies there have, however, been some attempts to present local beliefs without privileging more secular, technical accounts. Mahmouda Islam, for example, in her (1986) study of women's health and culture in rural Bangladesh, stresses how illness (*beram*) is socially rather than pathologically defined, connected to women being no longer able to do their work, rather than to particular physical symptoms or discomfort. Village people tend to ask why, rather than how people become ill, and explanations are found in terms of spirits, ritual impurity or non-observance of rites, or sorcery. Such explanations were certainly common in Kumirpur. Thus when the milk from Asha's cow suddenly dried up, she claimed it had been bewitched by someone jealous of her position as my interpreter. The infatuation of a young woman in the Mondols' gusti for a married man was put down to sorcery, and she was healed from it by the application of an amulet, given to her by a (Hindu) folk healer. These methods of healing coexist with other treatments: it was Dhiren, the main allopathic/homeopathic practitioner in Kumirpur who arranged the meeting of the Mondols' bewitched girl and the healer who treated her.

M. Islam (1986:191) goes some way towards criticizing the dominance of technical values, as she states 'modern medicine' is: 'ill adapted to provide social meaning to the experience of illness'. She also stresses the importance of the wider relationship in healing, and how in seeking causes folk healers spend time on the mental state and social context of the one who is ill, while socially 'western' medical provision tends to be impersonal and alienating. The balance struck is, however, an uneasy one. Medically, Islam concedes the Western approach to be 'immensely superior' (p. 191). The underlying rationale of the study (sponsored by the Ford Foundation) is to explore how health care provision in the rural areas could be improved. If one is not very careful, therefore, 'local culture' becomes another factor to be accommodated within the development frame of reference. Instead of being seen as essentially constitutive of the social environment, culture then becomes objectified as an obstacle which more appropriate (socially and culturally adapted) techniques could overcome.[6] This reflects in large part the bias of the discourse itself:

however sympathetically presented, it is difficult to convey local beliefs in a convincing way, they almost always appear 'irrational' beside 'Western' explanations.

Patricia and Roger Jeffery and Andrew Lyon (1989) also make a sensitive exploration of local concepts in their study of childbearing in North India. This is strengthened by their open confrontation of political questions. They locate pregnant women's and new mothers' lack of access to good health care in their wider social situations of subordination and dependency. Alongside this, and very importantly, they present an aspect that M. Islam inexplicably ignores: access to formally 'free' treatment in government hospitals varies sharply by class and social connections. In practice it is often extremely expensive, as patients' families have to provide food, medicines and often payments to medical staff in order to secure their attention. In Kumirpur certainly the condition of government hospitals ('you're more likely to get ill there than recover from something') and their expense were frequent complaints, and very significantly hindered people from going there for treatment. The Jefferys' study is important in pointing out the connections between the private sphere practice of childbearing, cultural and religious beliefs, and the public sphere of politics and the state. It does not resolve, but does to some extent expose, the inherent tension between an argument that takes analysis beyond the social surface, and a fair presentation of local forms of thought.

Perhaps the key to this is in the breadth of the Jefferys' vision. They offer a practical analysis, grounding childbearing in women's work and family structures, the articulation of fertility and sexuality, the sense of the body and spiritual beliefs, observance of pollution and shame, and linking in the nature of the state. As they comprehend such different levels and aspects of the same social reality, there is space to present their analytical perspectives alongside, in ways that sharpen, but do not undermine, their presentation of villagers' practices and beliefs. They make the crucial point that magical explanations are not uncritically accepted, but are open to doubt and controversy even within village society (p. 192). This is implicit in M. Islam's account also, as she observes that people refer to medicine as *chesta* (attempts) (p. 124) and try a wide range of approaches in the hopes that one will work.

A different perspective is advanced by Thérèse Blanchet in her study *Meanings and Rituals of Birth in Rural Bangladesh*. She points out how in village beliefs and rituals strict Islamic and Brahmanical traditions do not appear in pure form, but fused with Bengali folk culture. Women's link with fertility brings them particularly close to this folk tradition, with its 'spirits of the land', such that: 'We may speak here of a women's sub-culture, for behind their "purdah", in their polluted state as females, wives or mothers, women do not experience the world the way men do' (p. 17).

Here, Blanchet clearly identifies women as polluted, simply by the fact of being creatures that menstruate (women past menopause may therefore be exceptions, though their activities tend to keep them polluted, p. 36). At other times she seems to recognize some variation in degree of pollution, as it sometimes seems limited to (or intensified in?) particular times of actual menstruation or childbirth. In general, however, her picture of the local view is of pollution as part of female 'nature' (p. 35). Separate spheres reappear in ideological/cultural/biological form. Her introduction of the notion of a female 'sub-culture' further supports this binary opposition, though she does qualify this to some degree in recognizing differences in the Muslim belief system by class (pp. 19–20). While the idea of sub-culture aims to correct the image of a society subordinate simply to a dominant male perspective, it implicitly confirms the notion of male/female as an essential opposition and the definition of female as difference from the norm. This leaves no space to identify the processes through which inequality is constructed in society, or the struggles underlying the differential shaping of male and female, masculine and feminine, at different times and different places.

In place of a single, universal culture giving a coherent view of the world, or yet a dominant (male) culture with a corrective (female) sub-culture, there is a range of associated concepts and practices that are differently read, experienced, interpreted and fought over. People's religious and ritual participation needs to be reclaimed from the shadows to explore the points of debate and disjuncture, the places of doubt and those of colonizing assertion, which reveal key categories and may become a nexus for change.

Sexuality

In some ways the area of sexuality may be the predominant shadow cast by my study. Again, the reasons for this are mixed. First, there are the practical difficulties of asking about it, in getting reliable information, and of appearing to have an 'unhealthy' interest in it. Second, these problems reappear in writing up. Third, this text reflects the unwritten rules concerning the women and development discourse: to present women as far as possible as desexualized, economic agents. This is a reaction, of course, to the biological determinism which for many years identified women exclusively with sexuality and fertility, and used this to define them by difference from the (male) norm of economic and political actors. In this branch of writings on gender, instead of bringing men into sexuality, the focus has shifted almost entirely to the social and economic. This means missing out a crucial dimension: sex represents a defining, negative motif in Bangladesh society, it stands for chaos, disorder and loss of control. The differential association of male and female with this, including variations over time and in relationship, are crucial aspects of gender definition.

Sexuality represents a nexus of contradiction for conceptualizations of gender. At first sight, it seems the area where gender is at its most natural and inevitable. In Bangladesh, the predominant preoccupation is with heterosexual sex. Here, the couple are defined by irreducible difference: male and female. At the same time, sexuality itself calls into question the whole construction of secondary qualities built upon that difference. Most radically, gay and lesbian sex threatens the identification of male–female binary opposition as the basis of social structure. But even in heterosexual sex, females may shed conventional feminine characteristics of passivity and submergence in the family, to take on masculine qualities of aggression and self-will. In the ultimate intimacy, boundaries are breached and divisions dissolve. This threat of chaos is symbolized, among other ways, in the custom common to Hindus and Muslims, men and women, to bathe after sex, and so signal their re-entry to the world of order and convention.

The disruptive potential of sexuality is very extensive. Women's sexual joking, for example, is widely noted as ridiculing male organs and activities and so deflates men's presumed superiority. In rural Bangladesh this joking is a particularly well-developed cultural genre.[7] Witholding sex is also a frequent strategy of domestic resistance among wives and lovers everywhere. Making a sexualized appeal is also a common means that people – most usually girls and women – use to further their interests. While often successful, this is typically regarded as illegitimate. This would seem to represent social brakes on the power of sexuality: it may be highly effective, but it is also very high risk, with high penalties for what is perceived as 'misuse'. Alternatively, sexualized phrasing of other demands between sexual partners can be used to obscure unreasonable or exploitative aspects. Most damagingly, of course, illicit sex that results in pregnancy can threaten the entire family's honour. In extreme cases, this may be a deliberate act of sabotage – before she was pregnant, Jori, for example, was heard on several times to threaten her father with bringing the family down, in revenge for his treatment of her. The politics of sexuality clearly raises radical questions about the nature of power.

Concepts of honour and shame play a central part in the formation of sexuality and gender identities, and are in turn constitutive of society and politics. Abu Lughod (1986) makes an outstanding study of these concepts and the discourses that frame them amongst a Bedouin tribal group in Egypt. She sets sentiments common in ordinary speech which express values of honour and modesty, against poetic depictions of the self as weak and vulnerable, moved by deep feelings of love and longing (p. 35). Both discourses are formal, they are side by side, and they comment on one another (p. 244). While poetry is the means of expressing dissident personal feelings, and so is only spoken before intimates, it also enhances the ordinary discourse:

> Poetry as a discourse of defiance of the system symbolises freedom – the ultimate value of the system and the essential entailment of the honor code (p. 252).

A great strength of this study is the way Abu Lughod interweaves personal sentiment with political dimensions of honour and deference or autonomy. In Bangladesh, village life is flanked by the threat and fear of theft, fraud, and violence. A common word for 'clever' (*chalak*), which is often used approvingly, carries associations at least of sharp practice, and sometimes straight dishonesty, rather like 'crafty' in English. In Kumirpur it is commonly accepted that doors must be locked and double locked, produce will be stolen from the field if not guarded day and night, the powerful will cheat the less able of land, and prominent public figures are corrupt. At the same time, public figures are listened to, to some degree respected and continue in their local dominance. In some ways it seemed that the strong ethic of sexual morality in Kumirpur was made to bear the full weight of community virtue, though even so, extramarital sex was quite common, and everyone knew it to be. Sexuality, then, needs to be viewed in relation to these other border areas between order and disorder, the radical contradictions between rules and practice, and the differential ways they construe male and female.

In sexuality, the politics of gender and its relative autonomy from actual men and women are very clear. The boundary quality of sexuality gives it a unique power, which is often harnessed to other ends. The use of sexual images in advertising is one example of this, as is the way that Islamic Fundamentalists insist on the veil, making the strict chastity of their women's bodies the image of the community's, or the nation's, integrity. This significance of boundaries again evokes the categories inside and outside. Just as these do not correspond simply to set locations, they also are not conclusively identified with respectively female and male. Rather, they are values and meanings to be manipulated, asserted or defended in the production and reproduction of social identity. Maintaining and servicing such boundaries is often a key constituent of female roles (see Dubisch, [ed.], 1986). It is here, perhaps, that the association of women with the family (insiders) comes in, and perhaps in the area of boundary maintenance that the notion of pollution is significant. This would seem to give women a centrality and community significance very different from the common picture of men as the family representative to the outside world.

Concern with sexuality is of practical as well as analytical importance. It is, for example, a significant reason that girls are married within a few years of puberty if possible. It is a real reason for the tight restriction of mobility for newly married women, who are perceived as particularly risky, having recently had their dormant passions aroused.[8] It is also a major obstacle for single women in becoming self-reliant: rumours about their loss of virtue are inevitable and vicious; any new wealth is commonly put down to earnings from prostitution. In rural Bangladesh, as elsewhere, a single woman is an anomaly and something of a threat.

Their sexuality also makes women more vulnerable to physical attack. In 1986 a plan to extend the Family Planning network with the appointment of two new women workers in the Union to the north of Kumirpur had to be dropped because the Union Chairman there said that he could not guarantee their safety. Sexuality is, then, an area with direct implications for development projects that seek to bring women out and increase their economic activity. But still more importantly, ideals of female sexuality are a battleground between Islamic Fundamentalists and Moderates, as well as a central locus of divisions within the feminist movement itself. Models of sexuality represent key signifiers of social, economic and political difference, elements of major debate about the nature of Bangladesh and its women, what they are and who they may become.

Market domination

As noted above, the shadows cast by my study are not only the areas I neglected, but also inhere in the concepts and images that I used. Central to this is the model of the market.

Paradoxically, it is in the strength of the market metaphor that its weakness lies. The advantage in extending the concept of the market to women's activities is the dominance of the model: to bring women into the market means to bring them into the mainstream. To some degree, by pointing out the social elements in women's market involvement and their parallels in relations between men, the pure economic image of the market was itself questioned, as it was drawn into the context of other social interaction. But this was, I think, marginal. More fundamentally, phrasing the argument in terms of the market means replicating the central preoccupations and ideological package of the whole development enterprise.

The present dominance of market thinking in economic theory and practice does not need to be emphasized here. The consequences of this for Bangladesh economic policy are easy to see: under President Ershad, in particular, there has been large-scale privatization and repeated attempts to foster a more dynamic, production-oriented economy. The absence of reliable internal revenue and consequent state dependence on outside funds, would in any case undermine any attempt towards a more integrated approach of planned development. Added to this international donors have increasing influence on the direction of national policies (McCarthy and Feldman, 1984), and bring to these their strong ideological commitment to the rhetoric of economic efficiency and a market approach.

My use of the market model was clearly congruent with the growing penetration of international capital through aid intervention. Identification of (aid-funded) irrigation technology as the key motor of change further confirmed this, unintentionally echoing common images of an unchanging, passive, (feminine) 'traditional' society catalysed into 'modernizing' change by dynamic, active, (masculine) development intervention. Similarly, my emphasis on women's work and property mirrored the priority placed by the state and aid agencies on increased productivity and capital formation. Women's savings and credit schemes, as pioneered by the Grameen Bank and copied in numerous government and non-government programmes, are heralded as one of the great contemporary Bangladesh success stories, and are being eagerly exported around the world.[9] In forming a critique of the passive conceptualizations of Bangladeshi women, my study was ideally fitted to the tastes of the aid lobby. It repackaged women in Bangladesh in a highly acceptable way: exit the shy, weak, culture-bound daughters and wives; enter the active, enterprising, budding entrepreneurs, ripe for new investment.

A major implication of this, already glanced at above, is that I emphasized women's economic activity to the exclusion of other aspects of their lives. In terms of both the preoccupations of the literature on women in Bangladesh, and wider feminist theorizing about the dual importance of production and reproduction, my neglect of fertility and childbearing was the most glaring. The

Jefferys' book on childbearing in Uttar Pradesh makes clear how this is not only to miss a major part of women's roles and responsibilities, but also to fail to give a rounded picture of work itself, since childbearing is a part of this. Thus although I stated that production and reproduction were of equal importance, I in fact heavily privileged production in my presentation.[10]

In consequence of this, I was able to shuffle people between categories, but left the categories themselves largely intact. Thus in reaction to the status-of-women framework, I aimed to show differentiation and contradictory interests between women. For this, I brought women into discussions of class, in which social inequality is the central focus. To some degree, I also identified women as distinguished through family roles, particularly in discussion of household structure and marriage practices. But the movement was only one-way. None of this questioned the basic identification of men with the public sphere of work and class or explored how men are also shaped by gender constructions, and subject to familial authority and hierarchies of age and position. Instead, the non-economic tended to recede still further, and the identification of work and class as a discrete arena and of primary importance was implicitly reinforced.

The market model contributes to this by assuming a divorce between social and economic spheres. This is clearly symmetric with the international aid framework, which assumes a standard economic intervention can be applied across diverse social contexts. The ideal of the market is purely economic interaction, from which social links are excluded. In practice of course, this is never the case. Evidence from women's relationships and concerns with social status lead me to question whether, in rural Bangladesh, most people would divide their activities into 'social' and 'economic'. A common objection to this framework is the orientation in peasant societies towards consumption rather than profit. Work and home are not divided as in industrial capitalism, since the household represents, at least for peasants with landholdings in the medium range, the unit of both production and consumption.

Hints questioning the social/economic divide also appear in common speech. One aspect of this is the common use of economic imagery in describing social qualities. Thus someone's untrustworthiness may be expressed as 'his words have no worth'[11] in which the word for 'worth' is the common term for 'price' or 'cost' in the market place. The use of kin terminology in employment relationships is another instance of cross-over between economic and social spheres. Or take the kind of statement commonly made by poor women who no longer observe purdah: 'when there is nothing in the stomach, what place is there for shame?' This is usually taken as evidence that under stress economic override social considerations, while social concerns reappear with growing wealth, and women withdraw from outside work. It may be so, but such expressions and the forms of thinking that they reveal, need to be approached with a much more open mind: they should not be assumed to translate unproblematically into the categories confidently used in the development discourse. The fact that one can present village life through these categories says nothing about their validity in terms of local thinking or practice. Similarly, unless one knows how they are generally conceived, my recasting of activities usually termed social as economic has little reality external to the discourse through which it is produced.

A further aspect of this divorce between the social and economic is the way the market model assumes a world of freely transacting individuals. Implicitly, this is a male model, though it is formally non-gendered. In practice, this is of course, very far from the reality for either men or women. It does, however, seem that constructions of male gender roles tend to be more individualized than those of females. As James Baldwin (1986:21) lyrically describes the situation for Black Americans: 'A man fights for his manhood: that's the bottom line . . . Mama must feed her children – that's another bottom line.'

At the close of chapter 7 I noted the difficulty of dividing women's interests from those of their families and how the family engenders different perceptions of interests at different times, with the moulding of persons through their relationship to each other. People do not know themselves in isolation from others, notions of belonging and difference are part of the sense of self. Thus Geeta Somjee (1989:x–xi) states that in India, women and men are 'integral parts of wider ascriptive social units'. The problems of women cannot be looked at in isolation from the family, though nor is the family the root of all their problems. There is a danger of distortion:

> by introducing a culturally extraneous notion of women as individuals in an unqualified fashion, with their individual problems irrespective of the multiple relationships which give meaning to their being (Somjee, p. 23).

Whitehead (1984b:189) similarly generalizes from her field-work in Ghana that women are typically much less able than men to act: 'in a socially unencumbered way'. This 'male' model of market individualism is therefore particularly poorly fitted to capturing the complexity of how women experience their lives and options.

According to myth, the market represents a neutral mechanism for the circulation of goods and services: inequality is the result of more or less skilful market engagement. Any non-economic differentiation is outside the scope of concern: it exists prior to entry in the market and is suspended when engaging in it. In practice, of course, this is very far from being so. The women and development lobby has shown conclusively that the market not only responds to gender inequalities that already exist, but itself contributes to the further definition of gender relations. Female workers are typically concentrated in sectors with low productivity, low pay, poor working conditions and little security.[12] In a study of factories in Brazil, for example, Humphrey (1985) relates how tasks are labelled 'skilled' or 'unskilled' according to the gender of the people who do them: women's work is unskilled by definition. In Bangladesh also, gender segregation of the markets is not neutral, but gives men privileged access to the major resources. The tendency of this to reinforce constructions of female dependence and domestic orientation is clear.

This assault on the market ideology, subjecting it to the same kind of analysis as other social institutions, is essential. As it stands, the line it draws between 'social' and 'economic' obscures the social processes by which subjects are engendered. Ultimately, this identifies gender with biology, and implicitly female biology, since the male is taken as the norm. The radical potential inherent in taking gender seriously as a category of analysis and a factor in the constitution of social inequality disappears. Development discourse may thus safely appropriate feminist perspectives by assuming a sub-compartment for women, and carry on much as it was before.

Towards a new consciousness

Within development studies a concern with women is still quite new. It is still establishing its legitimacy and is vulnerable to attack. The danger, clearly, is that any challenge may weaken its basis, and encourage a reversion to a 'men only' view of development. In this final section I therefore want briefly to present some thoughts on practice. This returns to the issues raised in the first and second chapters, looking at the elements within the women and development discourse which tend towards colonialism, and suggesting how a focus on gender can escape them and restore to the discourse the plasticity and creativity that should be its key characteristics.

Mohanty makes an incisive attack on the colonialism inherent in much Western feminist writing on the Third World, and particularly on the women and development area. She states:

> Colonialism almost invariably implies a relation of structural domination and a suppression – often violent – of the heterogeneity of the subject(s) in question (p. 333).

The main force of her critique is directed at the universalizing assumptions of the literature. These involve a number of key characteristics. First, the literature takes women as its category of analysis, attributes to it a homogeneity predicated on a basic sameness of oppression (p. 337), and confuses its own construction of the category with an actually existing and coherent group of women sharing similar interests. Second, Mohanty states that through this bounded, peripheral Other of women in the Third World, Western feminists are themselves seeking self-definition and so are the real subjects of these studies. Third, key concepts such as marriage or the sexual division of labour are applied arbitrarily, and their local meanings assumed rather than explored. And finally, the writers identify gender as the origin of difference, suggesting that women exist previous to entry into social relations of the family, workplace etc., the effects of which on them are then observed.

The first two points clearly go together. It is through identifying women in the Third World as a category that writers can present themselves variously as 'sisters' in oppression by gender; representatives of a relatively developed (civilized?) culture; and/or virtuous exponents of humanitarian concern. Das recognizes self-representation by the West as fundamental in Mayo's outcry against the 'barbarism' of Indian men. Said (p. 3) similarly emphasizes how through Orientalism: 'European culture gained in strength and identity by setting itself off against the Orient as a sort of surrogate and even underground self.' European superiority was predicated on and demonstrated through Oriental inferiority, indeed the notions 'Western' and 'Oriental' were given coherence in and through their opposition to one another (p. 5). The corollary of this is clearly that if the category of the people observed is deconstructed, this implies also deconstructing the observers.

The category 'Bangladeshi women' then, is, as Mohanty points out, a creation of the discourse. This does not, of course, imply that women in Bangladesh cease to exist when no one is talking about them. Rather, it means that a statement which presents women in Bangladesh as a group having shared characteristics or interests is necessarily emphasizing some aspects and suppressing others. This means it creates an image, rather than directly presenting what is. This is equally true of indigenous formulations – religious, medical, legal, political – and those of development observers. To some extent, of course, development practice has already discovered this. Women's co-operatives in South Asia have, apparently to development agencies' surprise, been found to have exactly the same problems as their male equivalents in terms of domination by their wealthier members. The programmes changed, to form class-based groups among women as among men. Accordingly, almost all (though not all) studies now differentiate women by economic background, and perhaps by other features: religion, education, marital status and so on.

The examples from Kumirpur demonstrate that poor women are certainly not all the same, they do not necessarily identify common interests, they do not all face the same problems, they certainly do not all prioritize working together. They have sufficient similarity to be classified in one category, and that is about it. The same could be said of any number of further sub-divisions – poor Muslim women; female heads of households; city factory workers and so on. It is the interests of the discourse that identify them as a group. An example from another area of the aid business makes clear just how arbitrary this can be. A few years ago I met a British academic who had been commissioned by one of the major multilateral agencies to do a study on 'land-locked countries'. Without any apparent irony he spent some time earnestly explaining to me the important features that Nepal, Bhutan, Afghanistan, Zambia, Chad, and Paraguay had in common. This case is admittedly extreme, since the differences between these countries seem on the face of it greater than their similarities. The important point, however, is that he didn't see it. His commitment to the project (and the large consultancy fee it would earn him) meant that he really believed that this heterogenous collection represented a group with significant common interests when, in fact, the key interest holding them together was his own.

For writers, researchers, development consultants and aid officials, there is money in Bangladeshi women. While this is a crude point, it none the less needs to be made. Thus one aspect in the shift from a single category women to the multiple sub-divisions indicated above, may be the proliferation of these professionals and agencies, each eager to identify a particular client group as its own. Within this, to be sure, is a sincere wish to devise more appropriate programmes and accurate studies. But it is still the representation of them for us, and little of it touches the basic analytical issues which we and they have in common.

Of course, things are not as simple as that. Bangladesh is not, after all, an inert body on which development practitioners have their evil way. If we have an interest in development, so also have they. Since Independence, Bangladesh has appeared in a package labelled poverty for sale on the international market. Not for nothing did a leading Bangladeshi political scientist jokingly remark: 'Poverty is our main export'. This self-presentation is evident from the national government to the village level. One personal example can perhaps illustrate this. In summer 1989 I briefly worked in Bangladesh with an aid organization. I was concerned that I would not get the necessary information in the little time available. When doing research in Kumirpur there were constant 'interruptions': people asking about my family, criticizing what I was wearing, asking what we ate, what it was like to fly in a plane. But this time there was no problem. The people I met knew what I would be interested in and talked about that. So I was told very quickly their needs, what they had lost, the problems they faced, and what (they hoped) I could do about it.

Part of this was no doubt due to the briefing they had received from the regular aid worker. Part, perhaps, to their desperate situation. But more fundamentally, I believe it was evidence of the extent to which consciousness of being 'the third poorest country in the world' has become central to Bangladesh's national identity. Of course, I was a crucial part of this. The way those people presented themselves reflected above all their perceptions of me and of the relationship (donor–recipient) between us. What they told me was only a part of who they knew themselves to be: they presented that side of themselves that (quite correctly) they judged served our mutual interest. As the Indian colleague who was working with me remarked: they had been receiving relief a lot longer than we had been giving it. Said (p. 325) epitomizes this situation in his closing comments: 'the modern Orient, in short, participates in its own Orientalizing.'

Replacing 'women' by 'gender' as the focus of analysis is the way out of this conundrum. This does not simply widen the focus from women to include men, or even the relations between them. Rather, it removes the Other against whom the writer identifies him/herself. Attention shifts to the processes through which persons are constituted, and so problematizes the writer's identity, categories and explanatory concepts, as well as those of his/her subjects. As Linda Alcoff states in a letter to the American feminist journal, *Signs*:

> the construction of gender should be thought of as a fluid, ongoing process. To think of one's gender as a stable property and an objectively determinable property is to be the victim of ideology. Gender should not be thought of as an object with clear boundaries and properties at all.[13]

It is no coincidence that gender is much less straightforward as a focus than women: it resists repackaging its subjects for a new consumer's consumption, and draws attention instead to the inherence of power in ideas and action. In the long run, of course, talking more sensitively about gender will not be sustained, unless it also has an impact on development and social and political practice.

Stress on the process of how gender relations are constituted raises Mohanty's third point on the importance of exploring local meanings of key concepts. As I have stated above, I would want to expand on this, to stress that local meanings themselves vary with context, and are essentially provisional, diverse and conflictual. This in turn leads into Mohanty's (p. 340) final point, that writings on women in the Third World tend to identify gender difference as the origin of oppression, as if: 'men and women are already constituted as sexual–political subjects *prior* to their entry into the arena of social relations' whereas in fact: 'women are *produced through these very relations* as well as being implicated in forming these relations.' It is in following up these points on the social construction of gender difference that I suggest some conclusions from the Kumirpur study.

The stress on differences is a useful one, but it needs to be widened from looking at the differences between women, to those between notions of gender. This means a more sensitive comparative approach, looking not to classify societies as more or less unequal, as in the status of women debate, but to discover how and why differentiation takes place.[14] An important part of this is to make cross-regional studies: what appear explanations in one context need to be cross-checked against comparable cases. More fundamentally, it means mapping the differences between gender norms, between norms and practice, between the situations that culture prescribes and those in which people actually find themselves, and within gender identities, to see what these indicate of key processes in their constitution, and possible moments for change.

One line of approach is to take a number of entry points and then trace the different stages, each with their own options and pressures, which lead to particular outcomes. Thus, laws concerning property and inheritance prescribe male privilege and female dependence. Like a beam of light hitting a prism, these are diffracted through complexes of social custom, community pressure, class dynamics and micro-politics at the family level. Through these particular men and women gain or fail to gain access to certain pieces of land. Like another prism, the use they make of this again diffracts or reconcentrates the light, as it confirms or shifts gender identities, and class relations. A similar story, and of course a related one, could be told of marriage practices. Beginning this time from the bottom up, one could look at the different options that face particular husbands or wives, mothers or sons, senior members in a joint family or lone divorcees. In each case these could be traced back to personal character, arrangements of their marriage, the birth and gender of children, deaths or desertions, wealth or poverty, community and family pressures, law and cultural ideals.

Following the lines suggested by Poovey, difference can also be traced through confrontations between particular discourses: competition to define religious orthodoxy; disjuncture between social practice and the law (for example over dowries); the great family planning debate; competing demands for strict purdah and education or employment; push by industrial or agricultural employers for a cheaper workforce; trend towards small businesses building up pressure on male monopoly in the hat and so on. The central point is to recognize that difference is constituted through society: both when change happens, and when things stay the same. At the personal level, at each point (the birth of a child, its education or not, its going out to work or not, its marriage or not and so on) people's actions suggest their ideas about gender and class and also significantly structure relations for the future. At the same time, those actions are not free, but are heavily influenced by family politics, social and community pressure, the law and ultimately the state. Whether at the community, national or personal level, each point in the forming of identity involves a political process. It does not happen smoothly, but typically involves conflict, and more so the more change is involved. The long-term significance of change is never assured: it can be neutralized by classification as anomalous or exceptional, or colonized by incorporation into existing roles and the relations they express.

This process of negotiating gender norms is not about the opposition of men versus women. Rather, it represents the manoeuvring of particular interests against others. While at one level debates are about gender, at another gender may simply represent the idiom for other power struggles. In Bangladesh, the competing gender imagery in development and Islamic nationalist discourses is a clear case in point. At the same time, however, the outcomes of these struggles are clearly significant in shaping the range of options available to men and (particularly) women in future.

It is in the politics of identity that I think the way forward lies in terms of practice, as well as critical thought. This is strongly emphasized by the Italian–American feminist, Teresa De Lauretis. She states: 'Consciousness is not the result but the term of a process' (1988:8). As one's sense of oneself is always in relation to a particular historical context, it is also constantly changing. This recasts the notion of the personal as political, in terms of an understanding of one's identity as formed through interaction, in multiple and even self-contradictory ways (De Lauretis, p. 9). The sense of difference, not difference of the Female from the Male Other, but between women and within women, is central to her thought (pp. 14–15). This is clearly consistent with the focus on the constitution of gender in society for which I have been arguing.

As De Lauretis (1988:8) says, part of one's identity is formed through political commitment and struggle. There must, therefore, be organization of women and mobilization around women's issues. But there must, through this, be more critical analysis of the ways that these issues themselves reflect identity shaped through interaction with social institutions and the discourse they sustain and so are ultimately provisional (Alcoff). The classic means of drawing attention to discrimination, through monitoring women's participation in different arenas and access to key assets, can, of course, point up problem areas, and programmes may be able to remedy some inequalities. But this should not be all that is done. Rather, this should be a part of a larger development of critical consciousness, which expresses and embraces women's contradictory experience, using their identity as a problem, as a question, as resistance and a politics of change. The point is not simply to identify gaps and bring women in to the institutions that already exist. But to recognize how these institutions themselves engender male and female subjects, to show how family roles, religious myths, the division of labour, political rhetoric and development policies create women in opposition to men and the interests of power this serves.

The dominance of the development discourse in relation to women in Bangladesh does not make an alternative approach easy to launch. Vital, I think, is a multi-pronged guerilla attack. Anything else risks incorporation within the terms of the discourse with which it engages. This means, yes, serious academic studies of cultural institutions and social interaction, not just of the structural aspects, but of the common usage of engendered concepts and practices in song, poetry, propaganda (including from development agencies), painting, film, humour, advertisements, kin celebration. It means also more popular approaches, the presentation of disputes of gender definitions in drama and novels, the exploration of alternative images in music, exhibitions and videos. Of course, some of these things are already going on, side-stepping the development discourse, or hijacking one aspect of it. The essence, I think, is to be experimental, trying things out, getting people to think again, to question what is taken for granted, including the new orthodoxies that emerge. Perhaps the motif for feminism should be that of the jester, always aside from the main seat of power, pointing her finger at anomalies and incongruities, suggesting other ways of looking, and leaping nimbly away from the backlash her irreverence provokes.

For the last word in this study dedicated to 'arguing with the crocodile', I turn to the poet and political activist, June Jordan (1989:144), as she reflects on her visit to the Bahamas as a Black American woman, and her encounter there with another black woman, Olive, her hotel maid.

The plane's ready for takeoff. I fasten my seatbelt and let the tumult inside my head run free. Yes: race and class and gender remain as real as the weather. But what they must mean about the contact between two individuals is less obvious and, like the weather, not predictable.

And when these factors of race and class and gender absolutely collapse is whenever you try to use them as automatic concepts of connection. They may serve well as indicators of commonly felt conflict, but as elements of connection they seem about as reliable as precipitation probability for the day after the night before the day.

It occurs to me that much organizational grief could be avoided if people understood that partnership in misery does not necessarily provide partnership for change: *when we get the monsters off our backs all of us may want to run in very different directions.*

And not only that: even though both "Olive" and "I" live inside a conflict neither one of us has created, and even though both of us therefore hurt inside that conflict, I may be one of the monsters she needs to eliminate from her universe and, in a sense, she may be one of the monsters in mine.

Notes

1. 5.3 HB l/v j/s
2. 4.2 HM u/v j.
3. A mixture of spices, lime, betel nut and sometimes raw tobacco.
4. See Caplan (1985) on Hinduism; or Mernissi (1985) on Islam.
5. See Liddle and Joshi (1986) on Hinduism; Smith and Haddad (1982) or El Sadaawi (1982) on Islam; and Radford Ruether (1983) on Christianity.
6. This clearly raises associations of Alam and Matin's (1984) accusation noted in chapter 1 of 'a basically manipulative stance'.
7. See Arens and Van Beurden (1977) or Hartmann and Boyce (1983).
8. Jeffery et al. (1989:24–5) point out that while sexual intercourse is thought to ease men's *garm* (heat) it is thought to increase women's.
9. The Grameen Bank programmes do involve social development alongside the credit initiative.
10. This, of course, sets me in an honourable tradition, going back to Engels himself!
11. *Tar kothar dam nei.*
12. See Mies (1986); Agarwal (ed.) (1987) or Rogers (1980).
13. Quoted in editorial, *Signs* vol. 13(3) Spring 1988, p. 399.
14. In the different context of feminism and psychoanalysis, this point is made by Mitchel (1974).

Appendix A:
Glossary of Non-English Words and Acronyms

amon (t. *amon*):	early dry season paddy (harvested November–December); (transplanted amon)
aus:	monsoon paddy (harvested September)
bandhobi:	female friend
bari:	home, homestead, household
bichar:	community hearing/judgement
bigha:	unit of land, usually equal to one-third of an acre
biri:	local cigarette
bondhu:	male friend
boro:	late dry season paddy (harvested May–June)
borolok:	rich person
burqa:	over-garment worn by some Muslim women in observance of purdah
chal:	husked rice
chula:	hearth
Dada:	elder brother
dai:	midwife
dan:	gift
dhan:	paddy, unhusked rice
dheki:	wooden paddy-husking device
dhoti:	traditional Hindu male dress
dol:	group, gang, party, faction
doon:	wooden irrigation device
dorga:	burial shrine
genji:	vest
ghor jamai:	lit. 'son-in-law of the house'; marriage in which the groom resides with the bride in her parents' household
ghotok:	matchmaker
gorib:	poor
gram:	village
gur:	molasses
gusti:	patrilineal kin group
hat:	weekly/bi-weekly market
irri:	HYV paddy (irrigable)

izzat:	honour
jamai:	son-in-law
jati:	kind, caste
joetuk:	dowry
jomidar:	senior land tenure-holder, zamindar
khai kalasi:	fixed term land mortgage in which the amount to be repaid decreases each year
khana:	eating group (household)
lobh:	greed, lust
lojja:	modesty, shame
lungi:	traditional Muslim male dress for every day
Ma:	mother
madrassa:	Muslim religious school
Mama:	maternal uncle
matbor:	community leader
maund:	unit of weight, usually 37.5 kg
mauza:	revenue village
mehr:	Islamic dower, payable to wife on divorce
moktob:	Muslim religious infant school
mondol:	community leader
murri:	puffed rice
mushti chal:	handful of rice', a form of savings
naior:	visit home made by married daughter
para:	neighbourhood
pir:	Muslim holy man
pon:	marriage payment (bride price)
porer bari:	'other's house' – typically that of an employer or father-in-law
puja:	Hindu act of worship
salwar-kameez	loose trouser suit worn by girls
seer:	slightly less than 1 kg
shalish:	community hearing/judgement
somaj:	community
sudh-kot:	land mortgage in which full principal must be repaid
taka:	unit of currency. During the period of field work Tk40 = £1 sterling
tebhaga:	share-cropping contract where cultivator bears all costs and takes two thirds of harvest
union:	sub-division of upazila
upazila:	sub-district

Acronyms

BADC:	Bangladesh Agricultural Development Corporation
DTW:	Deep Tube-well
HTW:	Hand Tube-well
NGO:	Non-Governmental Organization
STW:	Shallow Tube-well

Appendix B:
Case Study Households

KEY

1) Numbers: First number indicates cluster to which households belong; second number, the households' centrality within the cluster (1 = most central).

2) Community: HM = Hindu Mahisyo; HB = Hindu Boisnob; HO = Hindu Other (Robidas/Bhoimali castes); ME = Muslim Exchange; ML = Muslim Local; Sa = Santal.

3) Class: u/s = upper/strong; u/v = upper/vulnerable; l/s = lower/strong; l/v = lower/vulnerable.

4) Household structure: j = joint; e = extended; s = separate; si = single.

5) Household members: (in relation to the named persons). d = daughter; s = son (or respectively niece/nephew in joint households); gs/d = grandson/daughter;
m. = married (in brackets if no longer household member).

6) Land: bg = bigha; o/o = owned/operated; s/i = shared in; s/o = shared out.

7) Occupations are agriculture or domestic work unless otherwise stated.

Number	Name		Resources
		Material:	11 bg o/o; no plough; few animals; HTW
1.1	Dhiren & Sukhi	Human:	2s, 1d school. Doctor
	HM u/v s	Social:	Close cluster – wife is daughter of former somaj head. As doctor, extensive cross-community links, local area
		Material:	1 bg s/o; 7 bg s/i; plough; 5 sheep
1.2	Narayan & Joia	Human:	1s school; 1d; (2 m.d)
	HM l/s s	Social:	Wife close cluster (with 1.1 & mother in village)
		Material:	3.5 bg o/o; no animals
1.3	Ziten & Chaya	Human:	2s small. STW/Bicycle mechanic
	HM l/s s	Social:	Fairly close cluster (particularly kin). Extensive through business

		Material:	2 bg s/i; no animals
1.4	Bisor & Gouri	Human:	3 adults s + 1 d-in-law; 2 gd; house
	HM l/v j		builder s; (1 m.d, died)
		Social:	Close cluster links
		Material:	55 bg o/o; 51 bg s/o; many animals; STW; HTW; motorcycle
2.1	Sajjur & Rashida	Human:	His parents, + brother and wife; 5s, 3d
	ME u/s j		school; (l m.d)
		Social:	Effective somaj head. Close cross-community cluster links
		Material:	62 bg o/o; 2.5 s/o; many animals; STW
2.2	Mannan	Human:	2 m.s + wives; 2 s school; 1 gs. (1 m.d).
	ME u/v j		Medicine shop. Registry Office clerk.
		Social:	Close cluster links – Sajjur is his brother-in-law
		Material:	22 bg o/o; 4 s/i; some animals
2.3	Hakim	Human:	1 m.s + wife; 1s; 3d school. (5 m.d.)
	ME u/v j	Social:	Close cluster links – Sajjur is his brother-in-law
		Material:	10 bg s/i; plough
2.4	Asha	Human:	Her parents – he old and lame; (l m. brother; 3 m. sisters)
	ME l/v s	Social:	Close cluster links
		Material:	0.5 bg (mortgage); no animals
2.5	Kitish & Parboti	Human:	2 s school; 1 baby d. Tailor. Rice
	HB l/s s		business
		Social:	Close cluster links
		Material:	No land; 6 goats
2.6	Budol & Susila	Human:	1s, 2d. Snack. Paddy. Rice business
	HB l/s s	Social:	Relatively independent
		Material:	No land; 6 goats
2.7	Gita	Human:	1s; 2d; (2 m.d). Rice business
	HB l/s si	Social:	Close cluster and kin links
		Material:	60 bg o/o; 45 s/o; DTW; STW; HTW; many animals; rice mill; motorcycle
3.1	Akhbar & Nilufa	Human:	His parents; gmother; 1 m. brother + 2
	ML u/s j		wives; 1 brother; 5 d school; (2 m. sisters). DTW 'manager'. Rice mill owner

		Social:	Close cluster links and increasingly active in local affairs

| 3.2a | Rohim
ML l/s e | Material:
Human:
Social: | 8 bg s/i; plough; 5 sheep; 10 fowl
Wife; sister; ld
Close cluster links |

| 3.2b | Karim
ML l/s s | Material:

Social: | 4 bg s/i; plough
Human: Wife; ls
Close cluster links (with numbers 3 & 2) |

| 3.3. | Soherab & Minu
ML l/s s | Material:
Human:

Social: | 3 bg o/o; 5 sheep
ls, 3d school. STW boring business.
Mina grows vegetables
Relatively independent |

| 3.4 | Abdul Khotib
ML l/s j | Material:
Human:

Social: | 5 bg o/o; 1 bg s/i; plough; fowl
Wife; 1 m. s + wife; 3 d school; 1 gd;
(3 m. s; 2 m. d). Spice business. Mosque official
Strong community links |

| 4.1 | Aynuddin
Mondol
ME u/s j | Material:

Human:

Social: | 42 bg o/o; 51 bg s/o; many animals; STW; HTW; rice mill; motorcycle
Wife; 2 m.s + wives; 2s school; 1 gs 1 gd; (3 m. s; 2 m. d). Machine oil. Spare parts. Salt businesses. Rice mill
Major local figure; strong cross-community and urban links |

| 4.2 | Purnima
HM u/v j | Material:

Human:

Social: | 10 bg o/o; 1 bg s/i; plough; some animals
Husband; 1 m.s + wife; 1s, 2d school; (3 m. d – 1 dead). Salt and curd business. Purnima very active
Wide cross-community links |

| 4.3 | Mira
HM l/s si | Material:
Human:
Social: | 6 bg s/o; 6 goats
Mother-in-law; 1s school
Close cross-community and kin links |

| 4.4 | Khalek & Kaniz
ME l/v s | Material:
Human:
Social: | 2 bg s/i; few animals s/i
3 s; 2d; (1 m.d)
Close economic but looser social links |

		Material:	121 bg o/o; 14 bg s/o; STW; HTW; many animals
5.1	Kangali Serkar HM u/s j	Human:	5 m. s + wives; 5 gs; 6 gd school; (1 m. d). Son teacher
		Social:	Somaj head. Teacher son active in local affairs
		Material:	2.5 bg o/o; 4.5 bg s/i; plough; some ducks; 3 s/i goats
5.2	Gonesh & Sorosi HM l/s s	Human:	1s; 2 d school. Murri business
		Social:	Relatively weak links
		Material:	3 bg mortgaged out; 2 bg s/i; calf; ducks
5.3	Onil & Bindi HB l/v s/j	Human:	2 s working; 1 s school. Onil ill; D and her family come and go; 2 gs; (1 other m.d). Murri business
		Social:	Fairly loose cluster links
		Material:	21 bg o/o; 18 bg s/i; 8 cattle; sheep; ducks; geese; HTW
5.4	Suresh & Maloti HM u/v s	Human:	2s; 4d school; (2 m.d). Paddy business. Teacher lodger
		Social:	Wide cross-community links and urban connections through business
		Material:	2 bg o/o; plough; few sheep/goats
5.5	Oni HM l/v si	Human:	1 adult s; 1 small s and d
		Social:	Oni close links with 5.4
		Material:	40 bg o/o; many animals; STW; HTW
6.1	Hasan Mullah ME u/v j	Human:	Wife; 2 m. s + wives; 2 s; 3 d school; 2 gs, 1 gd; (3 m. d) Social: Fairly independent. Strict Islam
		Material:	1 bg o/o; 2 bg s/i; plough; few other animals
6.2	Samad & Jori ME l/v s	Human:	Parents: 2 brothers 2 sisters – all but youngest do paid work – (2 m. brothers, 2 m. sisters)
		Social:	Samad close economic links but overall weak social integration
		Material:	0.5 bg o/o – half mortgaged; 0.5 bg s/i; few animals
6.3	Robi & Nondo HO l/v s	Human:	2s; 2d; (1 m. d). Shoe repair. Wine. Leather. Midwifery businesses
		Social:	Wide links but caste distance

		Material:	1.5 bg s/i; plough; 20 chickens
6.4	Bolai	Human:	Mother; wife; 3 brothers; sister; 1 s (all
	Sa l/v e		but s work as labourers)
		Social:	Economic links cross-community but social with other Santal groups
		Material:	1 pig s/i
6.5	Mahi	Human:	1 adult s; 1 niece
	Sa l/v si	Social:	Forced away after argument with others in household cluster

Bibliography

Abdullah, T. (1974) *Village Women as I Saw Them*. Dhaka: Ford Foundation.

Abdullah, T. and Zeidenstein, S. (1982) *Village Women of Bangladesh: Prospects for Change*. Oxford: Pergamon Press, vol. 4, Women in Development Series.

Abu-Lughod, L. (1986) *Veiled Sentiments: Honor and Poetry in a Bedouin Society*, Berkeley: University of California Press.

Acharya, M. and Bennett L. (1983) *Women and the Subsistence Sector: Economic Participation and Household Decision Making in Nepal*. World Bank Staff Working Paper No. 526.

Adnan, S. (1984) *Peasant Production and Capitalist Development: A Model with Reference to Bangladesh*. Cambridge: unpublished PhD thesis for the University of Cambridge.

—— (1989) 'Birds in a Cage: Institutional Change and Women's Position in Bangladesh'. Revised version of paper for International Union for the Scientific Study of Population, Oslo 1988.

Afshar, H. (ed.) (1985) *Women, Work and Ideology in the Third World*. London: Tavistock Publications.

Agarwal, B. (ed.) (1988) *Structures of Patriarchy. The State, the Community and the Household in Modernizing Asia*. London: Zed Books.

Ahmad, P. (1980) *Income Earning as Related to the Changing Status of Village Women in Bangladesh: A Case Study*. Dhaka: Women for Women Research and Study Group.

Ahmad, Q. K., Khan, M. A., Khan, S., Rahman, J. A. (eds.) (1985) *Situation of Women in Bangladesh*. Dhaka: Ministry of Social Welfare and Women's Affairs, Government of the People's Republic of Bangladesh.

Ahmed, N. (1968) *Peasant, Family and Social Status in East Pakistan*. Edinburgh: unpublished PhD thesis for the University of Edinburgh.

Ahmed, R. (1985) 'Women's Movement in Bangladesh and the Left's Understanding of the Woman Question'. Dhaka, *Journal of Social Studies* 30: 41–50.

Ahmed, R. and Naher, M. S. (1986) 'Changing Marriage Transactions and the Rise of the Demand System in Bangladesh'. Dhaka, *Journal of Social Studies* 33: 71–107.

—— (1987) *Brides and the Demand System in Bangladesh*. Dhaka: Centre for Social Studies, Dhaka University.

Akanda, L. and Shamim, I. (1984) *Women and Violence: A Comparative Study of Rural and Urban Violence on Women in Bangladesh*. Women's Issue 1. Dhaka: Women for Women.

Alam, S. (1985) 'Women and Poverty in Bangladesh'. *Women's Studies International Forum* 8 (4): 361–71.

Alam, S. and Matin, N. (1984) 'Limiting the Women's Issue in Bangladesh. The Western and Bangladesh legacy'. *South Asia Bulletin* IV (2): 1–10.

Alamgir, M. (1978) *Bangladesh: A Case of Below Poverty Level Equilibrium Trap*. Dhaka: Bangladesh Institute of Development Studies.

Alcoff, L. (1988) 'Cultural Feminism verus Post-Structuralism: The Identity Crisis in Feminist Theory' *Signs* 13 (3) Spring: 405–36.

Apthorpe, R. (1986) 'Development Policy Discourse' *Public Administration and Development* 6:377–89.

––––– 'Agriculture and Strategies: The Language of Development Policy' pp. 127–41, in Clay, E. and Schaffer, B. (eds.) *Room for Manoeuvre. An Exploration of Public Policy in Agriculture and Rural Development*. London: Heinemann Educational Books.

Arefeen, H. (1986) *Changing Agrarian Structure in Bangladesh: Shimulia, a Study of a Periurban Village*. Dhaka: Centre for Social studies, Dhaka University.

Arens, J. and Van Beurden, J. (1977) *Jhagrapur; Poor Peasants and Women in a Village in Bangladesh*. Birmingham: Third World Publications.

Arthur, W. and McNicholl, G. (1978) 'An Analytical Survey of Population and Development in Bangladesh'. *Population and Development Review* 4(1): 23–80.

Aziz, K. M. A. (1979) *Kinship in Bangladesh*. Dhaka: International Centre for Diarrhoeal Disease Research, Bangladesh. Monograph Series no. 1.

Baldwin, J. (1986) *Evidence of Things Not Seen*. London: Michael Joseph.

Banaji, J. (1972) 'For a Theory of Colonial Modes of Production'. *Economic and Political Weekly* VII (52): 2498–2502.

Banerjee, N. (1985) *Women Workers in the Unorganised Sector. The Calcutta Experience*. Hyderabad: Sangam Books (India).

BRAC (1980) *The Net: Power Structure in Ten Villages*. Dhaka: Bangladesh Rural Advancement Committee.

––––– (1983) *Who Gets What and Why. Resource Allocation in a Bangladesh Village*. Rural Study Series vol. 1. Dhaka: BRAC.

Bardhan, K. (1986) 'Women's Work, Welfare and Status. Forces of Tradition and Change in India.' *South Asia Bulletin* VI (1): 3–16.

Begum, Saleha and Greeley, M. (1979) 'Rural Women and the Rural Labour Market in Bangladesh: An Empirical Analysis'. *Bangladesh Journal of Agricultural Economics* 2(2): 35–55.

––––– (1988) *The Mechanization of Farm-Level Rice Processing and Displacement of Female Wage Labour in Bangladesh: The Need for and Nature of Effective Policy Response*. Final report for the Population Council, Contract No. C186.24F.

Begum, Suraiya (1989) *Poschim Banglar Rajnoitik Ongshogrohone Gramin Nari –Ekti Somikkha* (West Bengal Women's Political Participation – An Observation). Dhaka: Centre for Social Studies.

Beneria, L. (1979) 'Reproduction, Production and the Sexual Division of Labour.' *Cambridge Journal of Economics* 3.

––––– (ed.) (1982) *Women and Development. The Sexual Division of Labour in Rural Societies*. New York: Praeger.

Bertocci, P. (1970) *Elusive Villages: Social Structure and Community Organization in Rural East Pakistan*. Michigan: unpublished PhD thesis for Michigan State University.

––––– (1972) 'Community Structure and Social Rank in Two Villages in Bangladesh'. *Contributions to Indian Sociology* (n.s.) 6.

Bhuiyan, R. (1985) 'Legal Status of Women in Bangladesh', in Ahmad, Q. K. et al. (eds.) (1985).

Blanchet, T. (1984) *Meanings and Rituals in Birth in Rural Bangladesh*. Dhaka: University Press Ltd.

Blumberg, Rae Lesser and Hinderstein, Cara (1983) 'At the End of the Line: Women and US Foreign Aid in Asia, 1978–80', in K.A. Staudt and J. S. Jacquette (eds.)   (1983). *Women in Developing Countries: A Policy Focus*. New York: Haworth Press.

Boserup, E. (1970) *Women's Role in Economic Development*. London: Allen and Unwin.

Boyce, J. and Hartman B. (1983) *A Quiet Violence. View from a Bangladesh Village*. London: Zed Books.

Brijbhushan, J. (1980) *Muslim Women in Purdah and Out of It*. Dhaka: University Press Ltd, in association with Vikas Publishing House.

Briscoe, J. (1979) 'Energy Use and Social Structure in a Bangladesh Village'. *Population and Development Review* 5(4).

Butler, Flora, C. (1983) 'Incorporating Women into International Development Programmes: The Political Phenomenology of a Private Foundation'. Pp. 89–106 in   K. A. Staudt and J. S. Jacquette (eds.) (1983). *Women in Developing Countries: A   Policy Focus*. New York, Haworth Press.

Buvinic, M. (1986) 'Projects for Women in the Third World. Explaining their Misbehaviour'. *World Development* 14(5).

—— (1989) 'Investing in Poor Women: The Psychology of Donor Support'. *World Development* 17 (7).

Cain, M., Khanam, S., Nahar, S. (1979) 'Class, Patriarchy and the Structure of Women's Work in Bangladesh'. *Population and Development Review* 5(3).

Caplan, P. (1985) *Class and Gender in India. Women and their Organizations in a South Indian City*. London: Tavistock Publications.

—— (1988) 'Engendering Knowledge: The Politics of Ethnography'. *Anthropology Today* 4 (5); 4 (6).

Caplan, P. and Bujra, J. (eds.) (1978) *Women United, Women Divided. Cross-cultural Perspectives on Female Solidarity*. London: Tavistock Publications.

Center for Women and Development (1985) *Women and Politics in Bangladesh*. Dhaka: CWD.

Chaudhury, R., Ahmed, N. (1980) *Female Status in Bangladesh*. Dhaka: Bangladesh Institute of Development Studies.

Chen, L., Gesche, M., Ahmed, S., Chowdury, A., Mosley, W. (1974) *Maternal Mortality in Rural Bangladesh*. Dhaka: Ford Foundation.

Chen, L., Huq, E., D'Souza, S. (1981) 'Sex Bias in the Family Allocation of Food and Health Care in Rural Bangladesh'. *Population and Development Review* 7(1) March.

Chen, M. (1985) *A Quiet Revolution*. Cambridge, Ma: Schenkman Publishing House.

Custers, P. (1987) *Women in the Tebhaga Uprising: Rural Poor Women and Revolutionary Leadership (1946–47)*. Calcutta: Naya Prokash.

Das, F. Hauswirth (1932) *Purdah: The Status of Indian Women*. London: Kegan Paul, Trench, Trubner.

Day, L. B. (1909) *Bengal Peasant Life*. London: Macmillan.

De Lauretis, T. (1988) 'Feminist Studies/Critical Studies: Issues, Terms and Contexts', pp. 1–19 in De Lauretis (ed.).

—— (1988) (ed.) *Feminist Studies/Critical Studies*. Basingstoke: Macmillan.

De Vylder, S. (1982) *Agriculture in Chains – Bangladesh*. London: Zed Press.

Di Leonardo, M. (1987) 'The Female World of Cards and Holidays: Women, Families, and the Work of Kinship'. *Signs* 12 (3).

Dubisch, J. (ed.) (1986) *Gender and Power in Rural Greece*. Princeton: Princeton University Press.

Edholm, F., Harris, O., Young, K. (1977) 'Conceptualising Women.' *Critique of Anthropology* 9/10.

El Sadaawi, N. (1980) *The Hidden Face of Eve*. London: Zed Press.

―― (1982) *Women's Studies International Forum* 5 (2).

Elson, D. and Pearson, R. (1984) 'The Subordination of Women and the Internationalisation of Factory Production', in Young et al. (eds.) (1984).

Engels, F. (1972) *The Origin of the Family, Private Property, and the State*. London: Lawrence and Wishart.

Faaland, J. (ed.) (1981) *Aid and Influence. The Case of Bangladesh*. London: Macmillan.

Faaland, J. and Parkinson, J. R. (1976) *Bangladesh: The Test Case for Development*. London: C. Hurst.

Farouk, A. (1980) *Time Use of Rural Women (A Six Village Study in Bangladesh)*. Dhaka: Bureau of Economic Research, University of Dhaka.

Farouk, A. and Ali, A. (1975) *The Hardworking Poor*. Dhaka: Dhaka University Bureau of Economic Research.

Feldman, S. (1980) 'Rural Infrastructural Development in Bangladesh and its Potential Consequences for Reproductive Behaviour'. Dhaka, *Journal of Social Studies* (7).

Focault, M. (1981) *The History of Sexuality. Volume 1. An Introduction*. Harmondsworth: Penguin Books.

Geertz, C. (1988) *Works and Lives. The Anthropologist as Author*. Oxford: Polity Press.

Giddens, A. (1977) *Studies in Social and Political Theory*. London: Hutchinson.

Glaser, M. (1989) *Waters to the Swamp: Irrigation and Patterns of Accumulation and Agrarian Change in Bangladesh*. Bath: unpublished PhD thesis, University of Bath.

Greeley, M. (1983) 'Patriarchy and Poverty: A Bangladesh Case Study'. *South Asia Research* 3 (1).

―― (1985) *Rice in Bangladesh: Postharvest Losses, Technology and Employment*. Sussex: unpublished PhD for Sussex University.

Guhathakurta, M. (1985) 'Gender Violence in Bangladesh: the Role of the State'. Dhaka, *Journal of Social Studies* 30.

―― (1986) 'Bangladesher Unnoyone Boidesik Sahajjo O Nari Somaj' (Women and Foreign Aid in Bangladesh Development). *Somaj Nirikkon* (Social Studies) 22.

Hara, T. (1967) *Paribar and Kinship in a Muslim Rural Village in East Pakistan*. Canberra: unpublished PhD thesis for the Australian National University.

Harris, O. (1984) 'Households as Natural Units'. Pp. 136–55 in Young et al. (eds.) (1984).

Harris, O. and Young, K. (1981) 'Engendered Structures. Some Problems in the Analysis of Reproduction.' Pp. 109–47 in Llobera, J. and Kahn, J. (eds.) *Anthropological Analysis and Pre-capitalist Societies*. London: Macmillan.

Himmelweit, S. and Mohun, S. 'Domestic Labour and Capital' *Cambridge Journal of Economics* (1):

Hirschon, R. (ed.) (1984) *Women and Property – Women as Property*. London: Croom Helm.

Hossain, M. (1979) 'Nature of State Power in Bangladesh'. Dhaka: *Journal of Social Studies* 5.

Humphrey, J. (1985) 'Gender, Pay and Skill: Manual Workers in Brazilian Industry', in Afshar (ed.) (1985).

Huq, M. A. (1978) *Exploitation and the Rural Poor – A Working Paper on the Rural Power Structure in Bangladesh*. Comilla: Bangladesh Academy for Rural Development.

Inden, R. B and Nicholas, R. W. (1977) *Kinship in Bengali Culture*. Chicago: Chicago University Press.

IDS (1979) *Special Bulletin of Continuing Subordination of Women in the Development Process. IDS Bulletin* 10 (3) (University of Sussex Institute of Development Studies).

—— (1984) *Special Bulletin: Research on Rural Women. IDS Bulletin* 15(1).

Islam, A. K. M. A. (1974) *A Bangladesh Village: Conflict and Cohesion*. Cambridge, MA: Schenkman Publishing Co.

Islam, M. (1979) 'Women's Organizations and Programmes for Women' in Women for Women (ed.) (1979).

—— (1984) *Bibliography on Bangladesh Women with Annotation* (second edition). Dhaka: Women for Women.

—— (1985) *Women, Health and Culture*. Dhaka: Women for Women.

Islam, S. (ed.) (1982) *Exploring the Other Half: Field Research with Rural Women in Bangladesh*. Dhaka: Women for Women.

—— (1985) *Invisible Labour Force. Women in Poverty in Bangladesh*. Dhaka: The Asia Foundation.

Jack, J. C. (1916) *The Economic Life of a Bengal District*. Oxford: Clarendon Press, Oxford University Press.

Jahan, R. (1981) *Inside Seclusion: The Avarodhbasini of Rokeya Sakhawat Hossain*. Dhaka: Women for Women.

—— (1982) 'Purdah and Participation: Women in the Politics of Bangladesh'. pp. 262–83 in Papanek and Minault (eds.) (1982).

—— (1989) *Women and Development in Bangladesh: Challenges and Opportunities*. Dhaka: The Ford Foundation.

Jahan, R. and Papanek, H. (ed.) (1979) *Women and Development: Perspectives from South and South-east Asia*. Dhaka: Bangladesh Institute of Law and International Affairs.

Jahangir, B. K. (1979) *Differentiation, Polarisation and Confrontation in Rural Bangladesh*. Dhaka: Centre for Social Studies, Dhaka University.

—— (1982) *Rural Society, Power Structure and Class Practice*. Dhaka, Centre for Social Studies, Dhaka University.

—— (1986) *Problematics of Nationalism in Bangladesh*. Dhaka: Centre for Social Studies.

—— (1989) 'Political Economy of Development: Bangladesh Case'. *Journal of Social Studies* 45.

Jahangir, B., Jansen, E., Maal, B., Rahman, N. (1983) 'Dilemmas Involved in Defining and Delimiting Household Units in Rural Surveys in Bangladesh.' Dhaka, Journal of Social Studies 21.

Jannuzi, F. T. and Peach, J. T. (1980) *The Agrarian Structure of Bangladesh: An Impediment to Development*. Boulder, Colorado: Westview Press.

Jansen, E. G. (1986) *Rural Bangladesh: Competition for Scarce Resources*. London: Norwegian University Press/Oxford University Press.

Jansen, E., Dolman, A., Jerve, A. M. and Rahman, N. (1989) *The Country Boats of Bangladesh*. Dhaka: University Press Ltd.

Jeffery, P. (1979) *Frogs in a Well. Indian Women in Purdah*. London: Zed Press.

Jeffery, P., Jeffery, R., Lyon, A. (1989) *Labour Pains and Labour Power: Women and Childbearing in India*. London: Zed Books.

Jordan, J. (1989) *Moving Towards Home. Political Essays*. London: Virago.

Jorgensen, V. (1983) *Poor Women and Health in Bangladesh. Pregnancy and Health*. Lars Generyd, Informako: SIDA, Swedish International Development Agency.

Kabeer, N. (1985) 'Do Women Gain from High Fertility?' in Afshar (ed.) (1985).

—— (1989) 'The Quest for National Identity: Women, Islam and the State in Bangladesh'. *IDS Discussion paper* 268 October.

Karim, A. K. N. (1956) *Changing Society in India and Pakistan*. Dhaka: Oxford University Press.

Karve, I. (1953) *Kinship Organization in India*. Bombay: Asia Publishing House.

Khan, A. R. (1972) *The Economy of Bangladesh*. London: Macmillan.

—— (1977) 'Poverty and Inequality in Rural Bangladesh', in ILO *Poverty and Landlessness in Rural Asia*. Geneva: International Labour Office.

Khan, Z. R. (1985) 'Women's Economic Role: Insights from a Village in Bangladesh'. Dhaka, *Journal of Social Studies* 30.

Khuda, B-e-, (1982) *The Use of Time and Underemployment in Rural Bangladesh*. Dhaka: City Press.

Kishwar, M. (1986) 'Dowry: To Ensure her Happiness, Or to Disinherit Her?' *Manushi* 34.

—— (1988) 'Nature of Women's Mobilization in Rural India: An Exploratory Essay'. *Economic and Political Weekly* vol. XXII (52/53) December 24–31.

Kishwar, M. and Vanita R. (eds.) (1984) *In Search of Answers. Indian Women's Voices from Manushi*. London: Zed Press.

Klass, M. (1966) 'Marriage Rules in Bengal'. *American Anthropologist* 68.

Latif, A. and Chowdury, N. (1977) 'Land Ownership and Fertility in Two Areas of Bangladesh.' *Bangladesh Development Studies* V (2).

Lewis, D. (1990) *Technologies and Transactions*, unpublished PhD thesis, University of Bath.

Levy, R. (1957) *The Social Structure of Islam*. Cambridge: Cambridge University Press.

Liddle, J. and Joshi, R. (1985) 'Gender and Imperialism in British India'. *Economic and Political Weekly* XX (43) Review of Women's Studies.

—— (1986) *Daughters of Independence. Gender, Caste and Class in India*. London: Zed Books.

Lifschultz, L. (1979) *The Unfinished Revolution*. London: Zed Press.

Lindenbaum, S. (1968) 'Women and the Left Hand: Social Status and Symbolism in Pakistan'. *Mankind* 6.

—— (1974) *The Social and Economic Status of Women in Bangladesh*. Dhaka: Ford Foundation.

—— (1981) 'Implications for Women of Changing Marriage Transactions in Bangladesh'. *Studies in Family Planning* 12(11).

Lukes, S. (1974) *Power. A Radical View*. Studies in Sociology, British Sociological Association. London: Macmillan.

McCarthy, F. (1967) *Bengalee Village Women: Mediators Between Tradition and Development*. Michigan: unpublished MA, Michigan State University, Department of Sociology.

—— (1978) *The Status and Condition of Rural Women in Bangladesh*. Dhaka: Women's Section, Planning and Development Cell, Ministry of Agriculture and Forests.

—— (1981b) *Patterns of Involvement and Participation of Rural Women in Post-harvest Processing Operations*. Study No. 2. Dhaka: Women's Section, Ministry of Agriculture and Forests, and Regional Development Academy, Bogra.

—— (1984) 'The Target Group: Women in Rural Bangladesh'. Pp. 49–57 in Clay, E. and Schaffer, B. (eds.) *Room for Manoeuvre. An Exploration of Public Policy in Agriculture and Rural Development*. London: Heinemann Educational Books.

McCarthy, F. and Feldman, S. (1983a) 'Rural Women Discovered: New Sources of Capital and Labor in Bangladesh'. *Development and Change* 14(2).

—— (1983b) 'Purdah and Changing Patterns of Social Control Among Rural Women in Bangladesh.' *Journal of Marriage and the Family* 45(4).

—— (1984) *Rural Women and Development in Bangladesh. Selected Issues*. Oslo, Norway: NORAD, Ministry of Development Co-operations.

McGregor, J. A. (1991) *Poverty and Patronage: A Study of Credit and Development in Rural Bangladesh* Bath: University of Bath.

—— (1989) 'Boro Gafur and Choto Gafur: Development Interventions and Indigenous Institutions'. *Journal of Social Studies* 43.

Maher, V. (1976) 'Kin Clients and Accomplices: Relationships among Women in Morocco'. Pp. 52–75 in Barker, D. L. and Allen, S. (eds.) *Sexual Divisions and Society: Process and Change*. London: Tavistock.

—— (1984) 'Work, Consumption and Authority Within the Household: A Moroccan Case', in Young et al., (eds.) (1984).

Mani, L. (1986) 'Production of an Official Discourse on *Sati* in Early Nineteenth Century Bengal.' *Economic and Political Weekly* XXI (17) April, Women's Studies.

Martin, B. and Mohanty, C. T. (1988) 'Feminist Politics: What's Home Got To Do With It?', in De Lauretis (ed.)

Martius von Harder, G. (1981) *Women in Rural Bangladesh – An Empirical Study in Four Villages of Comilla District. Sozialökonomische Schriften zur Agrarentwicklung* 29/e. Saarbrucken.

Mayoux, L. (1983) *Women's Work and Economic Power in the Family: A Study of Two Villages in West Bengal*. Cambridge: unpublished PhD thesis, University of Cambridge.

Mernissi, F. (1985) *Beyond the Veil. Male–Female Dynamics in Muslim Society* (revised edition). London: Al Saqi Books.

Mies, M. (1979a) *Indian Women and Patriarchy*. New Delhi: Concept.

—— (1979b) 'Towards a Methodology of Women's Studies.' *ISS Occasional Papers* 77, The Hague.

—— (1986) *Patriarchy and Accumulation on a World Scale. Women in the International Division of Labour*. London: Zed Books.

Miranda, A. (1980) 'Nuptiality in Bangladesh'. Dhaka, *Journal of Social Studies* 9.

Mitchell, J. (1975) *Psychoanalysis and Feminism*. Harmondsworth: Penguin Books.

Mitchell, J. C. (1969) 'The Concept and Use of Social Networks', in Mitchell J. C. (ed.) *Social Networks in Urban Situations: Analyses of Personal Relationships in Central African Towns*. Manchester: Manchester University Press.

Mohanty, C. T. (1984) 'Under Western Eyes: Feminist Scholarship and Colonial Discourse'. *Boundary 2* (New York) Spring/Fall, XII (3).

Moore, M. and Dyson, T. (1983) 'Kinship Structure, Female Autonomy and Demographic Behaviour in India'. *Population and Development Review* 9(1).

Moser, C. (1989) 'Gender Planning in the Third World: Meeting Practical and Strategic Gender Needs'. *World Development* 17 (11).

Mukherjee R. (1971) *Six Villages of Bengal*. Bombay: Popular Prakashan.

Naher, M. S. (1985) 'Marriage Patterns: Customs and Changes in Rural Bangladesh'. Dhaka, *Journal of Social Studies* 30.

Nanda, B. (ed.) (1976) *Indian Women: From Purdah to Modernity*. New Delhi: Vikas.

Nath, J. (1986) *Dynamics of Socio-economic Change and the Role and Status of Women in Natunpur (Case Study of a Bangladesh Village)*. Dhaka: unpublished PhD University of Dhaka.

Nelson, N. (1979) *Why has Development Neglected Rural Women? A Review of the South Asian Literature*. Vol. 1, Women in Development Series. Oxford: Pergamon Press.

Netting, R., Wilk, R., Arnould, E. (1984) *Households. Comparative and Historical Studies of the Domestic Group*. Berkeley: University of California Press.

Nur Begum, N. (1988) *Pay or Purdah: Women and Income Earning in Rural Bangladesh*. (Reprinted) Dhaka: Winrock International Institute for Agricultural Development and Bangladesh Agricultural Research Council.

Oakley, A. (1974) *The Sociology of Housework*. Oxford: Martin Robertson.

—— (1976) *Housewife*. Harmondsworth: Penguin.

Pahl, R. (1984) *Divisions of Labour*. Oxford: Basil Blackwell.

Papanek, H. (1971) 'Purdah in Pakistan: Seclusion and Modern Occupations for Women'. *Journal of Marriage and the Family* 33 (3).

—— (1973) 'Purdah: Separate Worlds and Symbolic Shelter'. *Comparative Studies in Society and History* 15(3).

—— (1979a) 'Family Status Production, the "Work" and "Non-Work" of Women'. *Signs* 4(4).

Papanek, H. and Minault, G. (eds.) (1982) *Separate Worlds: Studies of Purdah in South Asia*. Delhi: Chanakya Publications.

Pastner, C. (1974) 'Accommodation to Purdah: The Female Perspective.' *Journal of Marriage and the Family* 36 (May).

Poovey, M. (1989) *Uneven Developments: The Ideological Work of Gender in Mid-Victorian England*. London: Virago.

Pryer, J. (1989) 'When Breadwinners Fall Ill: Preliminary Findings from a Case Study in Bangladesh'. *IDS Bulletin* 20 (2).

Quadir, S. A. (1960) *Village Dhaniswar: Three Generations of Man – Land Adjustment in an East Pakistan Village*. Comilla: Pakistan Academy for Rural Development.

Quasim, M., Saha, S., Bandana, S. (1981) *A Study on The Impact of Grameen Bank Project Operation on Landless Women*. Dhaka: Bangladesh Institute of Bank Management.

Radford Ruether, R. (1983) *Sexism and God-talk. Towards a Feminist Theology*. London: SCM.

Rahman, A. (1979) *Agrarian Structure and Capital Formation*. Cambridge: unpublished PhD thesis for the University of Cambridge.

Rahman, R. I. (1981) 'Women, Work and Wages in Rural Bangladesh'. *Journal of Social Studies* (Dhaka) 11.

—— (1986) *The Wage Employment Market for Rural Women in Bangladesh*. Dhaka: Bangladesh Institute of Development Studies.

Rahman, Z. (ed.) (1978) *The Status of Women in the Eye of the Law in Bangladesh*. Dhaka: Bangladesh Mahila Samiti.

Rajaraman, I. (1983) 'Economics of Bride Price and Dowry.' *Economic and Political Weekly* XVIII(8).

Reiter, R. R. (1975) *Toward an Anthropology of Women* New York: Monthly Review Press.

Rogers, B. (1980) *The Domestication of Women*. London: Kogan Page Ltd.

Rogers, S. C. (1975) 'Female Forms of Power and the Myth of Male Dominance: A Model of Female/Male Interaction in Peasant Society'. *American Ethnologist* 12 (4).

Rosaldo, M. (1980) 'The Use and Abuse of Anthropology: Reflections on Feminism and Cross Cultural Understanding'. *Signs* 5(3).

Rosen, L. (1984) *Bargaining for Reality: The Construction of Social Relations in a Muslim Community*. Chicago/London: Chicago University Press.

Roy, M. (1975) *Bengali Women*. London: Chicago University Press.

Rudra, A. (1978) 'Class Relations in Indian Agriculture'. *Economic and Political Weekly* XIII (22): 916–23; (23): 963–68; (24): 998–1004.

Said, E. W. (1985) *Orientalism*. London: Peregrine Books.

Sarkar, T. (1987) 'Nationalist Iconography: Images of Women in Nineteenth Century Bengali Literature'. *Economic and Political Weekly* XXII (47).

Sattar, E. (1974) *Women in Bangladesh: A Village Study*. Dhaka: Ford Foundation.

Sayers, J., Evans, M. and Redclift, N. (1987) *Engels Revisted. New Feminist Essays*. London: Tavistock Publications.

Schrijvers, J. (1986) *Mothers for Life. Motherhood and Marginalization in the North Central Province of Sri Lanka*. Delft: Eburon.

Scott, J. C. *Weapons of the Weak: Everyday Forms of Peasant Resistance*. New Haven/London: Yale University Press.

Sharma, U. (1978) 'Segregation and its Consequences in India: Rural Women in Himachal Pradesh', in Caplan and Bujra (ed.) (1978).

—— (1980a) *Women, Work and Property in North West India*. London: Tavistock Publications.

—— (1980b) 'Purdah and Public Space'. Pp. 213–239 in De Souza (ed.) (1980).

—— (1984a) 'Dowry in North India: Its Consequences for Women', in Hirschon (ed.) (1984).

—— (1984b) '"Family Status Production Work" What does it Produce?' Dhaka. *Journal of Social Studies* 24.

—— (1985a) *Women's Work, Class, and the Urban Household*. A Study of Shimla, North India. London: Tavistock Publications.

—— (1985b) 'Unmarried Women and the Household Economy: A Research Note'. Dhaka, *Journal of Social Studies* 20.

Siddiqui, K. (1982) *The Political Economy of Rural Poverty in Bangladesh*. Dhaka: National Institute of Local Government.

Signs (1988) vol. 13(3) Spring.

Smith, J. and Haddad, Y. (1982) *Women's Studies International Forum* vol. 5(2).

Smith, J., Wallerstein, I., Evers, H. (eds.) (1984) *Households and the World Economy*. London: Sage Publications.

Sobhan, R. (1982) 'The Crisis of External Dependence: Some Policy Options for Bangladesh'. Dhaka, *Journal of Social Studies* 18.

—— (ed.) (1990) *From Aid Dependence to Self-Reliance*. Development Options for Bangladesh.

Somjee, G. (1989) *Narrowing the Gender Gap*. London: Macmillan.

Standing, H. and Bandhyopadhya, B. (1985) 'Women's Employment and the Household. Some Findings from Calcutta'. *Economic and Political Weekly* XX (17) Review of Women's Studies.

Staudt, K. A. and Jacquette. J. S. (eds.) (1983) *Women in Developing Countries: A Policy Focus*. New York: Haworth Press.

Strathern, M. (1984) 'Subject or Object? Women and the Circulation of Valuables in Highlands New Guinea', in Hirschon (ed.).

—— (1987) 'Out of Context: The Persuasive Fictions of Anthropology'. *Current Anthropology* 28(3).

—— (ed.) (1987) *Dealing with Inequality. Analysing Gender Relations in Melanesia and Beyond*. Cambridge: Cambridge University Press.

Thorner, A. (1982) 'Semi-feudalism or Capitalism? – Contemporary Debate on Classes and Mode of Production in India'. *Economic and Political Weekly*, XVII (49); (50); and (51).

Thorp, J. (1978) *Power among the Farmers of Daripalla: A Bangladesh Village Study*. Dhaka: Caritas Bangladesh.

Van Schendel, W. (1981) *Peasant Mobility: The Odds of Life in Rural Bangladesh*. Assen, The Netherlands: Van Gorcum.

Vatuk, S. (1971) 'On a System of Private Savings among North Indian Village Women'. *Journal of African and Asian Studies* 6.

Vreede-de-Stuers, C. (1968) *Parda: A Study of Muslim Women's Life in Northern India*. New York: Humanities Press.

Wallace, B., Ahsan, R., Hussain, S. and Ahsan, E. (1987) *The Invisible Resource: Women and Work in Rural Bangladesh*. Boulder/London: Westview Press.

Westergaard, K. (1983) *Pauperization and Rural Women in Bangladesh: A Case Study*. Comilla, Bangladesh: Bangladesh Academy for Rural Development.

—— (1989) *Analytical Bibliography on Rural Development in Bangladesh. Studies on Women* (draft and revised draft reports). Dhaka: Bangladesh Institute of Development Studies; Copenhagen: Centre for Development Research.

Whitehead, A. (1977), review of J. Goody (1976). *Critique of Anthropology* 3(9–10).

—— (1979) 'Some Preliminary Notes on the Subordination of Women'. *IDS Bulletin* 10 (3).

—— (1981) 'A Conceptual Framework for the Analysis of the Effects of Technological Change on Rural Women'. *WEP Research Working Paper*. WEP 2-22/WP 79. ILO.

—— (1984a) '"I'm Hungry, Mum": the Politics of Domestic Budgetting' in Young et al. (eds) (1984).

—— (1984b) 'Men and Women, Kinship and Property: Some General Issues', in Hirschon (ed.) 1984.

Women for Women Research and Study Group (1975) *Women for Women: Bangladesh 1975*. Dhaka: University Press.

—— (1979) *The Situation of Women in Bangladesh*. Dhaka: Women's Development Programme, UNICEF.

Wood, G. D. (1978) 'Introduction'; 'The Political Process in Bangladesh'; "Class Differentiation and Power in Bondokgram: The Minifundist Case'; and 'Conclusion', in Huq (ed.) (1978).

—— (1980a) 'Rural Development in Bangladesh: Whose Framework?'. Dhaka. *Journal of Social Studies* 8.

—— (1980b) 'The Rural Poor in Bangladesh: A New Framework?' *Journal of Social Studies* 10.

────── (1981) 'Rural Class Formation in Bangladesh 1940–80'. *Bulletin of Concerned Asian Scholars* 13 (4).

World Bank (1984) *Bangladesh: Economic Trends and Development Administration. Volume 1: Main Report.*

Young, C. (1985) *Upholding the Veil: Hindu Women's Perceptions of Gender and Caste Indentity in Rural Pakistan.* Edinburgh: unpublished PhD for the University of Edinburgh.

Young, K., Wolkowitz, C. and McCullagh, R. (1984) (second edition) *Of Marriage and the Market. Women's Subordination Internationally and its Lessons.* London: Routledge and Kegan Paul.

Zaidi, S. M. H. (1970) *The Village Culture in Transition.* Honolulu: East–West Center Press, University of Hawaii.

Index

landholdings, 138; concentration of, 53; patterns in Kumirpur, 53, 54; sub-divided through inheritance, 57
landlessness, 6, 57, 67; rise in, 53
Liddle, J., 91
livestock: as risk insurance, 128; male ownership of, 126; marketing of, 127; trading of, 79; women's tending of, 128
loans, 38, 106; among women, 82, 83, 89; given on male authority, 46; interest-free, 63
Lokkhi, goddess, 123
Lyon, Andrew, 151

madrassa, building of, 42, 43
Maher, V., 79, 90, 115
Mahisyo caste, 34, 41, 43, 72, 108
Maloti, 65, 97, 100, 105, 122, 123, 134, 135
Mannan, 57, 86
market: as male space, 23, 73, 78; women in, 23, 70, 78-88; women's exclusion from, 70
market domination, 155-8
markets: access to, 46; interlocked, 57; segregated by gender, 46
marriage, 7, 14, 24, 27, 29, 36, 57, 63, 92, 95, 96, 97, 98, 100, 103, 130, 131, 134, 148, 150, 158, 162; arrangement of, 99-102; breakdown of, 112, 113, 136; court, 101; cross-caste, 108; *ghor jamai*, 104, 107, 113; Hindu-Muslim, 108; in Hinduism, 99; in Islam, 99; within natal village, 108
marriage payments, 102-7
Marx, Karl, 24
matchmakers, 99, 100
Matin, N., 19, 21, 22
Mayo, Katharine, 2, 158
Mayoux, L., 79
McCarthy, Florence, 19, 21, 89
mechanization: of agriculture, 30, 46, 76; of rice husking, 85
medical care, 150, 151
midwives, 136
migrant labour, 29, 61, 77, 124; and wage rates, 62
migration, 6, 19, 27, 56
Minu, 122, 124-5, 141
mobility, 38; of peasants, 36; of women, 35; social, 36, 37
Mohanty, C.T., 144, 158, 159, 161
moktob school, 42
Mondol kin group, 32, 33, 35, 42, 43, 88, 150
Mondol, Aynuddin, 42, 43, 105, 132
Morocco, 79, 90
Moser, Caroline, 19, 20

mothers-in-law, 109, 110, 111, 127, 136, 144
motorcycles, 47, 133
Mullah, Hasan, 42
murder of women, 104
Muslim community, 5, 6, 29, 30, 32, 33, 34, 40, 41, 42-3, 58, 73, 75, 78, 82, 87, 89, 90, 96, 99, 100, 102, 105, 108, 109, 113, 123, 129, 130, 134, 140, 145, 146, 147, 148, 149, 150
mutual help relationships between women, 88, 89

Nath, J., 79, 82
National Women's Organization, 15
nationalism, Bangladeshi, 11, 13
neighbours, role of, 88-91
networks, female, 91; reliance on, 93
Nilufar, 133
non-governmental organizations (NGOs), 15, 16, 48
Nondo, 136

office work of women, 95
orientalism, 3, 159, 160

paddy: amon, 49, 57, 58, 61, 63, 74; boro, 49, 57, 58, 59, 61, 63, 122
Pakistan, 29, 79, 90
Papanek, H., 114
Parboti, 76, 77, 78, 123
paternity cases, 116, 139, 146, 147
Percy Amendment, 20
personal assets of women, 126-9
politics of gender, 145-7
polygamy, 101, 149
Poovey, Mary, 11, 161
poverty, 47; as export of Bangladesh, 160
power, articulation of, 135-41
pregnancy, 116, 139, 150, 151, 153
property: and women, 129-35, 140; male privilege in, 107
property rights, 134; of women, 149
prostitution, 14, 21
Pryer, Jane, 112
purdah, 9, 21, 22, 23, 31, 35, 70, 78, 100, 122, 133, 151, 156, 162
Purnima, 109, 115, 124, 125, 146

Rahman, Sheikh Mujibur, 13, 14
Rahman, R., 83, 84
Rahman, General Ziaur, 14, 15
rape, 14
Rashida, 41, 130, 133
registration of land, 130, 132, 134, 139
religion, 17; folk, 21
religious practice, 147-52

rice: buying of, 77, 92; eating of, 40, 76,
    99; fluctuating prices of, 59; growing
    of, 74 (men and, 121); increased
    cropping of, 48, 49; production
    process of, 85; sale of, 72, 76, 81, 92,
    115, 123, 124
rice husking, 75, 76, 77, 81, 136, 137;
    mechanization of, 75, 76, 85
rice mills, 75, 76, 117
Robi, 136
Rohim, 57, 60, 62, 89
Rufia, 137, 138

Said, Edward, 3, 159, 160
Sajjur kin group, 32, 33, 35, 41, 64, 77, 87,
    88, 92, 99, 116, 127, 130, 133, 148
salaried work of women, 84, 96
Samad, 115-18, 139
Santal group, 29, 35, 47, 61, 79, 108, 127,
    130, 136; women as agricultural
    labourers, 60
savings co-operatives, 117, 155
savings of women, 83
separate spheres, model of, 22-5
Serkar, Kangali, 34, 35, 43, 86, 102, 111,
    121, 137
Serkar, Tanika, 11, 12, 146
sewing machines, 74, 121
sex: extramarital, 154; witholding of, 153
sexual abuse, 84, 102, 113
sexuality, 152-5; policing of, 137
Shakti, cult of, 22
shallow tube wells (STW), 48, 51, 52, 55,
    74, 76, 124
shame, 22, 67, 68
share-cropping, 7, 27, 38, 42, 46, 48, 52,
    55, 57-60, 63, 64, 66, 67, 116, 124, 131,
    134
share-cutting, 61, 62
share-tending of livestock, 81, 82, 87, 127,
    128
Sharma, Ursula, 3, 83, 88, 90, 114, 115,
    140
Shashthi, cult of, 22
sickness, 112, 150
Sierra Leone, 91
small business, growth of, 71-8
social capital, women's dependence on,
    126
somaj social unit, 32
Somjee, Geeta, 157
status of women, debate on, 24
stealing, 111, 114, 124, 153
suicide of women, 100, 104
Sukhi, 5, 41, 67, 86, 100, 101, 105, 123,
    130, 131, 132, 140
Suresh, 65, 100, 105, 122, 134

technology, 6, 16, 19, 29, 65; and effect on
    women, 92; in male hands, 46, 75
Tozimember, 33, 67, 68, 87, 147
traditional birth attendants, 73

USAID agency, 23, 70

Van Beurden, J., 21, 121
Van Schendel, W., 36, 103
Vatuk, S., 114
violence against women, 16, 21, 101, 104,
    111, 136, 137
visiting, importance of, 114

wage rates: for agricultural labour, 62; in
    relation to migrant labour, 62
waged labour, women's entry into, 24, 25
water: drinking, supply of, 50; fetching of,
    78, 89 (men and, 51) ; non-availability
    of, to poorer farmers, 52; sale of, 74
wedding gifts, 133
Whitehead, A., 140, 157
widows, 76, 79, 86, 92, 93, 111, 112, 139,
    146; remarriage of, 113
women: abandoned after liberation
    struggle, 14; as central to household
    relations, 66; as statutory minors, 107;
    in Bangladesh, research on, 15-21;
    revolt of, 137; role of, as
    intermediaries, 67
women's work, 21, 36, 66, 140; as topic of
    field studies, 20; central to marriage,
    97; debate on, 4; displaced by
    machinery, 75, 85; expressing class
    relations, 84; in household, 121;
    limited possibilities of, 84; related to
    power in household, 136
World Bank, 30

Young, C., 79, 90
Yunus, Prof. Muhammad, 20

Zeidenstein, 18, 70, 83, 84